Fair Enough?

Fair Enough? proposes and tests a new framework for studying attitudes toward redistributive social policies. These attitudes, the book argues, are shaped by at least two motives. First, people support policies that increase their own expected income. Second, they support policies that move the status quo closer to what is prescribed by shared norms of fairness. In most circumstances, saying the "fair thing" is easier than reasoning according to one's pocketbook. But there are important exceptions: when policies have large and certain pocketbook consequences, people take the self-interested position instead of the fair one. *Fair Enough?* builds on this simple framework to explain puzzling attitudinal trends in postindustrial democracies, including a decline in support for redistribution in Great Britain, the erosion of social solidarity in France, and a declining correlation between income and support for redistribution in the United States.

CHARLOTTE CAVAILLÉ is an assistant professor at the University of Michigan's Gerald R. Ford School of Public Policy.

T0371363

Cambridge Studies in Comparative Politics

General Editor

Kathleen Thelen, *Massachusetts Institute of Technology*

Associate Editors

Lisa Blaydes, *Stanford University*
Catherine Boone, *London School of Economics*
Thad Dunning, *University of California, Berkeley*
Anna Grzymala-Busse, *Stanford University*
Torben Iversen, *Harvard University*
Stathis Kalyvas, *University of Oxford*
Melanie Manion, *Duke University*
Prerna Singh, *Brown University*
Dan Slater, *University of Michigan*
Susan Stokes, *Yale University*
Tariq Thachil, *University of Pennsylvania*
Erik Wibbels, *University of Pennsylvania*

Series Founder

Peter Lange, *Duke University*

Editor Emeritus

Margaret Levi, *Stanford University*

Other Books in the Series

Christopher Adolph, *Bankers, Bureaucrats, and Central Bank Politics: The Myth of Neutrality*
Michael Albertus, *Autocracy and Redistribution: The Politics of Land Reform*
Michael Albertus, *Property without Rights: Origins and Consequences of the Property Rights Gap*
Santiago Anria, *When Movements Become Parties: The Bolivian MAS in Comparative Perspective*
Ben W. Ansell, *From the Ballot to the Blackboard: The Redistributive Political Economy of Education*
Ben W. Ansell and Johannes Lindvall, *Inward Conquest: The Political Origins of Modern Public Services*
Ben W. Ansell and David J. Samuels, *Inequality and Democratization: An Elite-Competition Approach*
Ana Arjona, *Rebelocracy: Social Order in the Colombian Civil War*
Leonardo R. Arriola, *Multi-Ethnic Coalitions in Africa: Business Financing of Opposition Election Campaigns*

(Continued after the index)

Fair Enough?

Support for Redistribution in the Age of Inequality

CHARLOTTE CAVAILLÉ

University of Michigan

Shaftesbury Road, Cambridge CB2 8EA, United Kingdom

One Liberty Plaza, 20th Floor, New York, NY 10006, USA

477 Williamstown Road, Port Melbourne, VIC 3207, Australia

314–321, 3rd Floor, Plot 3, Splendor Forum, Jasola District Centre,
New Delhi – 110025, India

103 Penang Road, #05–06/07, Visioncrest Commercial, Singapore 238467

Cambridge University Press is part of Cambridge University Press & Assessment,
a department of the University of Cambridge.

We share the University's mission to contribute to society through the pursuit of
education, learning and research at the highest international levels of excellence.

www.cambridge.org
Information on this title: www.cambridge.org/9781009366069

DOI: 10.1017/9781009366038

First published 2023

A catalogue record for this publication is available from the British Library

Library of Congress Cataloging-in-Publication Data
Names: Cavaillé, Charlotte, 1984– author.
Title: Fair enough? : Support for redistribution in the age of inequality /
Charlotte Cavaillé, University of Michigan, Ann Arbor.
Description: 1st edition. | New York : Cambridge University Press, 2023. |
Series: Cambridge studies in comparative politics | Includes
bibliographical references and index.
Identifiers: LCCN 2022058421 (print) | LCCN 2022058422 (ebook) |
ISBN 9781009366069 (hardback) | ISBN 9781009366038 (ebook)
Subjects: LCSH: Distribution (Economic theory) | Equality.
Classification: LCC HB523 .C39 2023 (print) | LCC HB523 (ebook) |
DDC 339.2–dc23/eng/20230302
LC record available at https://lccn.loc.gov/2022058421
LC ebook record available at https://lccn.loc.gov/2022058422

ISBN 978-1-009-36606-9 Hardback
ISBN 978-1-009-36604-5 Paperback

To Linda McNulty and Dominique Cavaillé.
C'est mine mais c'est aussi un peu yours.

Contents

Figures

Tables

Acknowledgments

Welfare states – love them or hate them, their existence is a constant source of wonder. How did some societies achieve social solidarity on such a mind-boggling scale? How resilient is the welfare state in the face of economic change, fiscal stress and immigration? How does the existence of such an institutional behemoth affect mass political behavior, EU politics or the development of financial sectors? I knew I had a keen interest in these topics but where to start?

A class with Jim Alt and Torben Iversen on the politics of redistribution provided the original spark. This class introduced me to the analytical clarity and tractability of formal theory. One model, (in)famously known as the "Meltzer and Richard model," stood out to me. According to this model, democracies have a built-in inequality moderator, one rooted in voters' self-interest. The idea that, to paraphrase Adam Smith, the democratic invisible hand would lead voters to selfishly pursue more collectively equal outcomes was an appealing starting point. I had no doubt that it was wrong, but I could not find a convincing explanation of where exactly the model fell short. Claims that people were neither rational nor selfish income maximizers made me suspicious as they often betrayed a misunderstanding of formal theory. Arguments that people were simply misinformed about inequality implicitly assumed that inequality, like rain, was an empirical fact, not a social construct. An emphasis on a cultural "second dimension" that would distract voters from issues of inequality and redistribution did not align with my personal experiences in France and Great Britain. Growing up in France, I vividly remember intensive coverage of factory closures and picketing workers whose actions were supported by a large share of the population. Vacationing in Northern England, I was struck by the difference in rhetoric: my grandparents' newspaper was full of references to "welfare scroungers." In other words, talks of inequality and redistribution were ubiquitous in both countries, though the tone in each was very different. This book represents a decade of work spent grappling with these issues.

I have a long list of people and institutions to thank for their support and guidance. The Center for European Studies at Harvard, then under the leadership of Patricia Craig, provided much-needed travel grants and office space. The Program on Inequality and Social Policy, also at Harvard, and the Institute for Advanced Study in Toulouse deserve special mention. This book, and its mix of social psychology, sociology, history, political philosophy and behavioral economics, is the direct product of these centers' multidisciplinary focus. I am especially grateful for the support and kindness of Pam Metz, Sandy Jencks, Michele Lamont, Kathy Edin, Paul Seabright, Ingela Alger, and Karine Van der Straeten. Between 2012 and 2018, Oxford was twice my home. During my time there, I benefited from the advice and support of David Rueda, David Soskice, Jane Gingrich, Ben Ansell, Desmond King and Andy Eggers. My stay at Campion Hall was when the writing process finally took off. I am grateful to Georgetown University for making it happen and to the Campion Hall Jesuit community for their friendship. At Georgetown University, I have benefited from the mentorship of Irfan Noorudin, Erik Voeten and Abe Newman. Kate Mcnamara and Nita Rudra went above and beyond, giving me the gift of intellectual and emotional support. Drafting the final manuscript was a tough exercise: There is very little left of the version that got me out of graduate school. My stay at the Center for the Study of Democratic Politics at Princeton University helped me finally see the light at the end of the tunnel. Special thanks go to Michele Epstein, Brandice Canes-Wrone, Markus Prior, Charles Cameron and Carles Boix. I am now at the Ford School at the University of Michigan and could not ask for a better home institution. I am especially grateful to John Ciorciari and Liz Gerber, who have provided stellar mentorship and advice on the final stage of this book project. I spent the summer of 2022 putting the final touches to the manuscript and, thanks to Ruth Dassonneville, was lucky to do so in the beautiful city of Montréal.

The ideas developed in the book have benefited from the inquisitive minds of an exceptional and humbling list of scholars. My interest in political economy blossomed under Peter Hall's guidance and I have been profoundly influenced by his take on what social scientists can say about the world. Peter's role as a dissertation chair and advisor has extended beyond intellectual development, providing crucial and tactful moral support when the "imposture syndrome" was kicking in. Kathleen Thelen and Arthur Spirling helped me out of so many conceptual and methodological ditches. Torben Iversen has had a strong influence on my thinking. I have become mildly addicted to the buzz I feel after talking to him, my head full of new ideas and still glowing from his contagious excitement. Julie Lynch pushed me to improve my definition of fairness reasoning. Kenneth Scheve, Jenna Bednar, Ken Kollman, Robert Franzese, Liz Gerber and Rob Mickey provided detailed feedback on an early version of the manuscript. I am especially thankful to three anonymous reviewers and to Alan Jacobs for helping me dramatically improve the final manuscript. Amy Turner and Linda McNulty helped with copy-editing. Linda even learned how to use Latex to help me clean my .bib file. As editor, Rachel Blaifeder has been a pleasure to work with.

I have been gifted with the friendship and intellectual support of many young scholars, including Anja Neundorf, Kris-Stella Trump, Kyle Jaros, Emily Clough, John Marshall, Noam Gidron, Alexander Hertel-Fernandez, Catherine Hausmann, Kenny Lowande, Neal Gong, Bocar Ba, Scott Abramson, Asya Magazinnik, Adeline Lo and Devi Mays. Alisha Holland has reached beyond the possible in combining the best of friendship and intellectual comradeship. She is an impressive scholar as well as a generous friend. Alix Lacoste, Victoria Del Campo and Alexis Schulman are, with Alisha, Kenny, Devi and many more, my big American family; I could not ask for a better one. It takes a village to be a happy outsider: Thank you from the bottom of my heart.

I would like to conclude with my friends and family on the other side of the Atlantic. Daniel Sabbagh was instrumental in getting me into academia. Jean Driscoll was a generous host during my time in England. Celine Borelle is one of the most beautiful souls I have ever met: Without her friendship, I would be missing out on so much of what life has to offer. My family deserves a lot of praise for putting up with an unavailable daughter and granddaughter, thousands of miles away. I miss my grandfather, Jacques Cavaillé, who passed away while this book was being written. My brother, Yann Cavaillé, has kept me entertained with his awesome music mixes and Korean adventures. He also designed this book's beautiful cover. My parents are the main actors of this saga. Raised by a French bourgeois father and an English working-class mother, I practiced cross-class and cross-country comparative politics from the moment I could formulate sentences. My mother, Linda McNulty, taught me to love numbers, and my father, Dominique Cavaillé, to love books. In the hope of conveying to them my admiration and love, I dedicate this book to my parents.

1

Demand for Redistribution in the Age of Inequality

If history is any guide, excessive economic inequality never goes down without a fight. Quite literally so: In the past, only mass warfare, a state collapse or catastrophic plagues have significantly altered the distribution of income and wealth (Scheidel, 2018). Could this time be different? With the spread and deepening of democratic institutions, political systems are better equipped today than in the past to reflect the economic interests of the majority of voters and peacefully address, even if imperfectly, high levels of income inequality.

This more optimistic take implicitly assumes that public opinion will act as a countervailing force to rising inequality. For many social scientists, this seems reasonable. As resources concentrate in the hands of a minority, it becomes increasingly advantageous for the poorer majority to redistribute income by taxing the richer minority to fund transfers and public goods (Meltzer and Richard, 1981). As a result, support for income redistribution is expected to increase with income inequality. This increase should be especially large among people at the bottom of the income ladder who have the most to gain from progressive taxation and redistributive spending. Scholars are not alone in expecting the public to react to rising inequality. Pundits and commentators make similar predictions, though, in their case, the motive they impute to voters is rarely economic self-interest. While left-leaning pundits point to voters' moral outrage in the face of "unfair" income differences,[1] right-leaning commentators tie growing support for income redistribution to envy and resentment.[2] Whether due to voters' material self-interest, moral outrage or envy, expectations converge: Greater wealth and income inequality should lead to greater demand for an egalitarian policy response.

---

[1] "Sorry Washington Post, Bernie Sanders Is Right about Economic Inequality" by John Nichols, in *The Nation*, July 2, 2019.

[2] "Income Inequality and Bullsh*t" by William Irwin, in *Psychology Today*, November 15, 2015.

Still, evidence of rising support for redistribution, especially among the worse off, is scant. As described in more detail in this introduction, the overall pattern is one of striking long–term stability. In the two Western countries with the sharpest increase in income inequality, Great Britain and the United States, any evidence of attitudinal change goes against expectations. In Great Britain, aggregate support for redistribution has not increased but *decreased*. In the United States, attitudinal differences between low-income and high-income voters are *decreasing*, not increasing. How can these contradictory empirical patterns be reconciled with reasonable assumptions regarding the economic determinants of redistributive preferences? What can we conclude regarding public opinion's role as a countervailing force to rising inequality?

This book aims to answer these questions. In Part I, I show that mass attitudes toward redistributive social policies are shaped by at least two motives: material self-interest and fairness reasoning. On the one hand, people support policies that, if implemented, would increase their own expected income. On the other hand, people also support policies that, if implemented, would move the status quo closer to what is prescribed by shared norms of fairness. Combined, these two motives help explain why people often hold redistributive preferences that seem to cut against their own economic interest, with the poor being sometimes opposed to, and the rich very often in favor of, redistributive social policies.

In Part II, I examine how fairness reasoning and material self-interest interact with contextual factors to help explain stability and change in attitudes toward redistributive social policies. I show how, in Western democracies, changes in partisan dynamics have combined with fiscal stress to erode support for key redistributive features of the welfare state. Overall, the evidence suggests that this time might not be so different after all. Without a strong egalitarian turn in mass attitudes toward redistributive policies, there are few reasons to expect the democratic process to bring about ambitious policy responses to rising inequality.

In this introductory chapter, I first present stylized facts regarding expected and observed trends in mass attitudes toward redistributive social policies. I then present the book's main argument and its relationship to the existing literature. I end with a brief description of the chapters to follow.

The Dynamics of Support for Redistribution: Expectations and Evidence

A common expectation is that greater economic inequality will be partially offset by higher demand for policies that redistribute across income groups. In what I will call the "benchmark model," Meltzer and Richard (1981) helpfully formalize a set of scope conditions and assumptions under which such expectation holds. This model is not designed to capture reality in its complexity. Instead, it provides an internally consistent theoretical benchmark against which to compare and assess the empirical evidence. Any mismatch between the evidence and the model's predictions can be investigated by probing the model further. What does it overlook? How often are scope conditions met? I start with a brief review of this benchmark model and then turn to evidence of attitudinal change in postindustrial democracies.

The Benchmark Model

In the benchmark model, redistributive policies take the form of a flat rate tax and a lump sum per capita transfer equal to total revenue divided by population size. Income inequality is a situation in which some people receive a share of income that is larger than their share of the population ("the rich"), while others receive a share that is smaller ("the poor"). Mechanically, when there is income inequality, the combination of a flat rate tax and a lump-sum transfer results in income redistribution. That's because the tax an individual pays is proportional to their share of national income (high for the rich, low for the poor), while the transfer they receive is proportional to their share of the population (the same for both rich and poor). As a result, the rich pay more in taxes than they receive in transfer. The converse is true for the poor.

A key parameter in this benchmark model is the difference between one's own market income and mean market income, defined as national market income divided by population size. Mathematically, anyone who receives a share of national income that is larger than their share of the population is someone whose own market income is higher than the mean market income. This person will always favor a 0% tax rate as any positive tax rate will result in a net loss, that is, a tax bill that is larger than the transfer received. Conversely, anyone whose market income is lower than the mean market income stands to benefit from a high tax rate. Assuming no administrative costs and disincentive effects, this person will even support a 100% tax rate as the transfer received (equal to mean market income) will always more than compensate for the individual market income lost to taxes.[3] With this redistributive set up, the closer someone is to the bottom of the income ladder, the more they stand to gain. Conversely, the closer someone is to the top, the more they stand to lose.

---

[3] This assumes no disincentive effects from taxation and no bureaucratic costs. Relaxing these assumptions does not change the intuition presented here.

The comparison between mean market income and *median* income[4] captures whether a *majority* would benefit from a higher tax rate. Indeed, if median market income is lower than mean market income, then a hypothetical 100% tax rate would advantage a majority of the population. If the difference between the median and the mean is large, that is, if a small minority receives the bulk of market income, then not only does a majority stand to benefit from a high tax rate, it stands to benefit a lot. For this majority group, the resulting lump-sum transfer will more than compensate for the higher tax bill. In other words, the number of people who stand to benefit from redistribution and the extent to which they stand to benefit increase with a top-heavy rise in income inequality.[5]

This benchmark model generates two testable predictions. The first one is a positive relationship between the mean-to-median market income ratio and aggregate support for redistribution. The second prediction is a comparatively larger increase in support for redistribution among those closer to the bottom of the income distribution and no increase in support for redistribution among those closer to the top. Importantly, and in accordance with Occam's razor, this model lays out the key institutional and individual-level assumptions (also called micro-foundations) that underpin the expectation of a pro-redistribution turn in countries with rising inequality.[6] These assumptions include a tax and transfer system designed to be redistributive and citizens who prefer more disposable income than less, are informed about rising income inequality and are aware of its implications for their own position as net winners or losers of redistribution. As I show in the following section, when brought to the data, this benchmark model does not perform very well. Building on this evidence, I then revisit some of the model's key assumptions.

Testing the Benchmark Model

The rise in income inequality started in the 1970s, a decade marked by the end of the postwar economic boom and by a crisis of profitability, investment and productivity, as well as stagflation. The policies adopted to address the

---

[4] Median income is the income of the individual who splits the population into a bottom poorer half and a top richer half.

[5] The concentration at the top pushes the mean income up without affecting the median, thus increasing the gap between the two.

[6] The benefits of engaging with this benchmark model go beyond analytical clarity and tractability. Western societies are built on the ideal of equal dignity, which stands in tension with the existence of income inequality. Given this, a model hypothesizing that democracies have a built-in inequality moderator rooted in voters' selfish pursuit of more equal outcomes is an appealing starting point. It is a way for researchers to join the public conversation without taking a position on the tension between democratic ideals and existing levels of economic inequality.

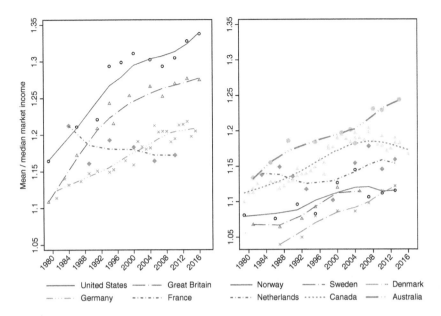

Figure 1.1 Mean-to-median market income
Plots the ratio of mean-to-median gross market income. To improve comparability across countries, the income measure only includes private – not public – pensions. Source: UNU–WIDER, World Income Inequality Database (WIID), www.wider .unu.edu/project/world-income-inequality-database-wii

crisis restored profits and crushed inflation while also contributing to rising economic inequality. These developments have affected some countries more than others. Figure 1.1 plots overtime changes in market income inequality using the mean-to-median income ratio. The figure on the left plots this ratio for all the countries examined with some detail in this book, namely the United States, Great Britain, France and Germany. The figure on the right plots the same ratio for a mix of countries for which similar data are available. The increase in income inequality is most striking in the United States and Great Britain. While positive, the rate of increase in Germany is comparatively lower. France is an outlier: Over the period, the ratio of mean-to-median income is mostly stable (another exception is the Netherlands). Overall, most countries are experiencing an increase in market income inequality.

The mean-to-median ratio obscures what is happening at the two ends of the income distribution. Figure 1.2 plots the average income (market income and public pensions) in the top decile (between the 90th and the 100th percentiles), divided by the average income in the second decile (between the 10th and the 20th percentiles). I focus on the second decile to address concerns that the first

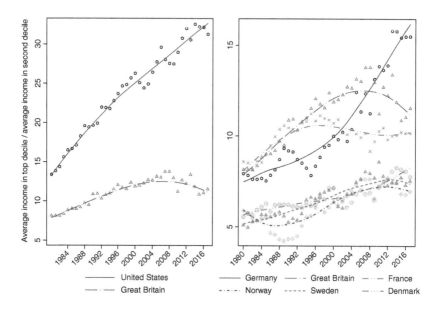

Figure 1.2 Mean market income of the rich relative to that of the poor
Plots the ratio of mean market income in the top decile to mean market income in the second decile. To extend the analysis beyond the working age population, the market income measure includes both public and private pensions. Excluding pensions returns a similar picture, with one exception: the increase in market income inequality in Great Britain is steeper (Atkinson, 2008).
Source: World Inequality Database (WID.world), https://wid.world/data/.

decile might consist of a very disparate group of individuals (e.g., long-term unemployed and students). As shown on the left-hand side, the United States is a clear outlier: Today, the average income in the top decile is thirty times that of the average income in the second decile, representing a tripling of the top-to-bottom income ratio since the early 1980s. In that regard, the evolution in Great Britain is far less dramatic; the average income in the top decile is "only" twelve times that in the second decile, representing a mere 50% increase in the top-to-bottom ratio relative to the 1980s.[7] The figure on the right-hand side plots trends in France, Germany and three Scandinavian countries (Great Britain is included as a benchmark, notice also the change in the *y*-axis). While most countries are experiencing an increase in income inequality, this increase is among the largest in Germany, with France again being the stable outlier.

In light of the trends plotted in Figures 1.1 and 1.2, the United States and Great Britain are ideal candidates for testing the benchmark model. Based on the latter, aggregate support for income redistribution should increase as in-

---

[7] There is also a noticeable reversal starting with the onset of the Great Recession.

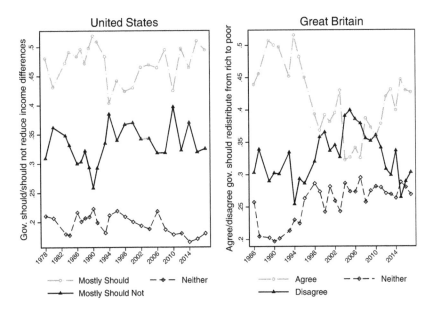

Figure 1.3 Demand for redistribution in the United States and Great Britain
Plots the share of respondents who express mostly support, mostly opposition or neither to a statement asking about income redistribution by the government. Left panel (US): "Some people think that the government ought to reduce the income differences between the rich and the poor, perhaps by raising the taxes of wealthy families or by giving income assistance to the poor (1). Others think the government should not concern itself with reducing this income difference between the rich and the poor (7). (...) What score between 1 and 7 comes closest to the way you feel?" Variable recoded as follows: 1 through 3 "mostly should concern itself," 4 "neither," 5 through 7 "mostly should not." Right panel (GB): "Government should redistribute income from the better off to those who are less well off." Answers recorded using a strongly agree (1)–strongly disagree (5) Likert scale. Variable recoded as follows: 1 and 2 "agree," 3 "neither," 4 and 5 "disagree." Source: GSS 1972–2018, weighted (left panel); BSAS 1983–2017, weighted (right panel).

come inequality increases, starting with the bottom half of the income distribution. Empirically, this implies an increase in the share of individuals who agree that "the government should redistribute income from the better off to those who are least well-off." Over time, we can also expect attitudinal differences between the top and the bottom of the income distribution to increase. Do we observe the expected increase in mass support for redistribution? Have the preferences of the rich and the poor diverged over time, especially so in the United States?

Overall, the evidence that trends in mass social policy preferences align with theoretical expectations is scant. As shown in Figure 1.3, in the United

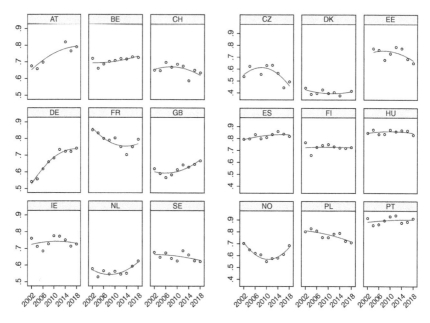

Figure 1.4 Demand for redistribution in postindustrial democracies
Plots the share of respondents who agree with the following statement: "The government should take measures to reduce differences in income levels." Answers were recorded using a strongly agree (1)–strongly disagree (5) Likert scale. In this figure, "strongly agree" and "agree" responses are combined.
Source: ESS 2002–2018, weighted.

States (left panel), the overall pattern is one of striking stability: Despite a sharp growth in income inequality since the 1970s, support for redistribution has remained very stable. In Great Britain (right panel), and against all expectations, the evidence points to a decline in support for redistribution (Georgiadis and Manning, 2012; Grasso et al., 2019). More generally, as shown in Figure 1.4, attitudinal stability is not specific to the United States: In most countries, the trend in support for redistribution is surprisingly flat. One exception is Germany, where support for income redistribution has gone up at the same time as income inequality has increased.

As the rich increasingly stand to lose from redistribution and the poor increasingly stand to win, is there any evidence of diverging attitudinal trends at each end of the income distribution? Figure 1.5 plots the share of respondents in the bottom income quintile who support income redistribution minus the share of respondents in the top quintile who also support it. In both countries, low-income respondents are more likely to support income redistribution than

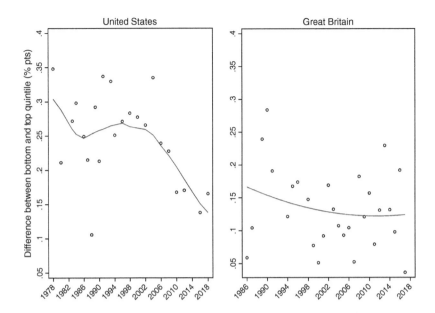

Figure 1.5 Demand for redistribution in the United States and Great Britain: Top versus bottom quintiles

Plots the difference between the share of individuals in the bottom quintile who agree with the policy principle of income redistribution and the share of individuals in the top quintile who also agree. For example, a positive value of 0.2 means that (1) the share of people in the bottom quintile who agree is larger than the share in the top quintile who agree and (2) the difference between the two group shares is equal to 20 percentage points. See Figure 1.3 for item wording. Income measures are described in Appendix A1.1.

US source: GSS, 1972–2018, weighted; GB source: BSAS 1983–2017, weighted.

high-income respondents. In Great Britain, this difference is stable over time. Strikingly, in the United States, the difference between the bottom and the top quintiles is decreasing.

To summarize, despite generational replacement, major recessions, large shifts in unemployment and changing policy paradigms (Hall, Kahler and Lake, 2013), support for redistribution is very stable. In our two most likely cases, Great Britain and the United States, any evidence of attitudinal change goes against common expectations: a decrease in aggregate support in Great Britain and a decrease in the attitudinal income gradient in the United States. Also noteworthy is the difference between Great Britain and Germany, two countries with similar increases in income inequality but with opposite attitudinal trends. Interestingly, France, despite no increase in income inequality, is one of the few countries (with the possible exception of Spain) to have experienced a nation-wide year-long social movement – *Les Gilets Jaunes* – focusing on economic issues and asking for more income redistribution. How to make sense of these puzzling patterns and country cases? Answering this question requires returning to the benchmark model's micro-foundations: What does the model get wrong, and how can it be amended to get things right?

The Argument Part 1: New Micro-Foundations

In Part I of this book, I relax two of the benchmark model's assumptions. One is the assumption that voters have a sophisticated understanding of their position as net winners or losers of changes to redistributive policy and that it affects their policy preferences. The other is the emphasis, in the form of a fixed rate tax and a lump-sum transfer, on policies' redistributive *consequences*. Relaxing these assumptions suggests a new set of micro-foundations, one in which fairness reasoning takes a leading role.

Fairness Reasoning

The benchmark model's assumption that people are well-informed, self-interested income maximizers is most helpful when economic stakes are quantifiable and large. In countries with mature welfare states, this is rarely the case. First, the redistributive implications of a given policy change are far from straightforward, and politicians, fearing a backlash from affected populations, have only limited incentives to provide clarifying cues. In addition, in countries with mature welfare states, many policy reforms have ambiguous implications (i.e., diffuse costs or benefits), meaning that, for many voters, redistribution is an uncertain or low-stakes issue, with few incentives to acquire the correct information regarding implications for their pocketbooks (Jacobs and Matthews, 2017; Roth, Settele and Wohlfart, 2022). In such a context, the assumption that voters are fully informed selfish income maximizers is heroic at best, requiring researchers to think more creatively about core behavioral motives guiding attitude formation and change.

In this book, I emphasize fairness reasoning as a behavioral motive well suited to the low personal stakes or high-uncertainty world of redistributive politics. Indeed, when it comes to preferences over broad categories of redistributive policies, it is often easier and more rewarding to reason according to fairness principles than to reason based on hypothetical implications for one's own pocketbook. People consequently support policies that move the status quo closer to what is prescribed by widely shared norms of fairness and oppose policies that move the status quo further away from what is fair. Because people hold different empirical beliefs regarding the fairness of the status quo, they also disagree over which policies to support or oppose. Given that beliefs about the fairness of the status quo are often disconnected from an individual's own position in the income distribution (more on this below), fairness reasoning only incidentally produces the types of policy preferences one might expect from self-interested citizens. Only when policies have large material consequences will people consider what is economically self-serving instead of what is fair. In a world of high uncertainty and low personal stakes, fairness considerations come first and self-regarding considerations about one's own pocketbook come second.

Before theorizing how fairness reasoning and material self-interest combine to shape attitudes toward redistributive social policies, I first provide a more precise definition of fairness reasoning and flesh out its consequences for how researchers conceptualize (and operationalize) attitudes toward redistributive social policies.

Two Norms of Fairness for Two Facets of Redistribution

I define fairness reasoning as the thought process through which individuals act as if a third-party judge ruling on the fairness of a given situation and acting to maximize fairness accordingly. In the context of this book, fairness is maximized by favoring a policy change that moves the status quo closer to what is prescribed by shared norms of fairness. I emphasize two norms of fairness. One is the proportionality norm, which prescribes that individual rewards be proportional to effort and talent. The other is the reciprocity norm, which prescribes that cooperative behavior be rewarded more than uncooperative behavior.

The proportionality norm underpins economic activity in a capitalist society. Consent is achieved when people believe that rewards are proportional to merit, itself a combination of personal decisions as a free agent, individual work ethic, acquired skills and innate talent. The reciprocity norm, in contrast, underpins social solidarity, that is, the provision by the group of basic material security for its members, lest the group not survive temporary material shocks. The successful provision of social solidarity implies group members who are willing contributors to a resource-pooling endeavor and feel no resentment toward those who benefit more than they contribute. This is achieved when people believe that the status quo abides by what the reciprocity norm prescribes, namely the belief that net beneficiaries are cooperators down on their luck, not free riders. In Western democracies, reasoning about the fairness of redistributive social policies consequently implies at least two types of fairness evaluation: (1) How fair is it for some to make (a lot) more money than others in the marketplace, and (2) how fair is it for some to receive more benefits than they pay in taxes? Each question calls to mind a different norm of fairness: the proportionality norm for the former and the reciprocity norm for the latter.

The benchmark model's emphasis on policies' redistributive *consequences*, while correct from an accounting perspective, overlooks this institutional and moral dualism. In doing so, it obscures important distinctions between at least two types of redistributive policies. One type includes policies that directly interfere with high-earning individuals' capacity to generate and keep market income. The other type includes policies that make social insurance redistributive. Policies that fit in the first category include progressive income taxes as well as industrial policies or corporate governance policies that affect the distribution of profits across stakeholders (also called pre-distribution policies). As a shorthand, I call this family of policies *redistribution from* policies because they mostly affect the accumulation of market income by "economic winners." Policies that fit in the second category include social programs that provide a safety net for those who cannot provide for themselves (e.g., means-tested transfers) as well as design features that regulate the extent to which access to generous social insurance programs is conditional on risk profiles and prior contributions (often described as social solidarity). As a shorthand, I call this family of policies *redistribution to* policies because they mostly affect the material conditions of "economic losers." In times of rising income inequality, both *redistribution from* and *redistribution to* policies contribute to more egalitarian outcomes.

The proportionality norm is most prevalent when reasoning about the fairness of *redistribution from* policies. *Redistribution from* policies that interfere with the "natural" allocation of income across economic actors are justified if this allocation is "unfair." In this context, "unfair" implies the belief that market rewards are not proportional to effort and talent. The reciprocity norm is most prevalent when reasoning about the fairness of *redistribution to* policies. *Redistribution to* policies, which redistributes resources to those who cannot provide for themselves (whether temporarily or not), are justified if pooled resources are allocated in a "fair" way. In this case, "fair" means the belief that *redistribution to* policies do not reward free riders more than cooperators.

Support for both types of redistributive policies is the highest among people who find market mechanisms unfair *and* believe that social insurance, especially its most redistributive features, benefit people who are not intentionally trying to "abuse the system." Relatedly, opposition to income redistribution as a whole is highest among people who find market mechanisms fair *and* believe that free riding is highly prevalent. Yet, as I will show in later chapters, most people exhibit a mix of beliefs, making them more likely to hold, for example, liberal preferences toward *redistribution from* policies and conservative preferences toward *redistribution to* policies (or vice versa).

Needless to say, the framework provided in this book should be understood as providing ideal types, not an exhaustive classification tool applicable to all existing norms of fairness, redistributive policies and their possible combinations. Take, for example, unemployment insurance: In most countries, it is designed to be fair according to both the proportionality norm (benefits are tied to contributions and thus to efforts and skills) and the reciprocity norm (the lucky subsidize the unlucky). Individual attitudes toward proposed reforms are consequently shaped by both people's perceptions of how much effort pays in the market place and one's beliefs about the prevalence of free riding. Still, as I will show throughout the book, the simplified framework I propose here has enough traction to justify overlooking some of these nuances.

Why Proportionality Beliefs Need Not Align with Reciprocity Beliefs

I trace the disconnect between proportionality beliefs (beliefs regarding deviations from what the proportionality norm prescribes) and reciprocity beliefs (beliefs regarding deviations from what the reciprocity norm prescribes) to differences between the moral economy of market economies and that of welfare states. Simply put, market economies are morally construed as an *individual* race, while welfare states are constructed as *collective* resource-pooling endeavors among citizens of the same country. One key implication is that, while welfare states imply group boundaries and interdependence, market economies do not. As a result, proportionality and reciprocity beliefs form each according to their own separate rationale.

Proportionality beliefs, I show, are partly self-serving: Individuals who are deemed losers in the individual economic race are more likely to interpret its rules as unfair, while winners are more likely to find it fair. Perceptions of the fairness of resource pooling follow a different logic: They are shaped by differences in how people intuitively reason about social dilemmas, membership and free riding. These differences in how people reason about these issues have little to do with people experiences as winners or losers of the economic race, explaining the disconnect between proportionality and reciprocity beliefs.

Empirically, this means that proportionality beliefs are correlated with one's own labor market position (e.g., income, occupation and skill level). Reciprocity beliefs, in contrast, are correlated with attitudes toward the death penalty, sentencing and discipline in school. These attitudes are commonly used to place people on a libertarian–authoritarian values scale. The disconnect between proportionality and reciprocity beliefs thus partly reflects the fact that liberal–authoritarian values and income are not correlated.

While people's policy preferences are often better predicted by their long-term beliefs about the fairness of the status quo than by a policy's implications for their own pocketbook, material self-interest still matters. First, the correlation between proportionality beliefs on the one hand, and earning capacity on the other, suggests that people form proportionality beliefs in a self-serving fashion, a point I will come back to when discussing how fairness beliefs form and change. Second, while material self-interest does not explain how reciprocity beliefs form, it helps understand *when* and for *whom* reciprocity beliefs matter the most and *when* and for *whom* they matter the least. I explain this latter point next.

Bringing Self-interest Back In

While economic stakes are small and uncertain for many people, for some people and in some contexts, redistributive policies do have large and quantifiable material implications. In such cases, the assumption that individuals behave in ways that maximize their income yields important predictive power. One simple way of conceptualizing the interaction between fairness reasoning and material self-interest is to think of attitude formation as following a two-step reasoning. First, fairness beliefs help people decide whether to support or oppose policies that seek to change the status quo. Second, material self-interest helps predict how much individuals deviate from what fairness reasoning prescribes. As a result, the policy preferences people ultimately settle on are a function of the type of fairness belief they start from on the one hand, and the policy's effect on their own disposable income on the other.

This is particularly relevant for *redistribution to* preferences. Remember that large portions of the morally conservative poor believe that *redistribution to* policies benefit undeserving recipients and that the prevalence of free riding is high. Because more low-income individuals benefit from *redistribution to* policies, they are also more likely, relative to high-income individuals, to adjust their support in a self-serving fashion. As a result, in surveys, the rich appear more driven by fairness concerns than the poor, who are much more likely to give the self-interested answer to a question about *redistribution to* policies.

A lot has been said about the irrational poor who vote against their interests. The argument and framework presented in the book show that this statement does not easily extend to redistributive preferences. On the one hand, low-income respondents are more likely to find the status quo unfair due to beliefs about the high prevalence of free riding. On the other hand, they are less likely to translate these beliefs into support for less generous *redistribution to* policies. High-income respondents, in contrast, are more likely to be morally liberal and to believe that *redistribution to* policies benefit deserving recipients. They are also more likely to translate these beliefs into support for generous and inclusive *redistribution to* policies. As a result, attitudes expressed by this group are rarely in line with their "objective" material self-interest, especially when compared to the attitudes of low-income respondents.

The Argument Part 2: Explaining Attitudinal Stability and Change

The goal of this book is to explain patterns of attitudinal stability and change in times of rising income inequality. Part II builds on the conceptual framework presented in Part I to theorize mechanisms of mass attitudinal change and document their role in the country cases discussed at the beginning of this chapter.

Based on this framework, attitudinal change results from the activation of one (or more) of three possible causal pathways.[8] One pathway is a change in the share of the population who, when asked about redistributive social policies, give the self-interested answer instead of the fair one (or vice versa). Such a change in the dominant mode of reasoning is most consequential when it affects cross-pressured individuals: those whose fairness-maximizing response differs substantively from their self-interested one. A second pathway is a change in the fairness rule people rely on when answering a given set of survey questions. This causal mechanism is best known in the literature under the umbrella expressions of *framing* or *priming* effect. It is most relevant when a given issue can be framed in ways that activate either proportionality concerns or reciprocity concerns. Because of differences in proportionality and reciprocity beliefs, answers can change depending on which norm is activated. A third pathway is a change in fairness beliefs. Unlike framing effects, which tend to only have temporary implications, a change in fairness beliefs has lasting and substantive consequences.

---

[8] As a friendly reminder, in this book, attitudinal change is a change in patterns of answers to *survey questions* about redistributive social policies, questions that have been asked repeatedly over time in large national and cross-national surveys.

Theorizing aggregate attitudinal change requires understanding the contextual factors that activate each of these three causal pathways. In this book, I discuss three activating factors. The first is fiscal stress, which affects attitudes through a reversal to self-interest among altruistic net contributors to *redistribution to* policies. The second consists of survey design and item wording, which affect attitudes through framing effects. The third is party competition dynamics, which affect attitudes by enabling changes in fairness beliefs. In Part II, I demonstrate how these activating factors help explain the puzzling patterns highlighted at the beginning of this chapter.

Fiscal Stress and the Erosion of Social Solidarity in France

In most countries, majority support for generous *redistribution to* policies is achieved through a combination of self-interested support among beneficiaries and altruistic support among those who, while not benefiting, nevertheless support it because it is the "fair thing to do." Fiscal stress, I argue, can trigger a reversion to self-interest among these altruistic supporters, leading to a decrease in support. As the threat of fiscal adjustment becomes more credible, people consider the implications for their own pocketbooks and increasingly favor letting the generosity of targeted policies mechanically erode. Absent fiscal stress, and because of fairness reasoning,[9] risk exposure and income are poor predictors of attitudes toward *redistribution to* policies. However, in times of fiscal stress, reversion to self-interest implies the re-emergence of a relationship between risk and income on the one hand, and support for more generous *redistribution to* policies on the other.

To test this argument, I focus on a most likely case, France, where tax increases are a credible threat. Since the 1990s, tax increases have occurred at regular intervals, always to deal with fiscal imbalances tied to social insurance.[10] Thanks to the availability of a rich decades-long longitudinal survey, I can examine the relation between fiscal stress generated by the Great Recession, and support for *redistribution to* policies, specifically willingness to pay for generous social transfers targeted to the poor and support for making access to social insurance unconditional on prior contributions.

The French case not only offers an ideal setting for testing a causal pathway, it also speaks to my argument's explanatory power. Given proportionality beliefs extremely critical of markets and inequality (documented in Part I), *Les*

---

[9] Indeed, a large subset of high-income and low-risk individuals trust that beneficiaries of *redistribution to* policies are "deserving" recipients.

[10] In contrast, in the United States, the threat of tax increases has remained elusive due to legislative gridlock and the country's ability to borrow at very low interest rates.

Gilets Jaunes movement's emphasis on more *redistribution from* is to be expected. Yet, as documented in Part II, these beliefs do not protect against the eroding effects of fiscal stress on support for *redistribution to* policies. The French case thus further highlights the need to distinguish between the two facets of demand for redistribution.

Great Britain: A Decrease in *Redistribution to*, not *from*

Policy debates about income redistribution are inherently multifaceted: They can emphasize fairly or unfairly taking from the rich, or fairly or unfairly giving to the poor. Empirically, this dualism has implications for how researchers interpret changes in answers to a survey item that asks about redistribution from the rich and redistribution to the poor in the same breath. This type of survey item is commonly found in longitudinal surveys and has become ubiquitous in studies of attitudinal change. In the book, I call this survey item the "traditional redistribution item." Because beliefs that make it fair to redistribute from the rich are distinct from beliefs that make it fair to redistribute to the poor, answers to this survey item can change depending on contextual primes and framing effects, making survey answers tricky to interpret.

I show that contextual primes tied to survey design partly explain the puzzling decline in the share of British respondents who agree that the "government should redistribute income from the better off to those who are less well off." In the British Social Attitudes Survey (BSAS), used in Figure 1.3, the redistribution item is included right after a block of survey items asking about free riding among the unemployed and the poor. Because reciprocity beliefs in Great Britain have much less egalitarian implications than proportionality beliefs, respondents primed to think about redistribution as a *redistribution to* policy express lower levels of support than when such prime is absent. As a result, the decline in support for redistribution documented in Figure 1.3 has to be interpreted with caution: It reflects a conservative shift in reciprocity beliefs (more on this below) and, consequently, a decline in support for *redistribution to* policies specifically, not *redistribution from* policies. As with the French case, these findings further highlight the pitfalls of conceiving of demand for redistribution in the singular.

Framing effects matter beyond survey design. Indeed, decades of research have shown that partisan competition, through priming and framing effects, shapes how people reason about a given redistributive issue (Zaller, 1992). Assuming a mid-to-long-run shift in partisan competition, it can also directly impact people's fairness beliefs, the third causal pathway examined in this book.

Partisan Dynamics and Belief Change in the United States and Great Britain

By fairness *beliefs*, I mean the subset of claims and considerations people hold that jointly shape their assessment of the status quo as barely deviating, deviating somewhat or deviating a lot from what the proportionality or reciprocity norms prescribe. For example, in the case of the proportionality norm, this includes the belief that "effort pays," that the education system is "meritocratic" or that "hiring is based on skills not personal connections." For some people, these beliefs might be only partially consistent, suggesting that these individuals do not have a clear sense of the fairness of the status quo. Yet, as I show in Chapter 3, most people answer survey items in ways that allow them to be ranked from holding "consistently unfair" considerations to "mostly unfair," to "mostly fair," to "consistently fair" considerations. To understand how people's "basket" of considerations change, I build on Zaller (1992) and argue that belief change happens at the intersection of (1) changes in one's discursive context, that is, the claims and considerations one is exposed to, and (2) one's propensity to accept and incorporate new claims into one's own basket or resist doing so despite exposure to new claims.

To identify systemic changes in people's discursive context, I focus on mid-to-long-term changes in party competition that affect how competing political parties talk about redistributive issues. People mirror these changes in predictable ways depending on their own exposure to elite messaging and partisan affinities. Furthermore, I show that people experiencing hardship are more likely to resist dissonant right-wing considerations about the fairness of market institutions and inequality and embrace consonant left-wing ones. The same logic applies to reciprocity beliefs: People who are moral liberals are more likely, relative to people who are moral authoritarians, to resist dissonant right-wing considerations about the prevalence of free riding and accept consonant left-wing ones regarding the deservingness of recipients. I trace these differences to cultural differences in how people reason about social dilemmas. These mechanisms of exposure and resistance help explain why proportionality beliefs correlate with income and why reciprocity beliefs correlate with liberal–authoritarian values.

This simple model of belief formation sheds new light on changes in mass attitudes on both sides of the Atlantic. In Great Britain, disagreement over how to better foster economic growth generated important tensions between the traditional left and the pro-market "Third Way," with the latter winning control of the Labour party in 1995. The first-past-the-post system meant that the traditional left was eclipsed by Tony Blair's winning coalition. The consequence of the demise of the traditional left in favor of the New Labour was a depoliticization of proportionality concerns in favor of a center–right bi-partisan consensus on the need to reform *redistribution to* policies. I document how mass attitudinal trends in Great Britain have mirrored these supply-side dynamics, that is, relative stability with regard to proportionality beliefs and a widely shared conservative shift in reciprocity beliefs. As reciprocity beliefs have become more conservative, support for cuts to welfare transfers has increased. In line with my argument, the impact on support for *redistribution to* policies is the largest among high-income respondents; low-income respondents, in contrast, maintain comparatively lower and stable support for cuts.

I contrast these trends with those found in Germany, where, after the Social Democratic Party (SPD's) shift to the right under Gerhard Schröder, the traditional left was, thanks to proportional representation, able to maintain its political relevance, with implications for the discursive context. This helps explain why in Germany attitudinal trends following Schröder's electoral victory have looked very different from that found in Great Britain after Blair's victory.

While Great Britain's main parties experienced a convergence on redistributive issues, in the United States, parties have famously polarized. In the United States, underpinning overall attitudinal stability is a pattern of mass partisan polarization that mirrors what is happening at the elite level. This is particularly true of reciprocity concerns, with the largest implications for the attitudes of high-income Democrats. I document a pro-redistribution shift in patterns of answers among high-income Democrats, a group increasingly likely to find minorities,[11] and low-income individuals in general, deserving recipients of *redistribution to* policies. Low-income Republicans, in contrast, have been much less likely to translate growing concerns over free riding and minorities' access to benefits into opposition to *redistribution to* policies. As a result, and against common expectations, the decline in the income gradient originates in growing support for redistribution among rich Democrats, not declining support among poor (often white) Republicans.

---

[11] It is by now well documented that in the United States, beliefs about the fairness of *redistribution to* policies are highly racialized: People disagree over the extent to which minorities, especially African Americans, are deserving beneficiaries of collectively pooled resources. Students of American politics have studied these beliefs under the umbrella term of symbolic racism (also called racial resentment). As shown by Enders and Scott (2019), and in line with the argument presented in this book, symbolic racism exists separately from adherence to liberal-conservative principles about government intervention and the fairness of market forces. See Chapter 8 for more detail.

Full Circle

In light of dramatic increases in income inequality, why aren't voters asking for more income redistribution? One explanation is fairness beliefs' stabilizing role as an *anchoring* proto-ideology in a context in which stakes are low or uncertain. Absent triggering factors, attitudinal stability is the norm. Rising inequality does not constitute a triggering factor for at least two reasons. First, for most people, income inequality is an abstract reality, meaningful only through the lenses of fairness reasoning and prior fairness beliefs. Only a subset of the population – the one that already finds market income unfair and already support redistribution – will experience a rise in income inequality as something needing to be addressed. Another reason is the existence of more than one type of fairness evaluation: In the realm of *redistribution to* policies in particular, there is no obvious theoretical or empirical connection between market income inequality and policy preferences.

A strong egalitarian turn in mass attitudes toward redistributive policies will require a pro-redistribution change in fairness beliefs, an increase in the share of people who support such policies out of material self-interest or both. Under what conditions might this happen? Will these conditions be met any time soon? Answers to these questions partly depend on political parties' positioning on redistributive issues as well as the state of the government's finances.

My argument suggests that party competition dynamics have provided a discursive environment inhospitable to a pro-redistribution turn. In the 1980s, in response to stagflation, a new consensus emerged built on the assumption that increasing the reach of market mechanisms, both geographically and in terms of what counts as tradable goods and services, could help improve paltry growth rates. Increasing the reach of market mechanisms does not imply deregulation. Instead, it requires a state-driven process of institution building, the paragon being the European single market. In the process of crafting more markets (Vogel, 2018), elites have affected the discursive context in ways unfavorable to egalitarian fairness beliefs, specifically proportionality beliefs. Indeed, over the past few decades, disagreement over the merits of markets (and the fairness of market income inequality) has become less common, decreasing the likelihood of mass changes in the belief that the status quo deviates from what the proportionality norm prescribes.

Contrast this relative depoliticization of *redistribution from* policies to what has happened with *redistribution to* policies: In both Great Britain and the United States, the redistributive features of the welfare state have been the target of extensive rhetorical and policy innovation ("from welfare to workfare," "flexicurity," welfare chauvinism, etc.). As a result, aggregate attitudinal change on the *redistribution to* dimension has mirrored patterns of elite convergence (in the case of Great Britain) and polarization (in the case of the United States). In the concluding chapter, I tentatively argue that the restructuring of electoral cleavages (from being centered on income and class to being centered on education and skills) has made it electorally less risky to debate the need for more or less *redistribution to* than to disagree over the need for more or less *redistribution from*.

In Great Britain, the drastic austerity measures taken to address fiscal stress have likely accelerated the erosion of support for *redistribution to* policies. In the United States, the threat of tax increases has remained elusive due to legislative gridlock and the country's ability to borrow at very low interest rates. This helps explains the importance of fairness reasoning among high-income Americans.

Based on the argument presented in this book, the Covid crisis opens contradictory possibilities. On the one hand, there is little doubt that beneficiaries of *redistribution to* policies are not opportunistic free riders. Yet large levels of public spending have likely triggered concerns over moral hazard. The resulting debt, if it becomes politicized, could erode nascent support for generous and inclusive social transfers and programs among Democrats. In the realm of pre-distribution and taxation policies, stock market rallies and successes of companies such as Amazon raise sharp fairness concerns that echo those heard after World War II against war profiteers (Scheve and Stasavage, 2012). Yet absent entrepreneurial politicians willing to play this populist left-wing card, we are unlikely to witness any sharp change in how people reason about *redistribution from* policies.

Existing Literature and Competing Theories

I am not the first person to emphasize the importance of fairness reasoning. There is, for example, a long line of work examining the role "beliefs in a just world" or perceptions of the origins of poverty (Alesina and La Ferrara, 2002) play in generating support for the status quo (Benabou and Tirole, 2006; Lerner, 1980). Still, these studies cannot account for important stylized facts, most importantly differences between support for *redistribution from* policies and support for *redistribution to* policies. In line with research by Hvidberg, Kreiner and Stantcheva (2020), I find that people most likely to win in the economic "race" are also more likely to find it fair. What this research overlooks is that these same economic winners are also central to redistributive coalitions that support *redistribution to* policies because they believe that this is the fair thing to do.

The part of the argument regarding the mediating role of material self-interest is closely related to work by Rueda and Stegmueller (2019) who argue that, because of declining marginal return to consumption, only the rich have the luxury to reason altruistically. I extend this reasoning in at least two ways. First, instead of altruism, I emphasize the role of fairness reasoning, which might or might not result in altruistic preferences. Indeed, for a subset of the population, retrenchment – and not expansion – is the "fair" policy. Second, I emphasize the role of uncertainty over the personal consequences of redistributive social policies. My argument generates new predictions, unaccounted for by Rueda and Stegmueller, such as why, for some policies (e.g., Earned Income Tax Credits), it is the rich who are divided based on what they believe to be fair, while for other policies (e.g., a wealth tax), it is the poor.

How does my argument compare with previous attempts at explaining the missing left turn? According to one set of contributions, there is no reason to expect higher inequality to translate into higher levels of support for redistribution because voters simply do not behave like rational actors seeking to maximize their own income (Bartels, 2005; Sears and Funk, 1991). In contrast, I show that reality is more nuanced and that material self-interest plays a key role. Other studies have examined how contextual factors, such as residential segregation, shape people's (mis-)perceptions of inequality and their own position in the income distribution (Cruces, Perez-Truglia and Tetaz, 2013; Sands, 2017; Sands and de Kadt, 2020). Such studies assume a very specific distribution of fairness beliefs, one in which the median voter finds the status quo unfair, as defined by the proportionality norm. Only then can one expect correcting people's perceptions of inequality to translate into growing demand for more egalitarian policies. Whether or not a majority perceives income inequality as a violation of the proportionality norm is something to be explained, not assumed.

Studies that connect lower or declining support for redistribution to the presence of poor minority groups suggest an alternative interpretation of the empirical patterns described in this book (Alesina and Glaeser, 2006). According to this line of work, the decline in support for redistribution documented in Great Britain follows from growing hostility toward immigration, which famously culminated in the Brexit vote. From this perspective, differences in reciprocity beliefs are mostly capturing differences in people's hostility to minorities. Throughout the book, I show that this line of reasoning under-delivers both empirically and theoretically. Empirically, a necessary condition for net contributors to withdraw their support for policies that redistribute to the poor is that they perceive immigrants as overrepresented among net beneficiaries. However, there is little correlation between the latter and demand for more or less *redistribution to*. One reason is that the perception that the modal recipient is an immigrant (shared by many) does not imply the belief that immigrants do not deserve to benefit from *redistribution to* policies (most common among moral conservatives). Beyond tautologically arguing that some people are more xenophobic than others, few contributions provide useful tools to unpack why people differ on the latter point. In contrast, the interpretative framework presented in this book helps explain why moral conservative are both less likely to find immigrants deserving and more concerned about moral hazard and free riding in general. In doing so, it unpacks an important overlap between "second dimension" attitudes and redistributive preferences overlooked by existing work. This overlap sheds a new light on the evolution of far-right nativist movements, one that helps unpack the fairness concerns central to these movements' success.

Outline

The rest of this book explains my argument in greater detail and provides empirical support for my claims. In Chapter 2, I define fairness reasoning, explaining what it is and why it matters. In Chapter 3, I flesh out and test fairness reasoning's implications for how researchers conceptualize and measure demand for redistribution broadly speaking. In Chapters 4 and 5, I bring material self-interest back into the picture. Chapter 4 shows that, while proportionality beliefs appear to be self-serving, reciprocity beliefs do not and instead overlap with attitudes and values associated with "second-dimension" preferences. Chapter 5 documents how fairness reasoning and material self-interest combine in predictable ways depending on individual characteristics and policy design. This concludes the book's first part.

Jointly, the chapters in Part I propose a new interpretative framework, selected first by combining knowledge from across the social sciences and second by examining how well this framework fits the data relative to existing interpretative frameworks. The strength of the demonstration hangs on the number of empirical facts better accounted for by one theory over the other.

Part II focuses on explaining patters of stability and change both at the individual and country levels. In Chapter 6, I lay out the framework's implications for changes in mass attitudes toward redistributive policies. I discuss three causal pathways and three related activating factors. One activating factor is fiscal stress, which affects attitudes through a change in the mix of motives. It is discussed in Chapter 7 using the case of France. Another is survey design, which affect observable attitudes through framing effects. The third factor is party competition dynamics, which can affect mass attitudes by changing fairness beliefs. Both are discussed in Chapter 8 with the case of Great Britain and the United States. Chapters 9 and 10 zoom in on individual-level belief change, documenting the role of material self-interest for proportionality beliefs and moral worldviews for reciprocity beliefs.

Empirically, I test the existence of hypothesized individual-level pathways using survey experiments and regression models that leverage within-individual variation. At the country level, I strive to provide plausible accounts of changes in mass social policy preferences in the United States, Great Britain, Germany and France. Plausibility is assessed by leveraging longitudinal data (causal arguments have clear implications for the sequencing of events), qualitative accounts of important critical junctures (e.g., a change in elite discourse following Tony Blair's election) and by addressing alternative explanations (e.g., the role of immigration, discussed in Chapter 6).[12]

Chapter 11 concludes by discussing this book's implications for understanding the public's heterogeneous response to rising income inequality.

Appendix

A1.1 Measuring Income

Great Britain: Measuring Income in the BSAS

BSAS respondents were asked to provide an assessment of household income from all sources by choosing among a list of income brackets. New top income brackets were regularly added throughout the years. First, I transform the income intervals into their common-currency midpoints (e.g., 2,000–3,000 becomes 2,500). Second, for the top category, I use the method recommended by Hout (2004), which imputes an income value that is a function of the number of respondents in the top category and the number of respondents in the bracket that precedes it. This information, combined with a few assumptions regarding the skew of the income distribution, seeks to compensate for underestimating income levels among those with the highest income in the sample. Finally, I multiply the estimate by the GDP deflator available on the Bank of England website and adjust for household size by dividing the resulting amount by the square root of the number of people living in the household. I then divide this

---

[12] The book draws on both small and large-N methodological traditions in political science. For a discussion of how these methodologies combine, see the online appendix available at www.charlottecavaille.com.

income measure into year-specific quintiles. Income trends in the BSAS are similar to those found in Labour Force Surveys: In the BSAS, the gap between the mean bottom quintile household income and the mean top quintile household income has increased from a multiple of 9 in 1986 to a multiple of 15 in 2009.

United States: Measuring Income in the GSS (and ANES)

Given the much sharper rise in inequality in the United States, I need a different empirical strategy than the one recommended by Hout (2004). Following McCarty, Poole and Rosenthal (2008), I use data on the actual distribution of household income to estimate the expected income within each categories in ways that better match the shape of the income distribution in a given year. Indeed, for some income categories, the midpoint might either over- or underestimate the average income of individuals in this category relative to the shape of the income distribution. The computation of these estimates is detailed in McCarty, Poole and Rosenthal (2008) (see the appendix in Chapter 3), and final individual measures were obtained through the program Matlab. This method for approximating income extrapolating from a categorical income variable assumes that the actual income is distributed following a log–normal distribution with a time-varying mean and variance obtained using labor force survey data. After imputing a continuous income measure for each respondent, I multiply this value by the GDP deflator available on the Federal Bank's website. I then adjust for household size following the US Census Bureau's recommendation to assign different weights to adults and children and to allow weights to decrease with each additional adult or child. I divide the resulting income measure into year-specific quintiles. As a robustness check, I also run the analysis using the year specific P20 and P80 measures provided by the Census Bureau to identify people in the top and bottom quintiles.

PART I

Demand for Redistribution: A Conceptual
Framework

2

What Is Fair?

For most citizens, informing oneself about and choosing the policy that aligns with one's own material interest is a demanding task. Only in the rare cases when high-stakes policy reforms have credible implications for a voter's pocketbook, can one reasonably expect such rational and egocentric behavior. If self-interested reasoning is the exception and not the rule, then what is the rule? Among all the possible rules, parsimony requires choosing one among those that matter the most. In this chapter, I make the case for fairness reasoning.

While fairness is a notion intuitively grasped by all, it is not easy to pinpoint what fairness is and what a positive analysis of fairness might look like. In this chapter, I start by defining fairness reasoning in broad functionalist terms, focusing on its role as a social technology that articulates the individual to the collective. I build on work in behavioral economics, anthropology and evolutionary psychology to argue that fairness reasoning is central to social life: It helps placate the centrifugal forces of envy and opportunism and, under the right conditions, fosters social order and cooperation while minimizing coercion (Levi, 1991).

From this general definition, I derive a simple way of conceptualizing and empirically documenting fairness reasoning "in action." A first step is to identify the shared principles people rely on when reasoning about the fairness of redistributive social policies. For this endeavor, experimental studies in social psychology and behavioral economics are particularly helpful: They carefully document the existence of a finite set of consent-inducing allocation principles (*norms of fairness* for short). Within Western democracies, there is quasi-universal agreement on what these norms prescribe. Instead, people differ in their empirical beliefs about the prevalence of norm-violating outcomes and behaviors (*fairness beliefs* for short). Fairness beliefs provide individuals with a proto-ideology through which to interpret the world and pick policies that maximize fairness. A second step in the study of fairness in action is consequently to measure such beliefs using survey data and document how they structure mass attitudes toward redistributive social policies.

The first step – identifying a finite set of fairness norms – is the focus of this chapter. The second step – measuring fairness beliefs – occupies most of Chapter 3.

Fairness Reasoning: An Overview

Humans are a social and cooperative species. "Without the invention of human society," writes Barrington Moore, "Homo Sapiens might well have become extinct long, long ago." The invention of society meant, among other things, the invention of morality. In line with other positivist studies of morality, I define morality in neo-functionalistic terms, that is, as a bundle of norms and behavioral traits "selected" over time for their capacity to suppress or regulate selfishness and make social life (and the goods it generates) possible, while still leaving some breathing space for the individual.[1] Put differently, moral systems are social technologies that help regulate the constant toggle between cooperation and opportunistic behavior characteristic of social life (Levi, 1991; Ostrom and Walker, 2003), ultimately contributing to social and institutional stability (Baumard, 2016; Binmore, 1994; Gintis et al., 2005; Graham, Haidt and Nosek, 2009; Tomasello, 2016). Like dark matter, a moral system cannot be directly observed or quantified. Instead, its presence is inferred from its effects on human behavior.

There are many types of moral systems. In this book, I am interested in moral systems that shape how members of a group cooperate and settle on an *uncontested* allocation of economic goods. These moral systems take the form of a shared commitment to the same principles of fairness alongside a shared understanding of the situations in which these principles can be called upon. Institutional stability implies that enough individuals share the same understanding of what is fair, care about maximizing fairness and share the perception that the status quo is fair according to this definition. When enough individuals share the same understanding of what is fair, care about maximizing fairness and share the perception that the status quo is unfair according to this definition, the likelihood of consensual institutional change increases. Instability and dissensus, in contrast, follow from one of two situations. One is a bimodal distribution of fairness beliefs without any widespread consensus on the fairness

---

[1] This neo-functionalist approach to issues of fairness and morality echoes recent contributions in evolutionary psychology and economics. Morality, in this line of work, is a "solution" to the problem of large-scale cooperation (Curry, Mullins and Whitehouse, 2019).

of the status quo. The other is a situation in which enough individuals in the group hold very different understandings of what is fair. In this latter case, the group's existence as a social entity is itself in question.

Broadly speaking, in the context of redistributive politics, a stable social order is one where there is a widely shared consensus that the solutions brought to two related ideal-typical resource allocation problems are "fair." In this case, the term "solution" describes the bundle of formal institutions and informal practices that constitute the status quo. The first of the two resource allocation problems was famously discussed by Rousseau in the *Discours sur l'Inégalité*. According to Rousseau, in societies built on the division of labor and private property, men envy each other, resenting those who have more or feeling pride knowing that they are envied by those who have less (see also McClendon, 2018). Social order implies the existence of formal and informal institutions that limit the public expression of envy and resentment. In Western liberal democracies, this problem comes with its own specific twist: Differences in material resources need to be reconciled with the normative claim that all members of the group are nevertheless equal in dignity and worth. I consequently call this first resource allocation problem the *inequality-among-equals* problem. The second problem to address is that of the provision by the group of basic material security for its members, lest the group not survive temporary material shocks. I call this ideal-typical problem the *social solidarity* problem. In practice, the social solidarity problem is at least partially solved when the majority of group members are willing *contributors to* the provision of some form of social insurance and do not feel resentment toward net beneficiaries of such resource and risk pooling (Levi, 1991). The existence of a shared understanding of what constitutes fair inequality and fair social solidarity (i.e., shared norms of fairness) helps regulate envy, minimize resentment and promote consensual resource sharing. Social stability is most likely when enough people believe that the status quo aligns with what these shared fairness norms prescribe.[2]

By definition, the existence of order-inducing moral systems implies the existence of a normative and behavioral imperative to abide by and enforce shared norms of fairness (Forst, 2014; Thévenot and Boltanski, 1991). As we will see in this chapter and in the next, there is ample evidence documenting its

---

[2] The fact that a moral system helps foster social order and cooperation does not mean that it is inherently good or that consent is so high that no power is being exercised. The moral system discussed throughout the book could indeed be described as an instance of Lukes' third face of power (Lukes, 2004) in the service of a hegemonic ruling class (Gramsci, Hoare and Smith, 1971). One limit of this latter literature is that it overlooks a degree of pluralism and discretion in how people engage in fairness reasoning. In that regard, I am closer to the work of Thévenot and Boltanski (1991) that highlights areas where fairness "logics" clash, generating space for critical discourse to emerge.

existence. As a shorthand, I call the individual-level manifestation of such imperative *fairness reasoning*. I define fairness reasoning as the thought process through which individuals reason as if a third-party judge ruling on the fairness of a given situation and on fairness-corrective measures.[3] In the following section, I turn to the task of identifying the finite set of widely agreed upon norms of fairness people use when engaging in fairness reasoning. This task first requires a description of the culturally specific and historically situated ways in which the two allocation problems play out in Western democracies.

Fairness Reasoning in Contemporary Western Societies

Social stability and resilient system of social solidarity are signs that a majority finds the existing combination of institutions and policies fair, or at least "fair enough," according to shared norms of fairness. What exactly does "fair" mean in the context of redistributive politics? Or to put it differently, what are the norms of fairness people rely on to justify their support or opposition to policies that address income inequality? Answering these questions first requires better defining the object of fairness reasoning, namely, redistributive policies and the status quo these policies seek to change.

Typology of Redistributive Policies

Governments can affect the distribution of income in a given society through three types of policies: pre-distribution policies, taxation policies and policies that change the design of the welfare state. The first affect how market income is generated and distributed. The second affect how much market income people get to keep. The third affect the extent to which social insurance is redistributive. Examples of the third type of policies include increasing the generosity of means-tested benefits, tweaking the relative mix of earnings-dependent and non–earnings-dependent benefits and expanding the legal definition of who is included in the welfare state. Great Britain's National Health Service (NHS) is one illustration of the redistributive impact of unconditional access: By making health care accessible to all irrespective of past contributions and legal status, the NHS redistributes extensively from the healthy to the sick as well as from the rich to the poor.

---

[3] Fairness reasoning is not alone in helping articulate the self and the group. Other examples include social identity, linked-fate reasoning or socio-tropic reasoning. However, unlike these latter concepts, fairness reasoning has yet to be included in political behavior tool box. This omission is in part due to the difficulty of defining, conceptualizing and operationalizing fairness concerns, an issue I take on in this chapter and in Chapter 3.

Pre-distribution and taxation policies affect the distribution of market income as generated by the "market economy." Policies that shape the extent to which social insurance is redistributive affect the distribution of social transfers provided by the "welfare state." The distinction between market income and the market economy on the one hand, and transfer income and the welfare state on the other, is central to Western democracies' social and political imaginary. Policies that affect market income are shaped by beliefs regarding the extent to which the market economy generates fair outcomes. Policies that make social insurance more redistributive are shaped by beliefs regarding the extent to which the welfare state generates fair outcomes. This dualism has important implications.

Institutional Dualism and Its Implications

A market economy is an "indifferent association, determined solely by personal preference and market capacity," one "open to whoever chooses to come in." In contrast, the welfare state helps people face the socioeconomic costs of their commodification through a resource-pooling endeavor of historically unprecedented scope. While markets are open, resource-pooling endeavors are closed. As a result, meaning and status derived from being a "productive" member of society has at least two distinct sources. One source is an individual's market value made visible to all by one's income. The other is an individual's membership in a group whose members owe each other mutual support. A quote by Walzer (1983) succinctly captures the latter relationship between membership, the welfare state and self-worth:

> Membership is important because of what the members of a political community owe to one another and to no one else, or to no one else in the same degree. And the first thing they owe is the communal provision of (...) welfare. This claim might be reversed: communal provision is important because it teaches us the value of membership. If we did not provide for one another, if we recognized no distinction between members and strangers, we would have no reason to form and maintain political communities. (p. 64)

A second important distinction between the two institutional realms is the famous free rider problem. While a central concern in the context of the welfare state, it is irrelevant to how people interact in a market economy. Indeed, resource pooling constitutes what researchers call a social dilemma, that is, a situation in which the collective interest does not align with the individual interest, thus generating an incentive to free ride. In the case of resource pooling, all members have an individual incentive to take advantage of the shared resource without contributing sufficiently to its maintenance. Contrast this with market institutions, themselves explicitly presented as aligning (and designed to align) the general interest with the individual interest. Writing in the eighteenth century, Adam Smith famously saw market institutions and the selfish pursuit of one's own material interest as liberating: It was a way to extract individuals from an unequal and oppressive web of interdependence and reciprocal rights and duties. Today, one might say that it is the market economy that, in the common imaginary, has successfully extracted itself from the web of interdependence and reciprocal rights and duties that define social solidarity. Put differently, the market economy has been expunged from the social solidarity problem; only the inequality-among-equals problem remains.[4]

As a result, the manufacturing of consent is achieved very differently depending on the institutional realm under consideration. In the market economy, mass consent implies the shared agreement that the status quo abides by what the *proportionality norm* prescribes, namely that rewards be proportional to merit, itself a combination of personal decisions as a free agent, individual work ethic, acquired skills and innate talent. Milton Friedman himself emphasized its centrality to the market economy's system of justification: "payment in accordance to product," he writes, is part of the "basic core of value judgments that are unthinkingly accepted by the great bulk of [a society's] members" and enables "resources to be allocated efficiently without compulsion" (p. 167). Yet, as argued earlier, people's experiences is two-faceted: What they experience as actors in the market economy is separate from what they experience as stakeholders in a resource-pooling effort embodied in the welfare state. This suggests the existence of a second norm, the *reciprocity norm*, which prescribes that all members of a group contribute to the collective effort and that free riding does not go unpunished.

Institutional dualism and normative pluralism thus have important implications for fairness reasoning and mass attitudes toward redistributive policies. On the one hand, policies that affect market income are by and large shaped by beliefs regarding the latter's fairness as defined by the proportionality norm (e.g., is market income roughly proportional to talent and effort or not?). On

---

[4] The market economy's existence as an autonomous institutional sphere separate from the welfare state and expunged of social solidarity concerns is partly reality, partly shared myth. Similarly, the claim that pre-distribution and taxation policies "interfere" (whether for good or bad reasons depending on one's political leanings) with the "natural" functioning of markets is a cultural construct (Vogel, 2018). Given that I am interested in people's beliefs about the status quo, whether or not this description of the status quo is true is irrelevant; what matters is that people share this representation of the world. Policy leaders have repeatedly sought to redefine markets in ways that emphasize social solidarity. One example is Obama's controversial "you did not build that" speech where he stated that economic entrepreneurs succeed as a result of others' help and work, partly through the government. The backlash was strong and immediate. See page 50 for a discussion of more successful instances.

the other hand, policies that affect the welfare state are by and large shaped by beliefs regarding its fairness as defined by the reciprocity norm (e.g., are net beneficiaries of social transfers mostly undeserving free riders or not?). For some people, both types of beliefs align to support pro- (or anti-)redistribution policies in both institutional spheres: Someone who believes that effort pays (i.e., the rich deserve their higher income) can also believe that net recipients of social transfers are undeserving free riders who could be self-reliant if they "really tried."[5]

However, the extent to which proportionality and reciprocity beliefs align is an outcome to explain, not something to assume a priori. To reiterate, while welfare states are constructed as *collective* resource-pooling endeavors among citizens of the same country, market economies are morally construed as an *individual* race; while welfare states imply group boundaries and interdependence, market economies do not. As will become clear later in the book, how people reason in a context in which interdependence and group boundaries are salient is very different from a context in which these are absent, resulting in a disconnect between proportionality and reciprocity beliefs. Simply put, believing that the status quo is fair according to one norm need not imply believing that the status quo is fair according to the other.

The distinction between deviations from what the proportionality norm prescribes for a fair distribution of market income on the one hand, and deviations from what the reciprocity norm prescribes for the fair distribution of social transfers on the other, is partly obscured by the generic terms available to discuss the fairness of a given situation and relatedly the fairness of the status quo. Specifically, two different outcomes can be similarly judged as fair (or unfair) despite the fact that each outcome calls to mind a different norm of fairness. Relatedly, the same concept of desert or deservingness can apply to very different fairness judgments (see Figure 2.1). As a result, researchers seeking to study fairness in action need to choose their words carefully.

---

[5] To further illustrate the importance of this dualism, a brief detour through private insurance can be illustrative. When assessing what counts as a "fair" premium, insurers can appeal to "actuarial fairness," that is, the principle according to which customers bearing high risks are charged higher premiums. Another principle is "solidaristic fairness," where "money from those lucky enough to avoid misfortune helps cover the costs of those unlucky enough to have to submit claims" (Kiviat, 2019). In the case of solidaristic fairness, the "fair" outcome is one in which high-risk individuals subsidize low-risk individuals, assuming the latter are truly "unlucky," meaning they have little control over the risk they face. In the case of actuarial fairness, such transfers are deemed "unfair" because they do not reflect the underlying risk distribution. With private insurance, private insurance, the two norms are in direct conflict. With redistribution, the distinction between the market economy and the welfare state means that they tend to affect distinct status quo policies, with implications for how people reason about redistirbution broadly defined.

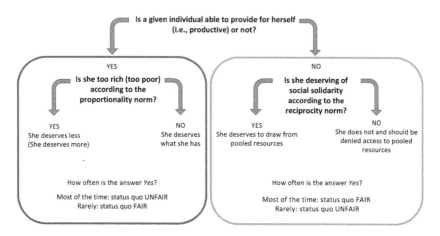

Figure 2.1 What is fair? Who is deserving?

In the remainder of this chapter, I review evidence in support of my argument. Specifically, I review studies that document the existence of a consent-inducing imperative to behave fairly as defined by the proportionality and reciprocity norms. While people agree on the two norms (what ought to be) they disagree over the extent to which the status quo conforms to what these two norms prescribe (what is). This implies that individuals hold different empirical beliefs regarding the nature of the status quo. The latter point will be examined in more detail in Chapters 3 and 4.

Norms of Fairness: Evidence

When reviewing the evidence, I focus on studies that document the existence of a *finite* set of norms understood in the *same* way by all involved and *behaviorally consequential* for all involved. Empirically, this implies two types of evidence: one documenting universal agreement over a given normative principle (Bicchieri, 2016) and the other documenting the absence of competing norms beyond the identified set.

Ethnographic studies, in which thick description helps explicate the reasoning behind actors' actions, have played a key role in documenting the importance of fairness reasoning. Yet such a research strategy suffers from the usual concerns about competing motives beyond fairness maximization, including material self-interest, or group-specific concerns (e.g., parochial altruims). Furthermore, these empirical strategies do not tell us if people are using the same, behaviorally constraining fairness *norms*, or merely that they are using the same fairness rhetoric.

Experimental methods in a controlled setting provide one solution. To understand how this works, one can think of a norm as a mathematical function: the output (Y) varies with the input (X) in predictable ways $(f(X) = Y)$. To study the norm $(f(X))$, researchers can rely on two main research strategies. One is to vary X experimentally and examine whether this change affects Y in systematic ways. This gives researchers information on the content of the norm as understood by all participants. Another strategy is to maximize or minimize the differences in how people understand the features of a given situation (X) and see how it affects the variance in Y. If all share the same X and apply the same norm $f(X)$, then they should all agree, resulting in a Y with a very small variance. Conversely, disagreement over X will be reflected in disagreement over Y.

There is by now a large literature across the social sciences that implements these strategies. Below, I review the most important studies, focusing first on the proportionality norm and then on the reciprocity norm. The same studies also show that emphasizing only these two norms covers a lot of ground: Relative to the proportionality and reciprocity norm, other distributive principles (e.g., equality or need) take a back seat.

What Constitutes Fair Inequality Among Equals? The Proportionality Norm

Aristotle famously provided the first known explication of the proportionality principle. According to Aristotle, for an unequal division of resources to be fair, individual rewards and punishments have to be proportional to individual contributions to good or bad outcomes.[6] Any division of resources that is not proportional to individual contributions is unfair based on this principle. In the context of a market economy, an individual contribution is any factor that (1) can be attributed to the decisions and actions of a given individual and (2) increases the market value of tradable goods and services. These factors include, effort, talent, skills and individual bets on the future such as saving and investment decisions (or failure to make such bets). There are two main sources of inequality in this framework: differences in individual contributions, assuming all have the same opportunity to make a value-increasing decision, and

---

[6] To follow up on the comparison with premium pricing in footnote 5, Aristotle was arguing for actuarial fairness, not solidaristic fairness, that is, reciprocity.

differences in the opportunity to make such value-increasing decisions (Almås et al., 2010; Cappelen et al., 2007, 2013; Konow, 2003). Most people find the former source of inequality fair and the latter unfair in line with the proportionality norm (Frohlich, Oppenheimer and Kurki, 2004; List, 2007; Miller and Komorita, 1995; Oxoby and Spraggon, 2008). This general pattern has been documented experimentally in many different contexts and with different types of individual contributions.

A stylized laboratory game called the Ultimatum Game (UG) provides strong evidence of the importance of the proportionality norm for manufacturing consent. The UG, first developed by Güth, Schmittberger and Schwarze (1982), is a two-player two-stage game, with a Proposer and a Responder. In its *baseline* form, the game proceeds as follows: the Proposer offers a division of a fixed sum to an anonymous Responder who then accepts or rejects the offer. If the Responder accepts, the sum is divided as originally proposed. If the Responder rejects, both players receive nothing. An income-maximizing Proposer should always offer the minimum amount and the Responder should always accept (lest they walk away with nothing). In practice, the Proposer offers on average a 60–40 split, and the Responder rejects half of the offers that are below an 80–20 split. In the *earned* variant of the UG, the Proposer has either earned the fixed sum to split with the Responder through her own effort or, in some designs, has earned the right to be the Proposer instead of the Responder. These studies return one consistent result: Proposers offer significantly less than the usual 40%, and Responders' rejection rates are much lower (Andersen et al., 2011; Levitt and List, 2007).

Differences between the *baseline* and *earned* conditions conform with the hypothesized existence of a norm according to which rewards should be proportional to merit. In the *baseline* condition, the fair thing to do is a 50/50 split, as none of the two players have earned the right to get more. One way to interpret the Proposer's modal 60/40 split is to conceptualize her decision as follow: She first starts with what the norm prescribes (50/50) and then, from this baseline, tries to maximize her payoff within the constraints set by the norm. Under the assumption of a shared norm, a rational actor seeking to maximize her payoff will pick something higher than 50, but not too high in order to avoid having the Responder enforce the norm by rejecting an offer that deviates too much from it.[7] In the *earned* condition, one player has worked for the right to have

---

[7] Early research has interpreted the convergence to something close to a 50/50 split as evidence of an equality norm. Instead, I follow Konow, Saijo and Akai (2008) in interpreting this evidence as merely the implementation of the proportionality norm in a context in which nobody deserve to receive more (or less) given that no effort was exerted and no individual decisions made.

more: The fair baseline split is an unequal split, with more rewards going to the most productive individual. Because both players abide by a similar fairness norm, the Proposer knows that she can be more selfish and yet avoid punishment. Indeed, no shared norms of fairness are broken when she does so, and the party with less has no reason to dissent: The outcome is fair. Overall, the existence of a shared proportionality norm, the knowledge that this norm is shared by all parties and the expectation that outcomes that deviate from what this norm prescribes will be met with discontent, best explains results from UGs (Bicchieri, 2005).

These experiments have been repeated across many Western societies, creating a patchwork of evidence for the existence of the proportionality norm as an order-inducing form of fairness reasoning that helps members of a group agree on a given resource allocation. As of this writing, the research community still lacks a comprehensive study that would assess the existence of the proportionality norm across a large sample of Western societies. Cross-national surveys provide a useful, albeit imperfect, substitute. If the proportionality norm is widely shared across postindustrial democracies, items that measure agreement with a statement in line with what the norm prescribes should receive overwhelming support. The closest available survey item that directly measures agreement with the proportionality norm is an item from the World Values Survey (WVS, waves 1–5) worded as follows:

> Imagine two secretaries, of the same age, doing practically the same job. One finds out that the other earns considerably more than she does. The better paid secretary, however, is quicker, more efficient and more reliable at her job. In your opinion, is it fair or not fair that one secretary is paid more than the other? (WVS, waves 1–5)

This question holds constant attributes one is not responsible for (age, tasks being given to accomplish) and only varies factors one has control over (i.e., effort). In all countries, more than four out of five respondents find it fair that one secretary is paid more than the other. Relatedly, the 2018 wave of the European Social Survey (ESS) asked respondents whether they agreed with the statement that a "society is fair when hard-working people earn more than others." On average, over 80% of respondents agree with this statement, with a high of 92% in Austria and a low of 70% in the Czech Republic.

A comparative study by Almås, Cappelen and Tungodden (2020) is also very informative. It presents two groups of respondents, one American and one Norwegian (both groups representative of the overall population),[8] with the same unequal outcome. This unequal outcome takes the form of a pair of real-life individuals (recruited on M-Turk) with unequal earnings. Participants in

---

[8] See also Konow, Saijo and Akai (2008) for evidence in Japan and the United States.

both countries were asked whether they wanted to redistribute income between the two individuals and, if so, how. Researchers experimentally varied the reason why earnings were unequally distributed across the two individuals. In one condition, which they call the *merit* condition, earnings were unequal because workers differed in productivity. In this case, the more productive individual got six dollars and the least productive zero dollars. In another condition, the *luck* condition, earnings were different as a result of the luck of the draw. In this case, the lucky winner got six dollars and the loser got nothing. The respondents had the option to leave the division of resources as such (6–0) or redistribute in one-dollar increments. This design ensures that American and Norwegian respondents hold the same priors regarding the causes of the difference in earnings. Assuming the same priors (X) and the same norm of fairness ($f(X)$), this should imply the same response (Y) in both countries.

When luck explained differences in earnings, an overwhelmingly majority of respondents chose some amount of redistribution, with 54% choosing to equalize incomes (3–3) in the United States and 78% choosing to do so in Norway. In the *merit* condition, the share of individuals who equalized dropped by about 40 percentage points in both countries, with the modal response being the 4–2 split (the most productive gets twice the amount received by the least productive). These results indicate that respondents in both countries contributed, through their actions, to implementing a distribution of resources roughly proportional to the work contributions. Against claims of American exceptionalism, a large majority of American respondents implemented some redistribution and more than half implemented full equality in the *luck* condition.

While reliance on the proportionality norm is widespread in both countries, there are still notable differences. In the *luck* condition, a smaller share of American respondents chose to equalize outcomes, despite inequality having little to do with differences in productivity. Similarly, in the *merit* condition, a larger share of Norwegians still chose the equal split despite differences in productivity. Could it be that Norwegians and Americans are relying on other country-specific norms beyond the proportionality norm? I turn to this issue next.

In Search of Competing Allocation Principles

While the conceptualization of fairness reasoning presented in this chapter does not imply the absence of competing allocation principles, it does elevate the proportionality principle to the status of dominant behaviorally binding norm. How reasonable is this assumption? The literature has identified a subset of competing allocation principles that could matter alongside proportionality. One is the equality norm ("if any difference, then equalize"). Differences between Norway and the United States could thus be due to Norwegians putting more weight on a norm of equality, explaining why a higher share chooses an equal split even in the *merit* condition.

Recent evidence suggests this is not the case. In a follow-up study, Cappelen et al. (2017) use neuroimaging data to show that, even among Norwegian respondents, the proportionality norm remains in the driver seat. They find that while deviations from a proportional income distribution generate strong reactions as measured by brain activity, deviations from an equal income distribution do not. The authors conclude that "concerns for outcome equality is of relatively little importance in situations in which income has been earned through work effort." They emphasize that these results are "particularly striking" since respondents are from "a Scandinavian country that is among the most egalitarian countries in the world."

More generally, even if some individuals seek to follow the equality principle, they are likely to be a small minority, undermining the equality principle's ability to manufacture consent. In 1991, the International Social Justice Project asked respondents in a small number of Western and Eastern European countries their attitudes toward the proportionality and equality principles. In all countries, around 90% of respondents agreed with the following statement, "(p)eople who work hard deserve to earn more than those who do not." Relatedly, about 80% agreed that "(i)t is fair if people have more money or wealth, but only if there are equal opportunities." In contrast, less than 20% on average agreed that "(t)he fairest way of distributing wealth and income would be to give everyone equal shares."

The 2018 wave of the ESS also included an item asking about fairness and equality. Respondents were asked whether they agreed with the following statement: "(a) society is fair when income and wealth are equally distributed among all people." In that case, close to half of respondents in the survey agreed, with a high of 72% in Slovenia and a low of 24% in Estonia. Yet, as Figure 2.2 illustrates, countries where agreement is high are also countries where a large share of the population believes that the education system and the job market are unfair, as defined by the proportionality norm. In other words, in these countries, most people hold beliefs that lead them to assess the status quo as unfair according to the proportionality norm. It is thus very likely that respondents who agree with the equality claim are not expressing support for a competing norm but merely expressing their belief that, given that income differences are unfair according to the proportionality norm, the only fair outcome, also according to the proportionality norm, is an equal distribution of income.

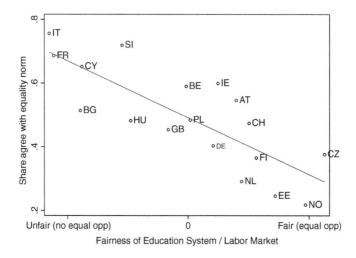

Figure 2.2 Agreement with equality norm and proportionality beliefs
Plots average agreement with the equality norm against average equal opportunity
beliefs. X-axis: mean of sum of two combined items (Cronbach's alpha: 0.77);
"(o)verall, everyone in [country] has a fair chance of achieving the level of education they seek" and "(o)verall, everyone in [country] has a fair chance of getting the
jobs they seek." Answers were recorded using a 0 [this statement does not apply at
all to country] to 10 [applies completely] scale. Y-axis: % respondents who agree
that "A society is fair when income and wealth are equally distributed among all
people." Answers recorded using a strongly agree (1) - strongly disagree (5) Likert
scale. In this figure, "strongly agree" and "agree" responses are combined.
Source: ESS 2018, weighted.

Let's now turn to the higher propensity for Americans to choose not to redistribute in the *luck* condition, despite the absence of differences in work contributions. This difference suggests that American respondents are less likely than
Norwegians to act to correct inequalities due to luck. Does this suggest the existence of a competing norm for fairness? My own reading of the evidence is that
the difference lies in how a random, but positive, outcome is interpreted. For
Norwegian, it is undeserved because unrelated to a decision to exert effort or to
skills. For Americans, given that all, in expectation could have been among the
"lucky" winners, such random positive outcome is not undeserved. According
to this logic, in expectation, the allocation is equal and thus fair. Compensating
the losers in the lottery would mean unfairly punishing the winners in an "equal
opportunity" race. Assuming this interpretation is correct, it points to possible
cultural differences within Western democracies in how individuals *apply* the
proportionality norm, especially when faced with a random outcome. Research

is required to better understand why such differences exist and with what consequences. For the purpose of this book, I will focus on the similarities (i.e., reliance on the proportionality norm is widespread in both countries) and leave the differences to follow-up research.

One last competing allocation principle often mentioned in the literature is efficiency. Evidence repeatedly shows that proportionality concerns are much more important than efficiency considerations (Almås, Cappelen and Tungodden, 2020; Durante, Putterman and Van der Weele, 2014). Most importantly, a closer look at the manifestation of the efficiency norm in public debates indicates that it is, by construct, subordinated to the proportionality norm. Indeed, one of the reasons invoked to explain why redistribution risks decreasing the "size of the pie" is that it can demotivate high achievers. This implicitly assumes that high income reflects higher levels of effort. In other words, anyone who explicitly expresses efficiency concerns is implicitly assuming that the status quo is fair as prescribed by the proportionality norm. Economists, in that regard, are not neutral proponents of efficient decentralized modes of coordination. Their work builds on deeply held beliefs about the latter's fairness.

The evidence reviewed in this section examines how individuals behave in situations where material rewards are unequally distributed. Taken jointly, results show that the proportionality norm is widely agreed upon by all, behaviorally consequential and faces limited competition from alternative allocation principles.

Unfair allocations are not limited to inequality-among-equals situations in which outcomes are unrelated to individual decisions. Another example is a situation in which social solidarity, that is, the pooling of resources to help individuals who can no longer provide for themselves, is plagued by free riding. Free riders are violating the reciprocity norm: the principle according to which prosocial behavior should be reciprocated in kind. In the following section, I review the evidence in support of the reciprocity norm as a universally shared and behaviorally relevant norm of fairness that helps manufacture consent, specifically the consensual provision of generous and redistributive social insurance.

What Constitutes Fair Resource Sharing? The Reciprocity Norm

Numerous studies have documented the importance of the reciprocity norm when people are engaged in joint cooperative endeavors (Axelrod, 1980; Ostrom and Walker, 2003). This norm is both simple to describe and surprisingly difficult to theorize. Simply stated, the norm turns people into conditional cooperators. People willingly contribute to a collective endeavor if they feel others are not free riding (positive reciprocity). They punish free riders by either ceasing to cooperate or by excluding them from accessing the goods generated by cooperation (negative reciprocity). Behavior attached to the reciprocity norm is thus inherently two-faceted and can be presented in one of two lights. The more positive light casts it as a form of conditional altruism: People's default position is to help others unless others are "antisocial" (Fong, Bowles and Gintis, 2006; Henrich et al., 2001). Viewed in a negative light, it is a form of conditional punishment: People's default position is to deny help to others unless they are prosocial.

Researchers have argued that the reciprocity norm is a powerful cooperation-inducing social technology: It helps solve the previously mentioned social solidarity problem by turning all group members into willing cooperators, despite the incentive to free ride (Berg, Dickhaut and McCabe, 1995; Falk, Fehr and Fischbacher, 2003). To unpack the relationship between the reciprocity norm and this cooperative equilibrium, behavioral economists rely on an ideal-typical game called the public goods game (PGG) (Bechtel and Scheve, 2014; Fehr and Gächter, 2000; Fischbacher, Gächter and Fehr, 2001; Ostrom and Walker, 2003). In this setup, participants independently (and privately) choose how many of their private tokens to put into a public pot. The collectively pooled tokens are multiplied by a fixed factor and then divided among players. Each subject gets to keep the tokens they do not contribute on top of their cut of the common pot. The multiplying factor is chosen to create a tension between collective interest and self-interest. On the one hand, the group's total payoff is maximized when everyone contributes all of their tokens to the public pot. On the other hand, each player could walk away contributing nothing (keeping their tokens) while still receiving their share of the collective pot. Ultimately, each player faces the same dilemma: Contributing more tokens is only beneficial if others are also contributing, but the more others contribute, the more beneficial it is to contribute zero tokens and "free ride" on others' contributions.

Results from studies with repeated iterations of the PGG show that, left to their own devices, individuals start by contributing a share of their tokens, but ultimately, end up contributing nothing. Detailed follow-up studies suggest a specific sequence of events. First, a significant share of players start with optimistic priors about what others will do (i.e., contribute) and consequently contribute tokens. Yet, after several rounds, having observed that not all players contribute and/or many players contribute only small amounts, players update their priors in a more pessimistic direction. Over multiple iterations, the final result is that nobody contributes to the common pot.[9] What the PGG captures is the group's joint failure to solve the tension between individual and collective interest.

A striking finding coming from this line of work is that under specific conditions, the exact opposite outcome occurs and the group converges to full cooperation, with everyone donating all of their tokens. These conditions include information on prior contributions, the ability to communicate and, most importantly, the ability to punish beyond simply refusing to cooperate. In most designs, the option to punish implies taking tokens away from someone who has not behaved in a reciprocal fashion, that is, someone who has contributed less than others. In some studies, this punishment also comes at a personal cost, with individual players having to give up some of their own tokens to have the option to punish players who did not contribute. With punishment, cooperation is much more likely to emerge. This happens through a four-step process. First, cooperation is jump-started by a group of "altruistic" individuals willing to take the risk of assuming that others will cooperate. Second, the introduction of punishment limits the share of individuals who decide to free ride in the first place and increases the share of individuals who believe that others will cooperate. Third, with punishment, a subset of individuals (which may or may not include the "altruistic" optimists in round one) pays the price of punishing people who free ride, forcing this latter group to change their behavior. Fourth, after punishment is observed, it leads more players to update their priors about the relative share of cooperators and free riders. Core to this dynamic is the existence of individuals willing to punish even if at their own expense, resulting in the shared expectations that free riding will not go unpunished.

Jointly, these results highlight the existence of a norm, particularly relevant to situations of mutual help and interdependence, that makes people react negatively to free riding and positively to prosocial behavior, and to expect others to do the same. As third-party judges seeking to enforce this norm, people will behave in ways that punish free riders and reward prosocial individuals.

To the extent that social insurance can be characterized as mutual assistance and resource pooling on an unprecedented scale, one can expect the reciprocity norm to be on people's minds when reasoning about social insurance. The best evidence comes from the literature on welfare and deservingness that

---

[9] Interestingly, evidence shows that the mismatch between expectations and actual contributions is due to actors hedging their bets: They would be willing to contribute large sums but, absent certainty that others will contribute the same amount, they ultimately decrease their exposure to loss by contributing a smaller amount. This "play-it-safe" strategy is what ultimately undermines the whole collective endeavor with each actor ending up seeming less cooperative than they actually are (Fischbacher and Gachter, 2010).

documents a baseline willingness to help those in need, conditional on evidence that a needy recipient is not a free rider. How do people know someone is a free rider? Assessments are particularly sensitive to what is known about an individual's choice set (constrained or not), agency (is one's behavior a conscious decision or not) and intentions (are they intentionally free riding) (Akbaş, Ariely and Yuksel, 2019; Fehr and Schmidt, 2006; Meier, 2007). Evidence that someone had the option to be self-reliant and did not take it is used to deny help, especially if this decision is understood as intentional. Jointly, this suggests that people are willing to engage in resource sharing if and only if it does not reward someone trying to "take advantage" of this willingness to help.

The cues most often used to detect free riding is information on job options, work effort and overall labor force attachment (Kootstra, 2016; Sniderman et al., 2014). In most countries with large welfare states, having a job is the best way to avoid being in need. In addition, given that this insurance component of the welfare state often relies heavily on the taxation of labor income (Kato, 2003), not working means both needing help and not contributing to resource sharing. The reasons for one's unemployed status are consequently up for scrutiny. Jobless but able-bodied individuals – who could in theory be working – raise the most suspicion. For example, Sniderman et al. (2014) show that negative assessments of immigrants in Denmark are tied to stereotypes about a group's time spent working: Least deserving are Muslim housewives who are perceived to draw more than they contribute due to their weak labor market attachment.

At first sight, the emphasis on work effort and earned income suggests an overlap between the reciprocity norm and the proportionality norm. Both rely on individual actions observed in the economic realm as inputs X into the fairness function $f(X)$. Specifically, individual effort in the economic realm is used sometimes as a numeraire to judge the amount of resources one should hold relative to another (proportionality norm) and other times as a cue to judge how secure one's access to shared resources is (reciprocity norm). Yet, because of institutional dualism and norm pluralism, the same Xs can lead to very different fairness judgments. Take, for example, the case of first-generation immigrants. As hardworking individuals, they are often perceived to be deserving of higher market incomes; yet, as low-skill economic migrants, they are also perceived as welfare shopper undeserving of means-tested social benefits. This difference follows from the fact that reasoning about the welfare state primes people to think about group boundaries and free riding, while reasoning about the market economy does not. Relatedly, what looks like the same X actually conveys very different information depending on the norm being used. For example, it might be fair, based on the reciprocity principle, to help a hardworking individual who is unemployed due to no fault of her own. This does not necessarily imply that it would also be fair to increase her wage (relative to others) when employed. Put differently, that she was fired due to a recession says nothing about the fairness of her wage, given her skill level, when employed.

As with the proportionality norm, systematic comparative studies documenting the relevant of the reciprocity norms across all postindustrial democracies are unavailable. One exception is a recent set of studies by Michael Bang Petersen and coauthors that experimentally show that the reciprocity norm is important in two most different cases, namely the United States and Denmark. Petersen et al. (2012) randomly assign representative samples of American and Danish respondents to one of three treatment conditions. All respondents are presented with a male welfare recipient and then asked: "To what extent do you disagree or agree that the eligibility requirements for social welfare should be tightened for persons like him?" In one treatment, no cues are provided about the recipient's labor market attachment and effort. In another treatment condition, respondents are told that he "never had a regular job" and that while "he is fit and healthy," he is not "motivated to get a job." In a third treatment condition, respondents are told that the recipient "always had a regular job" but was affected by a "work-related injury" and is "motivated to get back to work again." Assuming individuals in both countries reason in similar ways based on the reciprocity norm, there should be little to no difference in how respondents treat the deserving recipient relative to the undeserving one. Indeed, as the authors write, "despite decades of exposure to different cultures and welfare institutions, two sentences of information (...) make welfare support across the U.S. and Scandinavian samples substantially and statistically indistinguishable." One implication is that the well-known differences between the two countries stem less from differences in willingness to punish free riders in line with reciprocity than from differences in the beliefs that free riding is ubiquitous among net beneficiaries of social insurance. I come back to this issue in the next chapter.

In Search of Competing Allocation Principles

The last claim in need of examination is whether or not the reciprocity norm crowds out other competing allocation principles. One competing principle is need, which states that a fair outcome is one where the neediest gets access to shared resources first.[10] Overall, most decisions to allocate resources based on need appear implicitly or explicitly tied to evaluations of the *reasons* for need, that is, someone's deservingness as defined by the reciprocity norm (Skitka and Tetlock, 1993). Furthermore, while need might overrule deservingness when deciding to help a *specific* individual, one can reasonably expect need to take a back seat when reasoning at the group level. This does not imply that need plays no role: It most likely explains why, even in the least generous social system, there is always a residual system that enables survival.[11] To the extent that this book is interested in inequality and redistribution, my focus is not on the existence of such a residual net, but the extent to which voters are willing to increase its generosity and/or include recipients into the more generous social insurance programs that cover the majority of the population. This is when the reciprocity norm and, as a result, beliefs about the prevalence of free riding matter the most.

Given the importance of membership for the reciprocity norm, a second possible candidate among competing allocation principle relates to what researchers call parochial altruism. According to this principle, a fair outcome is one where only group members get benefits, while nonmembers are excluded. In practice, people advocating for the exclusion of outsiders from accessing benefits frame their concerns in reference to the reciprocity norm: Immigrants do not deserve benefits because they are "welfare shoppers," African Americans do not deserve welfare because they are "lazy" (Gilens, 1999). In other words, xenophobia and out-group still need to be justified meaning that the reciprocity norm both enables the expression of parochial altruism and constrains it. This suggests that parochial altruism is a key input in the formation of reciprocity beliefs: People with a dislike for seeing outsiders treated as if insiders will perceive the status quo as unfairly benefiting "free riding" others. I will discuss this issue at length in the chapters on the nature and origin of fairness beliefs (see Chapters 6 and 10 in particular) and consequently refrain from doing so here. It is enough for now to point out that parochial altruism does not constitute a competing norm; instead, it finds its rhetorical expression through the reciprocity norm.

The evidence reviewed in this section describes how individuals behave when having to cooperate to provide resources to those who cannot provide for themselves while minimizing incentives to free ride (the social solidarity problem). Taken jointly, results show that the reciprocity norm is widely

---

[10] For example, 75% of ESS (2018) respondents agree with the claim that "A society is fair when it takes care of those who are poor and in need regardless of what they give back to society."

[11] For an extensive discussion of the role of need in providing charity as a large scale in the nineteenth-century Europe, see Ewald (2014, book 1, chap 3).

shared and behaviorally consequential. In the context of redistributive politics, it crowds out other allocation principles.

Beyond Western Postindustrial Democracies

How universal is the definition of fairness reasoning provided in this chapter? There is tentative evidence indicating that the proportionality norm might be specific to Western market-based societies. Indeed, a recent study of children in Western and non-Western societies found that "while children from a modern Western society distributed the spoils of a joint enterprise precisely in proportion to productivity, children from a gerontocratic pastoralist society in Africa did not take merit into account at all." The authors go on to conclude that "the results suggest that some basic notions of distributive justice," such as the proportionality norm, "are not universal intuitions of the human species but rather culturally constructed behavioral norms." More intuitively, the overlap between the proportionality norm and market ideology is so extensive that one need not probe much to hypothesize that the proportionality norm is the moral DNA of Western market economies.[12]

An emerging consensus among social scientists is that the reciprocity norm is itself rooted in a more fundamental tit-for-tat behavior deeply ingrained in the human psyche (Axelrod and Dion, 1988). This line of research has identified the proximate psychological mechanisms that make such a tit-for-tat dynamic possible. Among these mechanisms are the capacity to grasp interdependence and reason as a collective "we" (Ostrom, 1998; Tomasello and Vaish, 2013). This fundamental form of sociotropic reasoning is required if individuals are to develop an intuitive grasp of the collective dilemma they face as a group (Baumard, 2016; Gintis, 2016). It also provides the basis for prosocial behaviors such as the famous "sense of duty" used to explain, for example, why people vote despite there being no direct benefits to the self. An abundant literature on trust (see Ostrom and Walker (2003) for a review) also finds that people have an intuitive understanding of moral hazard and are attentive to cues signaling whether or not one is being taken advantage of.

Still, assuming that the basic structure of the reciprocity norm is common to most cultures, its exact embodiment is likely to be culture specific. In other words, perceptions of "who is carrying their (fair) weight and who isn't" will follow culture-specific cues, suggesting some amount of variation also within Western democracies (e.g., more racialized cues in the United States than in

---

[12] Extending some of the studies to China, with a "meritocratic" educational system anchored in the proportionality norm, seems like a fruitful avenue for future research.

Europe). While evidence shows that some version of the reciprocity norm exists in most societies, the particular version discussed in this book is likely limited to countries with an expansive and relatively generous welfare state.

Institutional Dualism and Norms of Fairness over Time

How time invariant is the definition of fairness reasoning provided in this chapter? Are there alternative ways in which allocation institutions and norms of fairness might have combined in the past and might combine in the future? Scheve and Stasavage (2016) describe an instance in which the fairness of the market economy was assessed not only in reference to the proportionality norm but also in reference to the reciprocity norm. Total warfare, they argue, faces a free rider problem: Citizens' individual interest is to defect at the expense of the collective. In line with the reciprocity principle, their willingness to contribute their blood to the war effort is conditional on the belief that everyone is engaged in a similar sacrifice, that is, nobody is free riding (Levi, 1991). In such a context, large economic profits are perceived to violate the reciprocity norm: They reflect an actor's selfish economic gains at the expense of the collective (ultimate) sacrifice. In other words, during total warfare, the economic race is put on hold and economic production becomes another "front." According to Scheve and Stavasage, the ability to frame high-income earners as war profiteers who violate the reciprocity norm helps explain why some countries were able to introduce wealth taxation while others were not.

Relatedly, the reciprocity norm used to be much more salient in the economic realm in the 1960s and 1970s. Following WWII, wage labor became the norm. At the same time, long-term reconstruction and growth plans under the leadership of a powerful state turned workers into a distinct class of stakeholders (Przeworski and Sprague, 1986). Economic output was partly understood as a public good resulting from large-scale cooperation at the firm and country levels, under the coordinating power of the state and economic corporatism.[13] The organization of labor at the firm level was also different in that period. Wage-setting practices were often similar to those found in state bureaucracies: They underweighted individual factors such as productivity in favor of collective understanding of worth, such as seniority or a given occupation's centrality to economic production (Castel, 1995).[14] Over the past three

---

[13] These national-level cooperative compromises are well known to students of postwar capitalism.

[14] This institutional set up would ultimately lead Galbraith to develop his concept of "technostructure," in which managers co-opted labor against the interests of shareholders, with

decades, political and economic elites have shifted the emphasis from cooperation to competition: Growth models are now built on the principle that growth is at the intensive margin and that markets are much better at doing this than states and centralized collective bargaining. Governments thus endeavor to build institutional environments where these market mechanisms can unleash their full potential. This, in a nutshell, is the mandate of the European Union. The legitimacy of this "pro-market" shift is rooted in the belief that markets are fair as defined by the proportionality norm (if one is of right-wing leaning) or that they can be made fair with the state's help (if one is of social democrat leaning). Policymakers across the political spectrum have committed themselves to the proportionality norm at the expense of the types of reciprocity concerns that used to characterize previous growth strategies.

The "neoliberal" turn, often portrayed as a swing back toward "markets against society" Polanyi (1944), is consequently better described as "society in support of *fair* markets." This latter expression helps capture a form of discourse and policies according to which regulations, taxes and transfers are justified as ways to bring economic institutions closer to what is prescribed by the proportionality norm, namely a distribution of economic resources truly proportional to individual merit, instead of one based on the cooperation of different classes of stakeholders. Changes at the firm level have been especially dramatic. Merit-based pay is now the standard. Workplaces have "fissured" (Card, Heining and Kline, 2013; Weil, 2014), moving closer to Ronald Coase's ideal-typical example of smaller units trading bilaterally through contracts on a market. Large corporations have shed their role as direct employers of the people responsible for their products and services, in favor of outsourcing. The gig economy is the most recent stage in this development. These changes imply the concomitant retreat of reciprocity concerns and a renewed investment in the proportionality norm. One implication is the retreat of a type of critical discourse emphasizing labor's "fair share" of profits. Such a critique was enabled by the perception that economic growth was built on interdependence and cooperation between stakeholders. It withers when the engine of growth is attributed to single entrepreneurs or disembodied and decentralized "competitive market structures."

This brief discussion suggests a complementary relationship between institutional change on the one hand, and changes in the relative prevalence of a given fairness norm on the other. It is unfortunately beyond the scope of this book (and beyond the reach of the data used throughout) to unpack this

---

the ultimately goal being the reproduction of what he called the bureaucratic technostructure (Galbraith, 1967).

relationship. In the remainder of the book, I will focus on the formation of fairness beliefs, that is, beliefs regarding the extent to which the status quo aligns with what fairness norms prescribe and leave the study of changes in norms of fairness to other scholars to pursue.

Summary and Next Steps

In this chapter, I have reviewed experimental evidence documenting the "contours" of two norms of fairness, namely, the proportionality and reciprocity norms and their role in manufacturing consent in two types of situations: (1) situations in which some have more "earned" income than others and (2) situations in which some benefit from resource pooling more than others.

These experimental studies ensure that, within a given treatment condition, all respondents share the *same* understanding of the situation being evaluated. When people apply the same norm of fairness to the same situation, they will come to the same conclusion regarding the extent to which this situation deviates from what the norm prescribes. Outside the controlled conditions of the lab, there is no way to ensure that people will agree over the best way to characterize the basic features of a given situation. As a result, despite using the same norm to evaluate a situation, they will also disagree over its fairness. Documenting these disagreements and fleshing out their implications is the object of Chapter 3.

3

Unpacking Demand for Redistribution

When it comes to mass attitudes toward redistributive social policies, fairness reasoning manifests itself in at least two ways. One is the existence of fairness beliefs, defined as beliefs about the prevalence of outcomes and behaviors that violate shared norms of fairness. The other is people's reliance on these beliefs to interpret the world and form fairness-maximizing preferences. In this chapter, I propose a friendly horse race between existing conceptualizations of fairness reasoning and the one presented in this book. As we will see, the evidence overwhelmingly supports the latter.[1]

Fairness Reasoning and Demand for Redistribution: State of the Art

To understand the benefits of the conceptual work accomplished in Chapter 2, it is helpful to contrast it with existing work on the same topic: How much do we gain by shifting to the conceptual framework presented in this book?

Researchers who study attitudes toward redistributive social policies routinely highlight the importance of fairness concerns. According to the dominant line of work, support for redistribution is affected by the views people hold about "the causes of wealth and poverty," the extent to which individuals are "responsible for their own fate," and the "long-run rewards to personal

[1] This chapter builds on Cavaillé and Trump (2015). I am grateful to my coauthor, Kris-Stella Trump, and to the *Journal of Politics* for the permission to reproduce parts of the article's empirical results. Several differences between the original article and this chapter are worth pointing out. While the article uses the expressions *redistribution to* and *redistribution from* to describe two latent dimensions that emerge from a factor analysis, I use them to describe two types of redistributive *policies*. In addition, the chapter's main emphasis is on the measurement of fairness beliefs, something the original article does not touch upon. Third, when testing the argument, I use previous work on fairness concerns as a benchmark, a literature that was not discussed in the original article. These differences follow from uncovering the role fairness reasoning plays in producing the two latent dimensions mentioned in the original article.

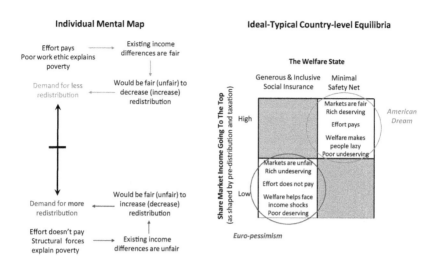

Figure 3.1 Fairness reasoning and demand for redistribution: Unidimensional approach

effort" (Benabou and Tirole, 2006; Lerner, 1980). In the words of Fong (2001), "the extent to which people control their own fate and ultimately get their just deserts are first-order determinants of attitudes toward inequality and redistribution," even "swamping the effects of own income and education." Similarly, Alesina and Angeletos (2005) emphasize the importance of beliefs about the role of effort for explaining both wealth and poverty. This perspective is sketched in Figure 3.1 (left-hand side).

According to Alesina and Angeletos (2005),[2] the individual-level relationship between demand for redistribution and the belief that effort pays helps explain why, in the aggregate, countries differ in their work-to-leisure ratio, levels of income inequality, as well as the share of GDP redistributed through taxes and social spending. Specifically, they identify two ideal-typical social equilibria: an American Dream equilibrium and a Euro-pessimistic equilibrium. In the American Dream equilibrium, people believe that effort pays and oppose pre-distribution policies, progressive taxation and the redistributive features of social insurance because these policies undermine fairness. Predistribution policies are unwarranted because economic institutions already reward effort. Similarly, taxing those who earn more market income is unfair given that they have worked harder and, consequently, deserve to keep what they have earned. Finally, social policy programs designed to redistributes to the chronically poor

---

[2] See also Benabou and Tirole (2006).

and unemployed are also unfair given that they transfer resources to people who choose to live off benefits instead of trying their best to improve their plight. In this equilibrium, the poor and unemployed are castigated as lazy, income redistribution is limited to offering a charity-like minimal income floor and total effort (annual hours worked) is high. As a result, income inequality is also high.

In the Euro-pessimistic equilibrium, people believe that "effort does not pay," and, consequently, are more supportive of predistribution policies, progressive taxation and social insurance that is generous and inclusive because these policies help maximize fairness. Specifically, predistribution policies help correct unbalanced labor relations, progressive taxation is fair because it affects the "undeserving" rich and the most redistributive features of social insurance help recipients who, despite efforts to escape poverty, fail to do so because of an unfair "economic system." In this equilibrium, the poor are less likely to be stigmatized as lazy, income redistribution is extensive and total effort is comparatively lower than that in the American Dream equilibrium. As a result, income inequality is also lower. These two equilibria are summarized in Figure 3.1 (right-hand side).

In large-N research, this unidimensional framework is operationalized using measurement strategies that combine reliance on single- and multiple-item indices. Specifically, when measuring support for more or less redistribution, scholars tend to rely on a single survey item, identified throughout this book as *the traditional redistribution item*. This item asks respondents whether they agree with a version of the following statement: "The government should redistribute income from the better off to those who are least well-off." Alternatively, researchers use dimension-reduction techniques to combine multiple survey items into a score interpreted as ranking respondents on a latent dimension from most left-wing/pro-redistribution to most right–wing/anti-redistribution (Alesina, Miano and Stantcheva, 2018). This latent dimension is also commonly described as capturing left–right preferences on "economic issues," or "government involvement in the economy" (Ansolabehere, Rodden and Snyder, 2008; Bornschier, 2010; Caughey, O'Grady and Warshaw, 2019; Poole and Rosenthal, 1997; Stoll, 2010; Zaller, 1992).[3]

To measure fairness concerns, researchers turn to survey items that directly ask respondents their beliefs about the causes of poverty and wealth and the extent to which effort pays. Researchers find that answers to these items predict answers to the traditional redistribution item as well as one's position on the latent left–right redistribution dimension. In some instances, they also doc-

---

[3] Empirically, answers to the traditional redistribution item tend to be very well predicted by one's position on this latent left–right redistributive dimension.

ument a correlation between average answers to these fairness items and levels of social spending both measured at the country level (Alesina and Angeletos, 2005).[4] This evidence provides support for the "does effort pay?" framework sketched in Figure 3.1.

In the following section, I contrast this framework to the one presented in this book. The latter assumes a very different mental map and, as a result, implies different measurement strategies and predicts different correlational patterns.

What Traditional Approaches Are Missing

The framework sketched in Figure 3.1 does not explicitly engage with the institutional dualism discussed in Chapter 2. While some policies redistribute by affecting the distribution of market income, others redistribute by making social insurance generous and accessible to all irrespective of past contributions. While market economies are morally construed as an *individual* race, welfare states are constructed as *collective* resource-pooling endeavors among citizens of the same country. Furthermore, generous social insurance raises free riding concerns that the distribution of marking income does not. These differences, I argued, imply at least two types of fairness norms and two types of fairness beliefs. Put differently, what counts as a fair allocation of market income is different from what counts as a fair allocation of social benefits. As a result, for many people, fairness reasoning implies a disconnect between support for policies that affect the distribution of market income and support for policies that shape the distribution of social benefits. As a shorthand, I call the former *redistribution from* policies and the latter *redistribution to* policies.

Redistribution from policies include predistribution and taxation policies that prevent a subset of actors from accumulating market income. I call them *redistribution from* policies because of their larger impact on the top of the *market* income distribution. *Redistribution to* policies describe policies that make social insurance generous and inclusive. I call them *redistribution to* policies because of their larger impact on the bottom of the *disposable* income distribution. Of course, many policies do not fit neatly in one category or the other (see footnote 5, page 58). Still, as this chapter demonstrates, this simplification provides much needed analytical leverage (Table 3.1).

---

[4] There is a large literature in political sociology exploring the relationship between welfare regimes on the one hand, and mass attitudes and beliefs on the other (Jaeger, 2006; Jaeger, 2009; Svallfors, 1997). In contrast to Alesina and Angeletos (2005), these studies struggle to find predictable patterns. In this chapter, I demonstrate that by assuming two norms of fairness and connecting each of them to a distinct institutional realm (market economy versus welfare state), a clear pattern emerges both within and between countries.

Table 3.1 Redistribution from *and* redistribution to *policies*

Redistribution from policies
A progressive wealth tax or closing tax loopholes that benefit rich corporations
A cap on CEO salary
New anti-trust legislation or regulations that increases drivers' bargaining power vis-a-vis a platform like Uber

Redistribution to policies
Increase in spending on social programs that maintain the living standards of the able-bodied unemployed
Making access to benefits unconditional on past contributions and/or on length of residency (if immigrant)
Decrease the ratio of earnings-dependent-to-non–earnings-dependent benefits

Both *redistribution from* and *redistribution to* policies are explicitly redistributive. Yet each raise distinct types of fairness concerns. As a result, ideological consistency across the two policy realms (e.g., support for both more *redistribution from* and more *redistribution to*) is the exception in need of an explanation, not something to assume a priori. This perspective, sketched on the left-hand side of Figure 3.2, stands in contrast to the mainstream conceptualization of demand for redistribution and fairness reasoning described in the previous section. The latter implicitly assumes that proportionality and reciprocity beliefs reinforce each other: The beliefs that the world is fair (unfair) according to the proportionality norm goes alongside the belief that the world is unfair (fair) according to the reciprocity norm. Specifically, if effort pays, then market income is distributed fairly and net beneficiaries of social transfers are free riders who are not trying hard enough to become self-reliant. Conversely, if effort does not pay, income differences are unfair and net beneficiaries cannot be blamed for a situation they cannot control. Relatedly, if the rich are deserving (undeserving) of their high earnings and should not (should) be taxed, then the poor are deserving (undeserving) of their plight and should not (should) be helped. In other words, in the traditional framework, fairness reasoning contributes to what scholars call "issue constraint" (Baldassarri and Gelman, 2008; Converse, 2006), that is, ideological consistency across beliefs and policy preferences within a given issue area broadly defined. In contrast, I expect individuals to sort across four ideal-typical proto-ideological profiles: consistently pro-redistribution (bottom-left quadrant in Figure 3.2), consistently anti-redistribution (top-right quadrant), in favor of more generous *redistribution to* but skeptical of more *redistribution from* (top-left quadrant) and inclined to support more *redistribution from* while opposed to more *redistribution to* (bottom-right quadrant).

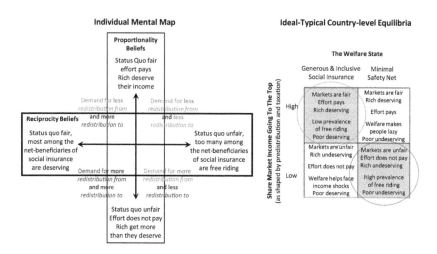

Figure 3.2   Fairness reasoning and demand for redistribution: Two-dimensional approach

Relatedly, the existence of two norms of fairness for two separate institutional spheres suggests not two but four ideal-typical social equilibria (right-hand side of Figure 3.2). To the high- and low-redistribution equilibria, hypothesized by the "does effort pay?" literature (top-right and bottom-left corners), I add two other combinations: one that limits income inequality at the top but fails to offer generous social insurance cover for the poor and the unemployed (bottom-right corner) and another that does not affect top income inequality but engages in large risk pooling through universal and generous social insurance (top-left quadrant). This is summarized on the right-hand side of Figure 3.2.

As I discuss next, the conceptual framework sketched in Figure 3.2 has implications for how researchers operationalize key concepts of interest.[5]

Implications for Measurement Strategies

If the conceptual framework sketched in Figure 3.2 is correct, then when trying to measure "demand for redistribution," researchers need to think care-

---

[5] The distinction between policies that prevent the accumulation of income at the top and those that prevent the formation of a destitute bottom is not exhaustive. First, it overlooks policies with an ambiguous impact on income redistribution (e.g., equal-pay-for-equal work reforms). Second, there exist policies that benefit the poor and yet occur in the realm of the market economy (e.g., minimum wage reform) and others that hurt the rich and occur in the realm of the welfare state (e.g., Obama's Cadillac tax). Nevertheless, as I demonstrate throughout the book, this framework strikes a useful balance between parsimony and accuracy.

fully about measurement strategies. Researchers interested in capturing voters' propensity to support redistributive social policies *broadly defined* would benefit from specifying which facet of redistribution they are most interested in: *redistribution to* or *redistirbution from*? The answer to this question will have implications for which survey items to pick. At a minimum, one should avoid ambiguously worded survey items that ask about both types of policies. Researchers interested in measuring support for a *specific* redistributive policy need to carefully consider the types of fairness beliefs being primed. First, many policies simultaneously take from those who have more and give to those who have less (e.g., a progressive payroll tax that funds a social program with unconditional need-based transfer). Such policies will prime both proportionality and reciprocity concerns, generating ambiguous opinions among people with inconsistent proportionality and reciprocity beliefs. Failure to ask about both types of beliefs will make it difficult to distinguish this subset of respondents from the rest.

The proposed framework also requires moving beyond single survey items that ask about effort or the causes of poverty. I have defined fairness beliefs as people's summary assessments of the status quo as deviating from what the proportionality and reciprocity norms prescribe. Such assessments can be conceptualized as a running tally of the many thoughts and considerations people hold that contribute to such fairness evaluations of the status quo. Measuring people's assessment of the status quo consequently requires relying on a battery of items that tap into thoughts and considerations relevant in light of the definition of the two norms of fairness. Using measurement strategies that leverage patterns of answers to such battery of items, researchers can then distinguish respondents based on the extent to which they hold "mostly unfair" or "mostly fair" norm-specific thoughts and considerations.

To proxy for an individual's proportionality beliefs, researchers can rely on at least three types of survey items. A first type includes items used by the "does effort pay?" literature. Respondents are asked the extent to which they believe that economic institutions reward talent and effort. These items need to be complemented with a second type of questions asking about the *prevalence* of norm-violating/conforming outcomes and behaviors. Indeed, the goal is to measure not only whether one believes that effort pays but also whether one believes that effort pays for most people, most of the time. A third type of items directly elicit respondents' perceptions of the size of the disconnect between existing income differences (what is) and fair income differences (what ought to be). Table 3.2 provides examples of survey items that can be used to measure proportionality beliefs.

Table 3.2 *Measuring proportionality beliefs*

1. *Fairness of economic institutions*
"In [COUNTRY], people get rewarded for their intelligence and skill.
  Agree/disagree?"[b]
"In [COUNTRY], people have equal opportunities to get ahead. Agree/disagree?"[b]
"In [COUNTRY], with hard work and a bit of luck most people can succeed
  financially. Agree/disagree?"[b]
"The economic system mostly benefits a privileged minority. Agree/disagree?"[b]
"The stock market is mostly there to help rich people get richer. Agree/disagree?"

2. *Prevalence of norm-violating outcomes*
"For people born in a rich (poor) family, hard work leads to economic success most
  of the time/some of the time/rarely/never?"[a]
"What share of people born in [COUNTRY] in a [POOR/RICH/MIDDLE CLASS]
  family get a fair shot at life? All/most/some/none"[b]
"In your opinion, what share of rich (poor) people are rich (poor) for reason that have
  nothing to do with how hard they work? All/most/some/none"

3. *Fairness of the income distribution*
"What is the income difference between a janitor/bricklayer and a doctor/CEO? In
  your opinion, should this difference be larger/smaller/stay the same?"[b]
"Are differences in market income too large/too small/about right?"[b]
"In [COUNTRY], income differences are legitimate reflections of differences in
  people's effort, talents and achievements. Agree/disagree?"[a]

[a] A version of these measurement items was asked in a purposely designed survey
described in Appendix A3.1. This survey will be discussed in the empirical analysis
presented later in this chapter as well as in Chapter 5.
[b] A version of these measurement items is available in national or cross-national
surveys, including the International Social Survey Program and the International Social
Justice Project (Wegener and Mason, 2010).

In the case of the reciprocity norm, norm violation takes the form of people
free riding on the common effort. To measure reciprocity beliefs, researchers
can ask respondents what they think about benefit recipients' tendency to cheat
"the system" and as well as their perceptions of the system's ability to successfully identify cheats. Also important are people's priors regarding how others behave when confronted with the option to free ride on shared resources,
something economists often call "moral hazard." Table 3.3 provides examples
of survey items that can be used to measure reciprocity beliefs.

A quick note on this list of items: notice how none of these items directly ask
about the proportionality or reciprocity norms per se, but elicit instead considerations about the nature of the world with respect to these norms. Studies that
overlook this simple distinction produce confusing results. A study by Sznycer
et al. (2017) titled "Support for redistribution is shaped by compassion, envy,

Table 3.3 *Measuring reciprocity beliefs*

---

1. *Prevalence of free riders in the recipient population*
"Most unemployed people are trying hard to find a job. Agree/disagree?"[b]
"People on benefits do not really have a choice. Agree/disagree?"[b]

2. *Failure to identify free riders*
"What share of social benefit cheats are successfully identified? Most/some/only a
few/none"[a]
"How often does welfare go to people who do not really deserve it? Most of the
time/some of the time/rarely"[a]
"What share of people who qualify are wrongly denied benefits? A
majority/some/only a few/none"[a]

3. *Human nature and moral hazard*
"Social benefits are too generous and make people lazy. Agree/disagree?"[b]
"To what extent can others be trusted to not abuse and cheat the system? Most of
the time/sometime/rarely/never"[b]

[a, b] See notes for Table 3.2.

and self-interest, but not a taste for fairness" illustrates this point. The authors
regressed participants' support for redistribution on variables designed to measure "endorsement of (...) fairness" in four countries. They find no evidence
that "a taste for fairness" predicts attitudes toward redistribution. One reason is
that the items used ask about what *ought to be* not what *is*. If the framework
presented in this book better describes the world, then one can reasonably expect all actors to agree on the ought. This means that when the goal is to explain
individual-level differences in policy preferences, such a measurement strategy
is bound to fail. A cursory review of studies that come to similar null results
(Wilensky, 1974; Wilensky et al., 1985) suggests that an inadequate measurement strategy is most often to blame.

In the remainder of the chapter, I use survey data to examine which of the
unidimensional or two-dimensional conceptualization of fairness reasoning and
demand for redistribution finds most support in the data.

Empirical Strategy

I start by testing which of the two hypothesized mental maps described in figures 3.1 and 3.2 (left-hand side) best fits the data using factor analysis. Specifically, I examine whether proportionality belief items and *redistribution from*
policy items load on the same latent factor, while reciprocity belief items and
redistribution to policy items load on a separate, only weakly correlated factor.
If the unidimensional framework better fits the data, then all items will load on

the same latent factor. Even if survey items load on separate factors, the unidimensional framework predicts that the two resulting factors should be highly correlated.

This analysis requires nationally representative survey data with a large set of measurement items that ask both about fairness beliefs and attitudes toward redistributive social policies. In addition, given that the framework is expected to apply to most market economies with a mature welfare state, these data should exist for a large set of Western democracies. Finally, to examine the claim that this framework captures something fundamental (i.e., time invariant) about the structure of public opinion, I also need data collected at different points in time.

International data-collection efforts such as the European Social Survey (ESS) and the International Social Survey Program (ISSP) meet most, though not all, of these criteria. The 2008 wave of the ESS includes a battery of items that tap into reciprocity beliefs and attitudes toward *redistribution to* policies. Some of these items are also available in the 2016 wave. Thanks to its module on social inequality (collected in 1992, 1999 and 2009), the ISSP provides a battery of items asking about deviations from the proportionality norm as well as a few items asking about *redistribution from* policies. To the best of my knowledge, no cross-national survey includes items that ask about both types of fairness beliefs. One exception is a single-country survey, namely the British Social Attitude Survey (BSAS), which includes both proportionality and reciprocity items.[6]

I start by analyzing the 2004 and 2016 waves of the BSAS. Specifically, I examine whether the underlying structure uncovered by factor analysis best aligns with Figure 3.1 or Figure 3.2 (or neither). Because cross-national surveys do not ask the same respondents about both reciprocity and proportionality beliefs, I cannot repeat this analysis in countries beyond Great Britain. Instead, I follow alternative empirical strategies designed to leverage the limited set of items available in both the ESS and the ISSP. When combined, these tests provide additional evidence that the patterns uncovered in the British context are not unique to this country.

Moving from the individual to the country level, I combine data from the ESS (2008) and the ISSP (2009) and examine whether, in line with the unidimensional approach, countries who find it fair to increase *redistribution from* the better off as prescribed by the proportionality norm also find it fair to in-

---

[6] British Social Attitudes, NatCen Social Research. For more information, see
www.bsa.natcen.ac.uk [Accessed 8 July 2022]. Data access through UK Data Service at
https://ukdataservice.ac.uk.

crease *redistribution to* the worse off as prescribed by the reciprocity norm. Against this expectation, I expect two additional clusters of countries to emerge: countries skeptical of more *redistribution from* policies but supportive of extending *redistribution to* on the one hand, and countries enthusiastic about more *redistribution from* but opposed to increasing *redistribution to* on the other.

The Structure of Redistributive Preferences in Great Britain

Since the late 1980s, the BSAS has repeatedly asked a battery of items aimed at measuring core political beliefs regarding income redistribution, labor relations, income inequality, social insurance, unemployment insurance and welfare recipients (Evans, Heath and Lalljee, 1996).[7] I focus my analysis on the 2004 wave as it includes a particularly large battery of questions on theses issues. For this analysis, I cast a wide net and include all items that I expect a priori to relate to at least one of the four concepts of interest, namely proportionality beliefs, reciprocity beliefs, attitudes toward *redistribution from* policies, and attitudes toward *redistribution to* policies.

Available items are listed in Table 3.4 alongside general comments regarding the type of beliefs and policy attitudes captured by each item. Note that I was not able to identify items that exclusively ask about *redistribution from* policies. Instead, I rely on an item that asks respondents how they would like to see additional tax revenue raised. Respondents can choose from among three options: a progressive tax (tax rate increases with income), a flat rate tax (tax rate is the same for all), or a lump-sum tax (tax amount is the same for all). I also include three different versions of the traditional redistribution question.

Best practice, when testing for the existence of a latent structure using survey data, is to divide the sample in two and run an exploratory factor analysis (EFA) on the first half of the dataset and a confirmatory factor analysis (CFA) on the second half. The EFA tests the plausibility of a unidimensional versus a multi-dimensional factor solution. By letting all survey items freely load on any latent factors in the data, an EFA provides information on whether inter-item correlations are larger for a distinct subset of items. To improve the interpretation of factor loadings, an EFA imposes structure on the relationship between

---

[7] When combined into multiple-item scales, these items have helped researchers place respondents on a "socialist versus laissez-faire – or left-right – dimension" as well as a "pro-welfare versus anti-welfarist" dimension (Park et al., 2012). To the best of my knowledge, there has been no attempt to use these items as part of a larger inquiry into the mental maps people use to reason about redistributive social issues.

Table 3.4 *Exploratory factor analysis of the BSAS*

General comments	Item wording	First Fact.	Second Fact.	Third Fact.	U. Sc.
Reciprocity beliefs					
Moral hazard (MH)	Benefits for unemployed people: too low and cause hardship vs. too high and discourage job seeking [dole]	**0.57**	0.23	-0.30	0.52
MH	The welfare state encourages people to stop helping each other [welfhelp]	**0.49**	0.02	0.28	0.67
MH	If welfare benefits weren't so generous, people would learn to stand on their own two feet [welffeet]	**0.87**	0.09	0.09	0.22
Fraud prevalence (FP)	Many people falsely claim benefits [falseclm]	**0.61**	0.00	-0.08	0.62
MH & FP	Many people who get welfare don't really deserve any help [sochelp]	**0.77**	-0.07	0.11	0.38
MH & FP	Most unemployed people could find a job if they really wanted one [unempjob]	**0.65**	0.06	0.10	0.56
FP	Most people on the dole are fiddling [dolefidl]	**0.77**	-0.02	0.06	0.39
MH & FP	Main reason people in need due to: laziness vs. lack of willpower [whyneed]	**0.57**	0.11	-0.06	0.66
Positive answer implies that recipients are deserving	Cutting welfare benefits would damage too many people's lives [damlives]	**0.65**	0.23	0.04	0.52
Proportionality beliefs					
Fairness of labor relations	Management will always try to get the better of employees if it gets the chance [indust4]	-0.16	**0.63**	-0.21	0.53
Equal opportunity	There is one law for rich and one for poor [richlaw]	-0.10	**0.77**	-0.09	0.38
Existing income differences: how fair? (HF?)	Working people do not get their fair share of nation's wealth [wealth]	0.04	**0.79**	-0.10	0.36
HF?	The gap between high and low incomes is too large [incomgap]	0.19	**0.53**	0.27	0.60
HF?	Differences in income in Britain are too large [incdiffs]	0.11	**0.77**	0.15	0.43

General comments	Item wording	First Fact.	Second Fact.	Third Fact.	U. Sc.
Positive answer implies inequality unrelated to effort	Inequality continues to exist because it benefits the rich and powerful [ineqrich]	0.03	**0.69**	−0.05	0.52
Positive answer implies inequality rewards effort	Large differences in income are necessary for Britain's prosperity [diffsnec]	−0.21	−0.26	−0.27	0.80
Redistribution to pol.					
Conditionality (C)	Limit immigrants' access to unemployment benefits (combined items) [acunbrec/acunrefu/acunbbr]	0.39	0.03	0.01	0.85
C	Limited access to unemployment benefits for those who do not work (combined items) [acunwshy/acunpoor/acunchil]	**0.51**	0.00	−0.08	0.73
Generosity (G)	The government should spend more on benefits for the poor [morewelf]	**0.40**	**0.47**	0.15	0.61
G	More spending on unemployment benefits [socspnd1]	**0.63**	0.23	−0.30	0.45
G	More spending on benefits for single parents [socspnd4]	0.34	0.16	−0.02	0.85
Redistribution from pol.					
	Assume gov needs to raise more taxes: how? Progressive tax vs. same rate for all vs. same amount for all [taxraise]	0.00	0.35	−0.02	0.87
Traditional red^o item	It is the responsibility of the government to reduce the differences in income [incdiff]	0.09	**0.79**	0.13	0.34
Implies support for less (vs. more) income red^o	Government should redistribute income from the better off to those who are least well-off [redistrb]	0.32	**0.58**	0.13	0.54
	Income redistribution from the better off to those who are less well off: too much vs. too little [redist]†	0.24	**0.60**	0.04	0.56

(continued)

Table 3.4 (cont.)

General comments	Item wording	First Fact.	Second Fact.	Third Fact.	U. Sc.
Miscellaneous items					
Social solidarity (SS). Positive answer implies recipients (R) are undeserving	It is not right that people benefit from services that they haven't helped to pay for [bnfrsec]	**0.62**	−0.12	0.28	0.51
SS. Positive answer implies R *deserving*	It is only right that taxes paid by the majority help support those in need [majtax]	**0.44**	0.25	0.00	0.73
SS	It is not fair that some people pay a lot of money in tax and hardly use the services [nousesec]	**0.48**	0.05	0.38	0.61
SS	People who buy private pensions/education/health care should pay the same (less) taxes as everyone else (combined items) [taxrpen/taxrnhs/taxreduc]	0.07	0.15	0.34	0.85
	Right or wrong that people with higher income can buy better health care/education (combined items) [buyhlth/buyeduc]	0.22	0.37	0.25	0.75
SS	More (less) taxes to fund more (less) social services [taxspend]	0.31	0.23	0.28	0.76
	Eigenvalue	7.32	3.98	0.99	
	Sample size	570			

Higher (lower) values imply more right-wing (left-wing) answers. Cell entries are factor loadings, with loadings greater or equal to 0.4 in absolute value highlighted in bold. The loadings are obtained from a varimax rotation of a principal component solution, yielding uncorrelated factors with unit variances; the correlations analyzed are the polychoric correlations of the ordinal survey responses. A first analysis was run with oblique rotations and found a correlation of 0.18 between the first and the second factors.

[†] The [redist] item is only available for a smaller subset of respondents. I ran the same EFA using this smaller sample (N = 463) and present for [redist] the factor loadings from this separate analysis. These factors loadings cannot be directly compared with other factor loadings presented in the table, which were obtained using the larger sample. Note, however, that the results are substantively the same when using this smaller sample.

Source: BSAS 2004.

the latent factors.[8] Switching to a CFA provides a more reliable estimate of the correlations between latent factors. Indeed, in contrast to EFA, CFA imposes constraints on the factor loadings, allowing to freely estimate the correlation between latent factors (Costello and Osborne, 2005; Matsunaga, 2010). In other words, an EFA tells us which items "go together," while a CFA tells us whether the latent factors underpinning each cluster of items are meaningfully correlated or not.[9]

Figure 3.4 presents results from the EFA.[10] I retain two factors that together explain close to 80% of the shared variance. The eigenvalues of the additional factors substantively drop after the second factor. The third factor is included for reference only.

Reciprocity beliefs are measured using items on perceptions of free riding and concerns over moral hazard. Responses to these questions load on the first factor, as do attitudes toward benefit conditionality, support for sharing resources with those who cannot provide for themselves and support for increasing spending on programs that benefit the jobless. Proportionality beliefs are measured using items that, jointly, capture the extent to which people perceive the distribution of market income as generated by a "fair" economic process. Responses to these items load on a separate factor. In line with expectation, the item asking about tax progressivity loads on the same latent factor as proportionality beliefs. Interestingly, attitudes toward income redistribution, as traditionally measured, most strongly load on this second factor, implying that answers to this item are best explained by differences in proportionality beliefs, not by differences in reciprocity beliefs.

Miscellaneous items included at the end of Table 3.4 provide additional information regarding the nature of the two latent factors. The first three items ask respondent whether they agree with the principle of risk pooling and resource sharing. Based on the argument presented in this book, agreement should be higher among people who are not concerned about free riding and lower among those who are. In line with expectations, three of these four items load on the same factor as reciprocity items. The fourth item combines three questions asking respondents whether people who rely on private education, health care and pensions should pay less taxes as a result. Attitudes on these issues do not appear to fit easily within the proto-ideological mental map hypothesized in

---

[8] In an EFA, the correlation between the latent factors is highly dependent on the rotation technique applied to extract the factor loadings.

[9] For example, if the EFA returns more than one factor, and the CFA shows that they are highly correlated, then it became harder, despite the existence of more than one factor, to reject the unidimensional mental map sketched in Figure 3.1.

[10] A detailed overview of the model-fitting procedure is available in Cavaillé and Trump (2015).

this book. General attitudes toward taxes and social spending also appear to be shaped by considerations not well captured by my framework.[11]

When performing the CFA on the second half of the sample, I only retain items from the EFA with a sufficiently large factor loading (0.4 or more). I examine whether constraining items to load on one factor severely affects the model fit, especially when compared with a model that allows the items to load on the two factors identified using the EFA. The results for the two-factor model are presented in Table 3.5. Model fit dramatically improves when switching from a model with one latent factor to a model with two latent factors. In line with the two-dimensional model of demand for redistribution sketched in Figure 3.2, the analysis shows no correlation between the two factors.

To reach an optimal goodness-of-fit, I have, for two items, relaxed the assumption that they load on one dimension only. One item asks respondents their support for more spending on welfare. The other item is a version of the traditional redistribution item. Note that this relationship between support for redistribution as traditionally measured and reciprocity beliefs is limited to one of the two available versions of the traditional redistribution item. Furthermore, in this case, the factor loading on the proportionality beliefs dimension is twice as large as the one on the reciprocity beliefs dimension.[12] All things considered, and against common expectations, answers to the traditional redistribution item appear only weakly correlated with beliefs about the work ethic of net beneficiaries of redistribution. Support for redistribution measured in this fashion is best interpreted as support for *redistribution from* not *redistribution to*.

Jointly, the results indicate that the two-dimensional conceptualization of fairness reasoning and demand for redistribution sketched in Figure 3.2 better fits the data than the unidimensional conceptualization sketched in Figure 3.1. Furthermore, the assumption that support for redistribution implies support for policies that take from the better off alongside support for policies that give to the worse off does not seem to hold. Research questions and designs that fail to address such heterogeneity run the risk of producing results difficult to interpret and build on.

What should one make of the fact that people support taking income from some without necessarily being in favor of giving it to others (or giving it to some without taking it from others)? This is only puzzling when assuming that people perceive a direct connection between policies that shape the distribution of market income and policies that affect how redistributive social insurance is.

---

[11] I will come back to this item in Chapter 7.

[12] As I will discuss in Chapter 8, this correlation with reciprocity beliefs is itself an artifact of item ordering specific to the BSAS.

Table 3.5 Confirmatory factor analysis of the BSAS

Item wording	First Fact.	Second Fact.
Reciprocity beliefs		
Benefits for unemployed people: too low and cause hardship vs. too high and discourage job seeking	0.53	
The welfare state encourages people to stop helping each other	0.44	
If welfare benefits weren't so generous, people would learn to stand on their own feet	0.87	
Many people falsely claim benefits	0.48	
Many people who get welfare don't really deserve any help	0.75	
Most unemployed people could find a job if they really wanted one	0.70	
Most people on the dole are fiddling	0.75	
Main reason people in need due to: laziness vs. lack of willpower	0.44	
Cutting welfare benefits would damage too many people's lives	0.65	
Redistribution to policies		
Limited access to unemployment benefits for those who have not paid much in taxes (combined items)	0.50	
The government should spend more on benefits for the poor	0.49	0.36
More spending on unemployment benefits	0.59	
Social solidarity		
It is not right that people benefit from services that they haven't helped to pay for	0.56	
It is only right that taxes paid by the majority help support those in need	0.51	
It is not fair that some people pay a lot of money in tax and hardly use the services	0.43	

(continued)

Table 3.5 (cont.)

Item wording	First Fact.	Second Fact.
Proportionality beliefs		
Management will always try to get the better of employees if it gets the chance		0.71
There is one law for rich and one for poor		0.80
Working people do not get their fair share of nation's wealth		0.81
The gap between high and low incomes is too large		0.47
Differences in income in Britain are too large		0.70
Inequality continues to exist because it benefits the rich and powerful		0.73
Redistribution from policies and traditional redistribution items		
Government needs to raise more taxes: same amount for all, same rate or progressive tax?		0.32
It is the responsibility of the government to reduce the differences in income		0.69
Government should redistribute income from the better off to those who are least well-off	0.30	0.67
Correlation coefficient between factors (95% CI)	0.06 [−0.2, 0.16]	
Standardized root mean squared residual assuming two dimensions (shown)	0.077	
Standardized root mean squared residual assuming one dimension	0.171	
Sample size	543	

Higher (lower) values imply more right-wing (left-wing) answers. The results are based on a confirmatory factor analysis; final model relaxes the assumption that the error terms for [incdiffs] and [incdiff] are uncorrelated. Additional goodness-of-fit measures: CFI = 0.85, RMSEA = 0.085. For full details on model selection, see the online appendix. Italicized questions are available over time (1986–2009) and are used later in the book to create an additive index.
Source: BSAS 2004.

In light of the institutional dualism discussed in Chapter 2 and given the importance of fairness reasoning, such assumption is unlikely to hold. In Chapter 7, I will discuss conditions under which people can start connecting the two policies. For now, results indicate that, in the low-stakes setting of a survey, when asked about policies with uncertain implications for their own pocketbook, people's reliance on fairness reasoning helps explain the disconnect between attitudes toward *redistribution from* and *redistribution to* policies.

As a robustness check, I replicate the 2004 BSAS results using the 2016 wave of the BSAS, which includes many of the same survey items. These results are available in the online appendix.[13] If this two-dimensional framework represents a stable feature of mass attitudes toward redistributive social policies, then the bulk of the results should easily replicate on a different dataset, even one collected more than a decade after the 2004 wave. The EFA of the 2016 data confirms the existence of two distinct latent factors, one anchored by items that ask about reciprocity beliefs, the other by items that ask about proportionality beliefs. In contrast to the analysis of the 2004 data, a CFA on the 2016 data does not reject the null that there is *no* correlation between the two latent factors. Still, while positive, the correlation remains substantively weak at 0.12. Similar to the 2004 data, allowing the traditional redistribution items to load on both factors improves model fit, though again, evidence indicates that survey responses to these items correlate more strongly with proportionality beliefs than reciprocity beliefs.

The BSAS was not specifically designed to test my argument and, as a result, items vary in how well they measure the types of beliefs and policy preferences I am most interested in. I consequently collected original data using survey items better suited to the task at hand and examined whether answers to these purposefully designed items are correlated with answers to a subset of the items available in the BSAS.[14] This exercise is described in detail in Appendix A3.1. The results confirm that the BSAS items used in the above analysis all load on the same dimension as items explicitly designed to ask about deviations from what the proportionality norm prescribes. For example, people who strongly agree that "working people do not get their fair share of nation's wealth" (a BSAS item) are also much more likely to disagree with the claim that "in Great Britain, income differences are legitimate reflections of differences in people's effort, talents and achievement." They are also much more likely to believe that, even if a poor person works hard, she never or rarely gets

---

[13] See footnote 12, page 24 for more information on where to find the online appendix.

[14] Respondents were recruited using an online panel and match the British population on education, age, gender and work status. Note, however, that this sample does not constitute a representative sample of the British population.

what she wants in contrast to a rich person who gets it "most of the time" or "always." Relatedly, I find that questions designed to ask about moral hazard, the work ethic of the poor and the prevalence of free riding among welfare recipients all load on the same latent factor. For example, agreement with the claim that "most unemployed people do not really try to find a job" (a BSAS item) is highly predictive of one's belief that half or more of welfare recipients cheat when applying for benefits. People who believe that "giving benefits to someone who does not qualify" is a more common mistake than "denying benefits to someone who does qualify" are also more likely to believe that "if benefits were not so generous, people would learn to stand on their own two feet" (a BSAS item).

As previously mentioned, the BSAS also lacks survey items designed to capture support for policies that redistribute market income away from those at the top of the income distribution (*redistribution from* policies). In this original survey, I asked respondents whether they support "increasing taxes on households with income over £100,000" to better fund the NHS. I then examined how attitudes toward this hypothetical tax relate to proportionality and reciprocity beliefs. To measure the latter, I used items similar to those listed in Table 3.5. In line with the two-dimensional framework, I find that individual-level differences in proportionality beliefs are highly predictive of support for this tax increase, while reciprocity beliefs are not.

Having found strong evidence for my framework using data from Great Britain, I now turn to evidence from other Western democracies.

Evidence Beyond Great Britain

As previously mentioned, data limitations preclude me from running the same analysis in countries beyond Great Britain. As a second best, I focus on testing empirical expectations adapted to the available data.

In 2008 and 2016, the ESS included a battery of items similar to the ones used in the British analysis to measure reciprocity beliefs. The items are listed in Table 3.6. The columns on the right reproduce results from an EFA performed on the pooled data. Both waves of the ESS also include a version of the traditional redistribution question worded as follows: "The government should take measures to reduce differences in income levels. Agree/disagree?" In the previous section, I found that, in order to predict whether people are supportive of income redistribution, as measured using the traditional redistribution item, one is better served by asking people what they think about the fairness of the market economy not what they think about the fairness of social solidarity. Below, I examine whether the same pattern holds in the ESS, namely a

Table 3.6 *Reciprocity beliefs measured using the ESS*

Item wording	ESS 2008	ESS 2016
Beliefs about the ubiquity of shirking		
Most unemployed people do not really try to find a job	0.54	0.65
Many manage to obtain benefits/services not entitled to	0.40	0.49
Employees often pretend they are sick to stay at home	0.47	NA
Beliefs about the disincentive effects of social benefits		
Social benefits/services make people lazy	0.77	0.80
Social benefits/services make people less willing look after themselves/family	0.80	NA
Social benefits/services make people less willing to care for one another	0.79	0.71
***Redistribution to* policies**		
Role of government to ensure a reasonable standard of living for the unemployed?	0.34	0.28
Eigenvalue	2.65	1.91

EFA on the pooled data. Countries included in the analysis are GB, FR, IE, BE, PT, DE, NL, CH, NO, AT, ES, FI, DK, SE, GR, as well as EE, HU, PL, SI, SK, and CZ. The latter countries were included because they are market economies with large welfare states. Note, however, that given half a century of Soviet occupation, the results for these countries should be analyzed with caution.
Source: ESS 2012 and 2016.

weak correlation between reciprocity beliefs and support for redistribution as traditionally measured.

To do so, I use items in Table 3.6 to compute individual factor scores that rank respondents according to how prevalent (and concerning) they believe free riding to be.[15] Table 3.7 (top panel) reports the predicted probability of disagreeing with the principle of income redistribution for a hypothetical individual with a reciprocity score equal to the 10th and 90th percentiles of scores in her country. I repeat this analysis using the 2016 data (bottom panel). In most countries and in both waves, moving from the 10th to the 90th percentiles on the reciprocity scores says little about one's level of opposition to income redistribution as traditionally measured. Put differently, knowing what someone thinks about the prevalence of free riding among welfare recipients says little about their agreement with the claim that government should redistribute

[15] I use factor scores derived from factor loadings obtained after separate country-by-country EFAs. Results are the same if I use an item response theory model to compute individual scores. The same applies if I use country-specific loadings or the same loadings for all countries.

Table 3.7 *Opposition to redistribution and reciprocity beliefs*

| | Probability of not agreeing that government should redistribute | | |
	Fair – free riding not a concern (10th percentile)	Unfair – too much free riding (90th percentile)	Delta
2008			
France	0.20	0.21	0.01
Germany	0.31	0.38	0.06
Sweden	0.29	0.45	0.16
Denmark	0.50	0.65	0.16
The Netherlands	0.42	0.48	0.06
Great Britain	0.39	0.43	0.04
Spain	0.20	0.20	0.00
Poland	0.21	0.28	0.07
2016			
France	0.24	0.25	0.01
Germany	0.23	0.32	0.09
Sweden	0.26	0.49	**0.23**
Denmark	na	na	na
The Netherlands	0.34	0.46	0.11
Great Britain	0.29	0.41	0.12
Spain	0.10	0.22	0.13
Poland	0.24	0.32	0.08

Reports predicted opposition to redistribution as measured using the traditional redistribution item. People who agree and strongly agree that the government should redistribute income are coded as 0. Other response categories are coded as 1. Estimates are computed using coefficients from a regression of the binary outcome on reciprocity belief scores computed used items in Table 3.6.

income from the most to the least worse off. There is one notable exception to this pattern, Sweden, with a differential equal to 23 percentage points (presented in bold in the table) for the year 2016.

In addition to the traditional redistribution question, the 2008 wave of the ESS includes two items related to perceptions of market income inequality: "for a society to be fair, differences in people's standard of living should be small" and "large differences in people's incomes are acceptable to properly reward differences in talents and efforts." We can reasonably expect people committed to small income differences to also think that existing income differences are unfair. As already mentioned, agreement with the second claim implicitly assumes that market insitutions successfully reward talent and effort. In other words, based on the framework proposed in this book, these two items should covary with the traditional redistribution item but should not load on the same factor as the reciprocity items listed in Table 3.6. In the online appendix, I show that this is indeed the case (see also Table 3 in Cavaillé and Trump, 2015). However, note that in the Swedish case, inter-item correlation is higher, suggesting that, for this country, a unidimensional framework might be sufficient to parsimoniously describe the structure of mass attitudes toward redistributive social policies.

Unfortunately, the United States is not included in the ESS. In addition, American surveys such as the General Social Survey or the American National Election Survey rarely include the relevant set of fairness items. Furthermore, as I will discuss in Part 2, available reciprocity items are racialized (they ask about the deservingness of African Americans) making it difficult to compare with empirical patterns found using European survey data. Proportionality items are also few and far apart and most often ask about what *ought* to be, not what *is* (Gross and Manrique-Vallier, 2012). One exception is a data collection effort by the PEW Research Institute, which, from the late 1980s to 2012, regularly asked respondents a set of questions about the fairness of the income distribution and industrial relations as defined by the proportionality norm. These include the following items: "do you agree/disagree" that "success in life is pretty much determined by forces outside our control," "hard work offers little guarantee of success," "there is too much power concentrated in the hands of a few big companies," "business corporations make too much profit," and "business corporations generally strike a fair balance between making profits and serving the public interest."

I combine these items into an index using weights recovered from an EFA. I examine whether people's beliefs about the returns to hard work and about business power predict whether or not they agree with the claim that "(p)oor people have become too dependent on government assistance programs." I run the analysis on the pooled data, as well as on single survey years. Irrespective of which sample I use, the results are the same: knowing how people feel about the fairness of the status quo as defined by the proportionality norm says nothing about their beliefs about the poor's reliance on government "handouts"; the correlation between the two is indistinguishable from zero (see Appendix A3.2). These results suggest that, in line with the two-dimensional framework hypothesized in this book, the ways in which people in the United States reason about the fairness of social solidarity differ from how they reason about the fairness of the economic sphere.

Another observable implication derived from the two-dimensional framework, but unaccounted for by the unidimensional framework, is worth discussing. In the unidimensional framework, people who believe that effort pays also believe that the rich are deserving and the poor undeserving. Conversely, people who think effort does not pay are more likely to find the rich unde-serving and the poor deserving. In contrast, the two-dimensional framework implies that perceptions of the deservingness of the poor are not the mirror im-age of perceptions of the deservingness of the rich. Indeed, according to the two-dimensional framework, in countries with a market economy, fairness rea-soning based on the proportionality norm regulates resentment toward those who have more than others. In countries with a large welfare state, fairness rea-soning based on the reciprocity norm regulates resentment toward those who are drawing more from the collective effort than they are contributing to it. As a result, perceptions of the poor are shaped not only by perceptions of the extent to which effort pays but also by free riding and membership concerns, which, as I will show in more detail in the next chapter, follow their own logic.

This mismatch between perceptions of the rich and the poor was famously documented, though not explained, by Kluegel et al. (1995). More recently, Fong and Poutvaara (2019) find that "36% of German respondents and 42% of U.S. respondents give different answers about the role of effort and circum-stances beyond one's control when being asked about reasons for high and low incomes."[16] These differences, while puzzling in the context of the unidimen-sional approach, are to be expected in the context of the two-dimensional one.[17]

Country-Level Analysis

To circumvent the lack of individual-level data, I now shift the analysis to the country level. Doing so allows me to match country-level estimates computed using one dataset to country-level estimates computed using another. Specif-ically, I combine data from the previously described 2008 wave of the ESS with data from the 2009 wave of the ISSP, which includes items asking about the fairness of the status quo as defined by the proportionality norm. I exam-ine whether the disconnect documented at the individual level extends to the country level.

---

[16] Echoing the results described in this chapter, the authors argue that this mismatch helps explain why one in five German respondents and two in three American respondents "either support increasing transfers to those with low incomes but oppose increasing taxes on those with high incomes, or oppose increasing transfers to those with low incomes but support increasing taxes on those with high incomes."

[17] One might offer a simpler interpretation: This disconnect is due to differences in stereotypes about the rich and the poor. Relatedly, and following Lupu and Pontusson (2011), people reason about the "middle-top comparison" in one way and the "middle-bottom comparison" in another. While descriptively correct, both claims do not constitute an alternative interpretation: They have little to say about the origins of this disconnect. In contrast, I argue that the disconnect has at least two sources: institutional dualism and normative pluralism.

First, a few words on the ISSP items, which are listed in Table 3.8.[18] The first measurement item proxies for perceived dissatisfaction with existing income differences. It combines answers to a set of questions asking about the perceived and preferred income of a fixed set of occupations. Specifically, I regress items capturing preferred income (what ought to be) over items capturing perceived income (what is). The resulting regression coefficient is equal to 1 if respondents believe that existing income differences align with their preferred income differences. The closer the coefficient is to zero, the more the respondent believes that existing income differences (as they perceive them) deviate from their preferred benchmark. The second item captures the extent to which people think blue-collar workers are underpaid. I focus on this occupational category as embodying the quintessential hardworking individual: Respondents who believe that this individual is underpaid are less likely to believe that effort alone is enough.[19] The third item is a dummy variable equal to 1 if a respondent perceives the society she lives in to be highly unequal, that is, a few rich at the top and most people at the bottom. Items 4 and 5 directly ask about inequality, while items 6 and 7 ask about the role of wealth and effort to get ahead in the country respondents live in. The last two items ask more specifically about *redistribution from* policies: Item 8 is the ISSP's version of the traditional redistribution item, while item 9 asks about support for more progressive taxation. I included these two items based on prior evidence that they load on the same latent factor as proportionality beliefs.

Table 3.8 includes factor loadings from an EFA on the pooled data: all items load on the same latent factor. I also repeat the analysis on the 1999 wave of the ISSP, which includes many of the same items.[20] For both waves, I compute factor scores that measure individual differences in how much people find income differences unfair and support redistribution. I then aggregate these scores at the country level.

Figure 3.3 compares country averages computed using the 2009 wave with country averages computed using the 1999 wave. The correlation between the 1999 country averages and the 2009 averages is 0.90 (N=13). Figure 3.3 also includes the same analysis using the 2008 and 2016 waves of the ESS. Specifically, I use the items in Table 3.6 to compute factor scores measuring individual differences in the extent to which people believe the unemployed and the poor are free riding and oppose transfers that benefit this group. In this case, the cor-

---

[18] See also the online appendix for more detailed information.
[19] Note that the correlation between items 1 and 2 is between 0.3 and 0.5 depending on the country.
[20] Note that in 1999, respondents were asked about income differences for eleven occupations, while in 2009 they were only asked about five occupations.

Table 3.8 *Measuring proportionality beliefs using the ISSP*

	2009	1999
1. Labor income: IS versus OUGHT	0.37	0.31
2. Blue-collar worker income: IS versus OUGHT	0.42	0.40
3. Shape of society	0.46	0.50
4. Income differences are too large	0.77	0.78
5. Inequality continues to exist because it benefits the rich and powerful	NA	0.51
6. Wealth important to get ahead	*0.24*	0.21
7. Effort important to get ahead	*0.13*	NA
8. Government should reduce income differences	0.74	0.76
9. High incomes should pay more taxes than low income	0.45	0.55
Eigenvalue	1.97	2.30

EFA on the pooled data using a polychoric correlation matrix adapted to ordinal variables. Note the small factor loading on items 6 and 7, items which are often used in the "does effort pay?" literature. See Appendix A3.2 for more details.
Source: ISSP 1999 and 2009.

relation between the two waves is 0.86 (N=19). Fairness beliefs appear to be a stable component of a country's attitudinal landscape.

Figure 3.4 combines the 2008 wave of the ESS and the 2009 wave of the ISSP. Note that the ESS does not include the United States. To place this country with regard to the reciprocity norm, I have relied on data collected independently by Clem Brooks and available in Svallfors (2012). Brooks' results show that response patterns in the United States are similar to those found in Great Britain. I consequently assign the same British score to the United States.

Overall, very few countries align along the traditional left–right axis (from the bottom-left to the top-right), which runs from consistently pro-redistribution beliefs (fair according to reciprocity, unfair according to proportionality) to consistently anti-redistribution beliefs (unfair according to reciprocity, fair according to proportionality). If anything, the key axis appears to be one running from fair to unfair according to both norms. Overall, the two-dimensional structure found at the individual level is also found at the country level, echoing the ideal-typical setup sketched in Figure 3.2 (right panel).

Given the imperfection of available items, this evidence remains tentative. Nevertheless, it highlights the limits of existing approaches to fairness reasoning as well as the benefits of the two-dimensional framework. First, notice how, despite very different institutional setups, Denmark, Norway and the United States are in the same ballpark when it comes to proportionality beliefs. Scandinavians find their economic system fair and rightly so: mobility rates are much

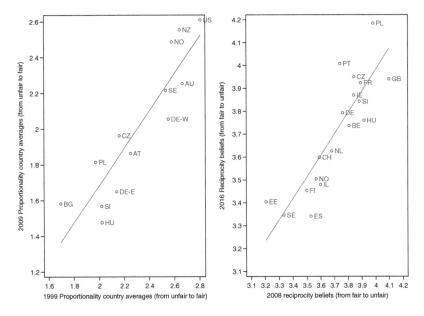

Figure 3.3 Fairness beliefs: Cross-country stability and change
Plots average proportionality (left panel) and reciprocity (right panel) beliefs measured at two different time periods separated by roughly a decade. See text for more details on the measures.
Source: ESS 2008 and 2016, ISSP 1999 and 2009, weighted.

higher and differences in market income lower. As a result, in these countries, support for income redistribution, as traditionally measured, is often lower than one might expect (see Chaper 1, Figure 1.4). Where these countries differ from the United States is in terms of their reciprocity beliefs: Scandinavian countries express high trust and comparatively much lower concerns about free riding and moral hazard, while the United States (and Great Britain) are much more likely to perceive unemployed workers as undeserving and be concerned about shirking. There is a similar split among countries who find the economic system and income inequality unfair. France and most postcommunist countries are closer to the United States and Great Britain than to Scandinavian countries in terms of their level of concern about free riding. The exceptions are Baltic countries who appear satisfied with how welfare spending is disbursed in their country.

These results cast a new light on possible ideal-typical social equilibria and how to identify them empirically. In the Scandinavian case, it appears that high levels of social spending are not predicated on the beliefs that effort does not pay; this is against expectations in Benabou and Tirole (2006) and Alesina and

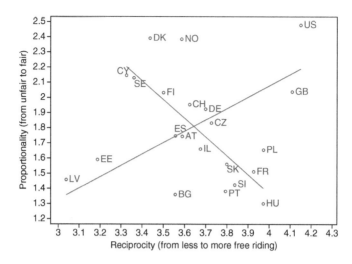

Figure 3.4 Fairness beliefs: Cross-country correlation
Plots average proportionality beliefs against average reciprocity beliefs measured in 2008 and 2009. See text for more details on the measures. Note that the U.S. score on the X-axis is approximated using Svallfors (2012).
Source: ESS 2008 and ISSP 2009, weighted.

La Ferrara (2005). Instead, they are predicated on the belief that the abuse of social spending and free riding is the exception, not the norm. This unique combination of fairness beliefs is particularly hospitable to the Scandinavian model of an export-driven economy and flexicurity, heralded as the ideal combination of market efficiency and social solidarity. This raises the broader question of whether the flexicurity model can be imported to other countries that do not share this combination of mass fairness beliefs.

When examining the existence of two social equilibria, the "does effort pay?" literature has focused on the relation between the share of the population who agrees that effort pays and social spending as a share of GDP. However, the two-dimensional framework presented and tested here suggests that this analysis obscures more than it reveals. First, cross-national differences in mass beliefs about the relationship between effort and income likely best explain differences in policies that shape market and tax institutions. The latter need not be correlated with social spending. On that front, Scandinavian countries have undergone significant institutional change, with very flexible labor laws (the "flex" in flexicurity) and a significant decrease in marginal tax rates in the 1990s. From the perspective of the "American Dream" versus "Euro-pessimistic" diptych, these changes are easy to overlook. In contrast, the two-dimensional approach hypothesizes such a combination. Whether these market and taxation reforms will ultimately translate into more market income inequality (the top-right quadrant in Figure 3.2) remains to be seen.

Second, cross-national differences in social spending are likely best explained by cross-national differences in reciprocity beliefs, not proportionality beliefs. A country like France, which taxes high incomes and regulates the market based on the belief that effort does not pay, appears to be less enthusiastic about deepening the redistributive features of social insurance. While this has not resulted in dramatic welfare cuts (a situation captured in the bottom-right quadrant in Figure 3.2), it might nevertheless preclude welfare reforms that seek to better meet the needs of the growing contingent of labor market "outsiders" (Emmenegger et al., 2012; Rueda, 2007; Saint-Paul, 1999).[21]

Summary and Next Steps

I started this inquiry in Chapter 1, by describing the benchmark model that identifies some of the key assumptions underpinning the expectation of a pro-redistribution shift in times of rising inequality. In Chapters 2 and 3, I departed from the benchmark model's emphasis on redistributive *outcomes* and grappled instead with the ways in which people experience inequality and redistribution as market income earners on the one hand, and stakeholders in a resource pooling endeavor on the other. Relaxing the assumption that voters are fully informed, I emphasized the key role of fairness reasoning in the form of policy preferences that covary with people's fairness beliefs. Fairness beliefs provide people with mental maps to simplify and make the world legible. Getting these mental maps right is an important step in the study of support for redistributive social policies.

The evidence presented in Chapter 3 not only documents the existence of fairness beliefs but also suggests revisiting mainstream conceptualizations and operationalizations of demand for redistribution. From the point of view of a third-party judge, reasoning about the fairness of redistributive social policies calls to mind two types of evaluations: Is it fair to take from those who have more? Is it fair to give to those who contribute less? Because people provide different answers to each question, demand for *redistribution from*, that is, support for policies that limit top-income inequality, is distinct from the willingness to contribute to *redistribution to*, that is, support for policies that cover the

---

[21] There is also an interesting difference between Baltic countries and countries like Poland or Hungary. The latter have famously experienced a populist wave, while the former have not. One might hypothesize that reciprocity beliefs may have an important role to play, something I leave for others to investigate.

needs of those who cannot provide for themselves. Measurement strategies that overlook this distinction risk leading researchers to contradictory or confusing results.

Next, I turn my attention to another of the benchmark model's assumptions, namely, the (plausible) claim that people prefer more disposable income than less.

Appendix

A3.1 Original Data Collection: Overview

The survey was completed online over a two months period (July and August 2019), using a sample provided by Dynata (www.dynata.com/). I requested a sample of 1,200 respondents living in England and Wales and 800 respondents living in Scotland. Quotas were used to approximate regional rates for age, gender, education and employment situation. The survey was conducted as open enrollment, whereby eligible panel members who log in to the Dynata website were offered a chance to partake in this survey. Surveys were completed using the Qualtrics online platform. Participants received a modest payment from Dynata for completing their survey. The oversampling of Scottish respondents was to examine whether fairness beliefs varied regionally. While I did found some differences, these were substantively small (e.g., around 0.1 SD). In the next analysis, I focus on the whole sample.

Given that this sample is not representative, the results cannot be interpreted with the same confidence as when using the BSAS sample. The main goal of this survey was to further probe the interpretation of the concepts discussed in Chapter 3 (i.e., proportionality beliefs, reciprocity beliefs and their relationship to attitudes toward *redistribution from* and *redistribution to* policies). In light of this goal, the lack of representativity is less concerning. Indeed, the aim is not to make population-level claims regarding the latent structure of the British public's beliefs and attitudes, but to examine whether inter-item patterns of correlation align with the interpretative framework discussed in Chapter 3. In this survey, I was able to include purposefully designed survey item alongside BSAS items. By examining whether these items correlate in expected way, I provide further evidence that they are capturing the hypothesized concepts of interest.

A main drawback of the BSAS is the absence of survey items specifically asking about *redistribution from* policies. The Dynata survey addresses this gap. I use answers to questions listed in the first part of Table A3.1 to build a variable measuring proportionality beliefs. This variable ranks respondents'

Table A3.1 *Items wording: Dynata survey*

Item wording	Fac. Sc.
Proportionality beliefs	
In the UK, income differences are legitimate reflections of differences in people's effort, talents and achievements (strongly disagree to strongly agree)	0.57
Working people do not get their fair share of the nation's wealth (strongly disagree to strongly agree)	0.48
In the UK, if people from a wealthy/poor background work hard, they never/once in a while/often/very often/most of the time/always get what they want (answers were combined to measure a respondent's assessment of differences in life chances between someone who is wealthy and someone who is poor.)	0.62
Imagine two British teenagers. One is born in a wealthy family, and the other is born in a poor family. Both want to be doctors one day. They are both hard workers and have similar grades at school. What are their respective chances of becoming doctors? (the teenager born in a poor family is much less likely/less likely/as likely/more likely/much more likely than the teenager born in a wealthy family.)	0.53
Eigenvalue	1.21
Reciprocity beliefs	
In the UK, too many people benefit from social services that they haven't helped to pay for (strongly disagree to strongly agree)	0.76
Most unemployed people do not really try to find a job (strongly disagree to strongly agree)	0.65
If social benefits weren't so generous, people would learn to stand on their own two feet (strongly disagree to strongly agree)	0.75
In your opinion, how many of your compatriots claim social benefits to which they are not entitled? (only a few/some/many (about half)/a lot/almost all)	0.34
In your opinion, of all the people applying for social benefits, how many misrepresent whether they qualify for the benefit? (only a few/some/many (about half)/a lot/almost all)	0.48
Thinking about mistakes the DWP makes when giving social benefits, which do you think is most common? (deny/give benefits to someone who qualifies/does not)	0.47
Eigenvalue	2.14

EFA on the pooled data. The factor loadings are obtained from a varimax rotation of a principal factors solution; the correlations analyzed are the polychoric correlations of the ordinal variables.
Source: Dynata 2019.

proportionality beliefs from "mostly unfair" (rewards are not proportional to merit) to "mostly fair" (rewards are proportional to merit), using weights derived from an EFA detailed in the same table.

I then examine how this variable predicts support for a tax on households with income over £100,000. Based on my argument, support for this tax on high incomes should not vary with reciprocity beliefs. To test this hypothesis, respondents were also asked a set of questions on free riding and moral hazard. These items are listed in the second part of Table A3.1. I use answers to these questions to build a variable measuring reciprocity beliefs. This variable ranks respondents' reciprocity beliefs from "mostly fair" (the prevalence of free riding is low) to "mostly unfair" (the prevalence of free riding is high), using weights derived from an EFA also detailed in the same table. As Figure A3.1 shows, while proportionality beliefs are predictive of answers to this tax item, reciprocity beliefs are not.

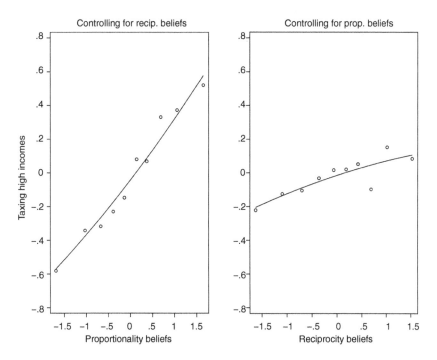

Figure A3.1 Opposition to taxing the rich and fairness beliefs
Binned scatter plots (individual-level analysis). The variable on the X-axis is split into ten bins. The line represents a quadratic fit computed using the full underlying data. Individual scores are calculated using weights recovered from an EFA. Variables have been standardized. Higher values are associated with opposition to taxes and anti-redistribution fairness beliefs.
Source: Dynata 2019.

A3.2 United States: Analysis of the PEW Items

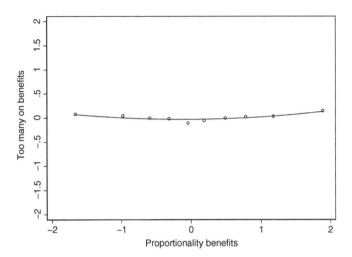

Figure A3.2 Perception of welfare recipients and proportionality beliefs in the United States
Binned scatter plot (individual-level analysis). See page 75 for item wordings. Individual X-axis scores are calculated using weights recovered from an EFA. Variables have been standardized. Higher values are associated with negative attitudes toward people on welfare and anti-redistribution proportionality beliefs.
Source: PEW Research Center, Value Survey 1987–2012, pooled data.

4

As If Self-interested? The Correlates
of Fairness Beliefs

Up to now, I have discussed the nature of fairness reasoning and its implications for redistributive preferences in isolation from other competing motives such as material self-interest. In Chapters 4 and 5, I bring material self-interest back into the picture. Chapter 5 examines the conditions under which people are informed of the pocketbook consequences of a given redistributive policy and act according to their material self-interest *in spite of* what fairness reasoning prescribes. In Chapter 4, I take on a different issue: To what extent do people, when seeking to do the fair thing, also end up doing the self-interested thing? This question raises the possibility that fairness reasoning and fairness beliefs lead people to opinions that align with their economic interest. If this is the case, amending the benchmark model to account for fairness reasoning, while more accurate, might not necessarily improve the model's overall predictive power.

The evidence presented in this chapter suggests that the tension between fairness reasoning and material self-interest is most acute in the case of reciprocity beliefs and support for *redistribution to* policies and less so for proportionality beliefs and support for *redistribution from* policies. Specifically, while proportionality beliefs correlate with someone's earning potential and exposure to economic risk, reciprocity beliefs do not. One reason, I show, is the robust correlation between reciprocity beliefs, on the one hand, and liberal-authoritarian values, on the other. As a result, there is a large share of low-income individuals who find a decline in *redistribution to* fair despite being more likely to be adversely affected by it. Conversely, there is a large share of high-income individuals who find an increase in *redistribution to* fair despite being unlikely to benefit from it.

What explains these correlations? Answering this question requires a theory of belief formation, something I will tackle in Part II of the book. In this chapter, I focus on correlations alone and what they tell us about fairness reasoning as a potential shortcut for people to reason *as if* concerned about their own pocketbook.

Do Individual Economic Conditions Predict Fairness Beliefs?

Redistribution from policies prevent people who have valuable skills and prior wealth from receiving a disproportionate share of economic resources. *Redistribution to* policies take the form of generous transfers from those who are in the good state of the world – employed, economically secure – to those who are currently in the bad state of the world – unemployed, economically insecure. This means that people with low-income, limited educational attainment and working in economically insecure occupations are more likely to benefit from both types of policies. I consequently start by examining the correlation between people's fairness beliefs on the one hand, and their economic situation on the other.

For this analysis, I return to the BSAS introduced in Chapter 3. To increase sample size, I pool two consecutive waves (2003 and 2004). To measure individual differences in proportionality and reciprocity beliefs, I focus on the subset of survey items that are available in both waves and combine them using weights recovered from an EFA. These items are listed in Table 3.5 (see italicized items). In the case of proportionality beliefs, higher scores indicate a higher likelihood of disagreement with statements such as "working people do not get their fair share of nation's wealth," or "there is one law for the rich and one law for the poor." In the case of reciprocity beliefs, higher scores indicate a higher likelihood of agreement with claims such as "the welfare state encourages people to stop helping each other" or "most people on the dole are fiddling."[1]

To measure educational attainment, I rely on a variable that classifies respondents based on the highest degree obtained. The income variable is described in Appendix A1.1. Combined, income and education levels provide a rough proxy of one's earning capacity. To proxy for the likelihood that one will end

---

[1] Note that, in the case of proportionality beliefs, I also include the traditional redistribution item among the survey items used to compute individual scores. That's because, relative to reciprocity items, fewer proportionality items were asked in both waves (four items versus six). Adding the traditional redistribution item helps close this gap. As discussed in Chapter 3, the traditional redistribution item strongly loads on the same dimension as other proportionality items. For symmetry, I also add to the reciprocity items a questions on government support for the unemployed (Table 3.6, bottom line). Note that results remain the same without these two policy-centric items.

up unemployed, I rely on three different measures. One is whether or not someone is unemployed at the time of the data collection. The other is a measure of the occupational unemployment rate computed using labor force survey data obtained through Eurostat and following the measurement strategy developed by Rehm (2009). Specifically, I pool three years of labor force survey data to compute unemployment rates for occupations defined at the three-digit level. The occupational unemployment rate is the ratio of individuals unemployed in this occupation over the total number of individuals classified as belonging to this occupation. Finally, I use a measure of risk developed by Iversen and Soskice (2001) that assesses how specific the skills required by a given occupation are. The more specific the skills, the harder it is, when faced with a layoff, to switch to other occupations. Note that this measure is only available for occupations identified at the two-digit level.

I regress fairness beliefs on income, education and unemployment risk. Results are presented in Table 4.1 in Columns (1) through (8). As shown in Column (1), more income implies more conservative proportionality beliefs. In contrast, income is not correlated with reciprocity beliefs (Column (5)). Comparing Columns (5) and (6), part of the reason for the absence of a correlation appears to be the role of education: the more education, the more one holds pro-redistribution reciprocity beliefs. In contrast, education is associated with anti-redistribution proportionality beliefs (see Column (2)). With regard to measures of risk exposure (Columns (3) and (7)), being in a high unemployment occupation implies more pro-redistribution proportionality beliefs but has no relationship to reciprocity beliefs. Overall, when it comes to reciprocity beliefs, measures of risk exposure have limited predictive power with one main exception: Unemployed individuals (less than 3% of the sample) are more likely to express pro-redistribution reciprocity beliefs than employed individuals. To sum up, one's position as a winner or loser of the economic "race" helps predict whether one finds this race fair. In contrast, with the exception of being unemployed, one's position as a potential beneficiary of social solidarity does not predict whether one believes that social solidarity is unfairly benefiting free riders.

To examine if this conclusion extends beyond Great Britain, I turn to the ISSP and ESS introduced in Chapter 3. Due to data constraints, I focus on two empirical regularities documented in the British case. One is the fact that income correlates with proportionality beliefs but does not correlate with reciprocity beliefs. The second is the fact that more education implies more anti-redistribution proportionality beliefs alongside more pro-redistribution reciprocity beliefs. The results, presented in Appendix A4.1, show that, in most countries, the patterns found for Great Britain replicate.

Table 4.1 *Economic predictors of proportionality and reciprocity beliefs*

	(1)	(2)	(3)	(4)	(5)	(6)	(7)	(8)	(9)
	Proportionality beliefs					Reciprocity beliefs			
	b/se	b/se	b/se	b/se	b/se	b/se	b/se	b/se	b/se
Income (log)	.64***	.51***		.51***	.01	.25***		.17**	.19***
	(.05)	(.05)		(.06)	(.05)	(.05)		(.05)	(.05)
Education CSE or equivalent		.05		.04		.05		.02	.11
		(.08)		(.08)		(.08)		(.08)	(.07)
O-levels		.19**		.18**		−.19**		−.22**	−.08
		(.06)		(.06)		(.07)		(.07)	(.06)
A-levels		.26***		.23**		−.27***		−.28***	−.03
		(.08)		(.08)		(.08)		(.08)	(.07)
Some higher education		.35***		.31***		−.31***		−.33***	−.098
		(.08)		(.08)		(.08)		(.08)	(.07)
University degree		.41***		.37***		−.80***		−.80***	−.27***
		(.07)		(.08)		(.08)		(.08)	(.07)
Occupational unemployment rate			−.40***	−.18***			.08	−.02	−.07
			(.05)	(.05)			(.05)	(.05)	(.01)
Unemployed			−.25	.06			−.80***	−.70***	−.61***
			(.05)	(.05)			(.05)	(.05)	(.04)
Skill specificity			−.09*	−.06			−.06	−.08*	−.09*
			(.04)	(.04)			(.04)	(.04)	(.03)
LAVs									−.80***
									(.03)
Cons	−.03	−.22***	.08**	−.25***	.01	.25***	.06	.32***	1.89***
	(.02)	(.04)	(.03)	(.05)	(.02)	(.04)	(.03)	(.05)	(.08)
N	2059	2059	2059	2059	2059	2059	2059	2059	2027
ll	−2808	−2787	−2864	−2779	−2916	−2845	−2896	−2829	−2468
r^2	.10	.12	.05	.12	.0	.07	.02	.08	.32

Higher values imply more anti-redistribution fairness beliefs. Outcome variables are standardized. Continuous predictors are demeaned and divided by 2 standard deviations. Coefficients can consequently be interpreted as a β standard deviation(s) change in Y following a 2 SD change in X. Significance levels: * $p<.05$, ** $p<.01$ *** $p<.001$.
Source: BSAS 2003–2004, pooled.

Reciprocity Beliefs: If Not Economic
Conditions Then What?

Why do individual economic conditions predict differences in proportionality beliefs but not differences in reciprocity beliefs? As I document in this section, part of the answer lies in the overlap between fairness beliefs and the two dimensions of political conflict in postindustrial democracies. Specifically, while proportionality beliefs are constitutive of the first economic/redistributive dimension, reciprocity beliefs fall along the "second dimension," a dimension of political conflict often described as "non-economic." In Part II, I trace this overlap to differences in how people reason about solutions to social dilemmas and the monitoring of free riding. For now, my goal is simply to document the overlap between reciprocity beliefs and this "second dimension" in the form of a robust and substantive correlation between reciprocity beliefs on the one hand, and liberal–authoritarian values on the other.

I use the expression "second dimension" with some caution. Indeed, while there is a general consensus regarding the nature of the first economic/ redistributive dimension, this consensus does not extend to the second dimension. Some researchers boil the latter down to whatever noneconomic issue is most salient in their country and period of interest, for example, immigration (Ford and Jennings, 2020), government intervention in favor of minority groups (Miller and Schofield, 2003), nationalism (Shayo, 2009), abortion or gay rights (Weeden and Kurzban, 2014). Others emphasize the shared "cultural preferences" or "values" that underpin people's attitudes toward these issues, distinguishing between "liberals" and "authoritarians" (Kitschelt, 1997). Given how constitutive of the second dimension issues of immigration and multiculturalism have become, it is now common to talk of "cosmopolitan liberals" and "parochial authoritarians" (Kitschelt and Rehm, 2014).[2] Throughout the book, I will speak of liberal–authoritarian values, or LAVs for short, as measured using items about order and discipline. Absent a clear understanding of what this second dimension is, my emphasis is on the survey items themselves, which capture how much people agree with an "authoritarian" approach to order and discipline.

Table 4.2 lists items commonly used to measure LAVs and available in the BSAS. I combine these items using factor scores recovered from a factor analysis. Figure 4.1 uses the 2016 wave of the BSAS and binned scatter plots to

---

[2] Other expressions include "communitarian" versus "liberal" (Bornschier, 2010), "materialist" versus "post-materialist" (Inglehart, 2007) or "open" versus "closed" (Johnston, Lavine and Federico, 2017).

Table 4.2 *Items wording: LAVs and anti-immigrant sentiment*

BSAS
Liberal–authoritarian values

People who break the law should be given stiffer sentences
For some crimes, the death penalty is the most appropriate sentence
Young people today do not have enough respect for traditional British values
Schools should teach children to obey authority

ESS

Anti-immigrant sentiment	*Liberal–authoritarian values*
Immigration bad or good for this country's economy	Schools should teach children to obey authority
Country's cultural life undermined or enriched by immigrants	People who break the law should receive much harsher sentences
Immigrants make this country worse or better place to live	Terrorist suspect should be in prison until police is satisfied
Allow many/few immigrants of different race/ethnic group from majority	
Allow many/few immigrants from poorer countries outside Europe	
Allow many/few immigrants of the same race/ethnic group as majority	

---

illustrate the correlation between reciprocity beliefs and LAVs. The left panel reproduces results from Chapter 3: More anti-redistribution proportionality beliefs does not translate into more anti-redistribution reciprocity beliefs. Any evidence of a correlation between proportionality and reciprocity beliefs is limited to a small subset of left-wing respondents (score 1 standard deviation (SD) or more below the mean). In contrast, the relationship between LAVs and reciprocity beliefs (right panel) is positive. As shown in Table 4.1 Column (9), once individual LAVs are included, the relationship between education and reciprocity beliefs disappears. In other words, the higher prevalence of pro-redistribution reciprocity beliefs among the higher educated is nearly entirely explained by the latter's more liberal values.

How much weight should we put on the overlap between reciprocity beliefs and measures of second dimension attitudes? If the correlation described above can be easily interpreted in light of existing theories of belief and attitude formation, then the answer is "not much." If, in contrast, this correlation is robust to alternative interpretations, then a theory on the nature and origins of reciprocity belief will have to address it head on. Next, I examine two such alternative interpretations and show that none can explain why reciprocity beliefs correlate with LAVs.

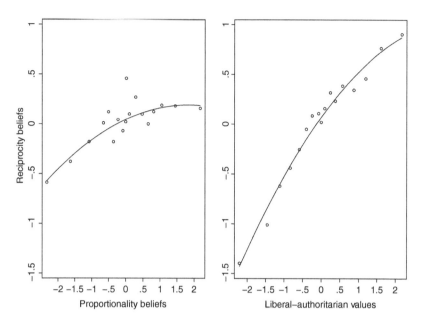

Figure 4.1 Reciprocity beliefs and liberal–authoritarian values
Binned scatter plots (individual-level analysis). The variable on the X-axis is split into twenty bins. The line represents a quadratic fit computed using the full underlying data. Individual scores are calculated using weights recovered from an EFA. Variables have been standardized. Higher values are associated with anti-redistribution fairness beliefs.
Source: BSAS 2016.

It's Immigration Stupid

Because the second dimension encompasses disagreement over immigration (Ford and Jennings, 2020), a plausible explanation of the previously described correlation is that reciprocity beliefs are capturing hostility to immigrants, themselves perceived to be overrepresented among benefit recipients (Alesina and Glaeser, 2006). This would suggest that the correlation documented in Figure 4.1 (right panel) is an artifact of the well-known correlation between LAVs and anti-immigrant sentiment, with anti-immigrant sentiment doing most of the heavy lifting. If reciprocity beliefs are mostly capturing hostility to immigrants in a context in which the poor and the unemployed are stereotyped as racially "other," then high hostility among low-educated beneficiaries of *redistribution to* policies might explain why reciprocity beliefs do not correlate with income and unemployment risk.

Assuming anti-immigrant sentiment is driving the relationship documented in Figure 4.1, the positive correlation between free riding beliefs and LAVs should disappear once controlling for anti-immigrant sentiment. Unfortunately, the BSAS used in Figure 4.1 does not include items that ask about immigration and immigrants. As an alternative, I turn to the ESS already introduced in Chapter 3, which includes reciprocity items similar to those available in the BSAS (see Table 3.6 for item wording). Furthermore, the ESS also includes a battery of items asking about anti-immigrant sentiment and LAVs. These are listed in Table 4.2.

Figure 4.2 presents binned scatter plots examining average reciprocity beliefs according to individual scores on the LAV scale, with and without controlling for anti-immigrant sentiment (left and center panels). The top panel uses British data, and the bottom panel presents the same analysis for Germany. In

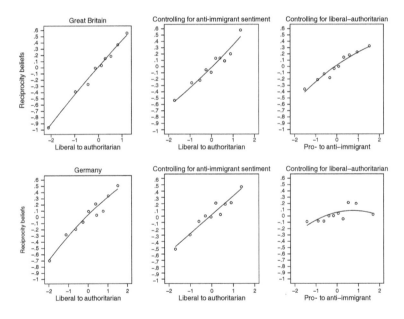

Figure 4.2 Reciprocity beliefs and anti-immigrant sentiment
Binned scatter plots (individual-level analysis). The variable on the X-axis is split into ten bins. Individual scores are computed using an EFA. Scores have been standardized using the country-specific mean and SD. Higher values are associated with conservative beliefs (i.e., high prevalence of free riding, authoritarian values, and anti-immigrant sentiment). Interpretation: In Great Britain 1 SD increase in the LAV score is equal to about half a SD increase in the reciprocity belief score (top-left panel).
Source: ESS 2008.

Great Britain, the two predictors explain roughly a similar share of the variance in reciprocity beliefs. In Germany, reciprocity beliefs are correlated with LAVs only: Any correlation between anti-immigrant sentiment and free riding beliefs disappears once the LAV index is included (bottom-right panel). A separate analysis reveals that, in many Western democracies, the pattern is somewhere between the one in Germany and the one in Great Britain.[3] In other words, the correlation between reciprocity beliefs and LAVs is not simply an artifact of differences in anti-immigrant sentiment.

Status threat

Another potential explanation for the lack of correlation between economic conditions and reciprocity beliefs emphasizes the role of status threat concerns (or ego protection). According to this line of reasoning, while pro-redistribution proportionality beliefs (i.e., "effort does not pay" and "differences in market income are unfair") are ego boosting for the poor, pro-redistribution reciprocity beliefs ("welfare recipients are deserving" and "benefits do not make people lazy") are not, thus explaining the disconnect between the two types of beliefs.

Indeed, for individuals of lower income and lower social status, assuming that the world is fair according to the proportionality norm also means grappling with the fact that their own income level signals less talent, fewer abilities and lower merit. For high-income individuals, believing the world is unfair according to the proportionality norm means accepting that they themselves may not be as talented or meritorious as their economic success suggests. One straightforward hypothesis is that individuals try to minimize the psychological cost of acknowledging lower merit and choose their fairness beliefs accordingly. The correlations documented in Table 4.1 are consistent with this explanation.

When it comes to reciprocity beliefs, ethnographic work finds that holding pessimistic beliefs about the high prevalence of free riding has ego-protecting properties (Lamont, 2002; Sherman, 2009). By presenting "other" recipients as "scroungers," individuals build a symbolic boundary that distinguishes them from norm-violating free riders and increases the perceived social distance between themselves and others at the bottom of the deservingness ladder. According to Lamont and Molnar (2002), this process of social distancing provides an "essential medium through which people acquire status" and self-esteem.[4] Jointly, this evidence suggests that being economically and socially proximate

---

[3] Additional country figures are available in the online appendix.
[4] See also Chase and Walker (2013), Gubrium and Lødemel (2013) and Garthwaite (2016).

to the poor and the unemployed can increase the propensity to present the latter as undeserving. To the extent that people from lower status tend to hold less liberal values, then the correlation between reciprocity beliefs and LAVs could itself be an artifact of status concerns.

To explore this possibility, I rely on an occupation-centric social stratification scale developed by Lambert and Prandy (2012). It captures how socially proximate someone is to those at the bottom of the status hierarchy. Lambert and his colleagues rely on census data to build a contingency table where the rows indicate the range of one partner's occupation and the columns indicate the range of the other partner's occupation. The cells contain the number of occurrences of each combination in the population.[5] Lambert and coauthors then use these data to rank occupations from least to most socially proximate on the basis of the likelihood that members of two occupations live under the same roof. Different scales are calculated for men and women, "since holding the same occupation may have different implications for a person's social position, depending on their gender" (Bergman and Joye, 2001, p. 36).[6] On one end of the scale are professional occupations such as doctors or lawyers (who receive higher scores on the scale), and on the other end are low-skill occupations, such as janitors or care workers (who receive lower scores).

Using detailed occupational information, I match BSAS respondents to their occupational scores. Regressing fairness beliefs on the occupational social distance score, I find that an increase in social distance is associated with more anti-redistribution proportionality beliefs and more pro-redistribution reciprocity beliefs (see Appendix A4.2). This aligns with the status threat interpretation of the difference between the determinants of proportionality beliefs and that of reciprocity beliefs.

Still, given that people with higher education levels have both higher status and more liberal values, this result could still be an artifact of the correlation between reciprocity beliefs and LAVs. To address this possibility, I zoom in on individuals with a tertiary degree (N= 621) and examine whether, within this group, social distance still predicts reciprocity beliefs. Due to a smaller sample size, I do not rely on binned scatter plots and use predicted values derived from a linear regression instead: The linear assumption helps compensate for the smaller number of observations.[7]

Figure 4.3 plots the relationship between LAVs, reciprocity beliefs and proportionality beliefs on the one hand, and occupational ranking on the other.

---

[5] Partnership is defined here as both marriage and cohabitation.

[6] For issues relating to "diagonal" effects (e.g., farmer will most likely marry a farmer) and multidimensionality, see Lambert and Prandy (2012) as well as www.camsis.stir.ac.uk/.

[7] Note, however, that I find similar results using using both kernel and locally linear regressions.

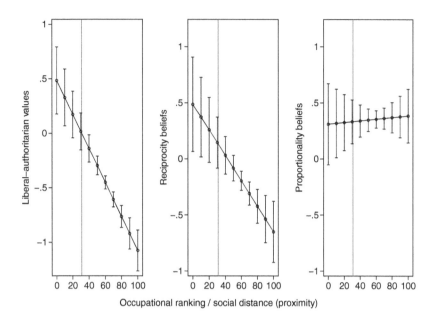

Figure 4.3 Occupational ranking and fairness beliefs: Tertiary education only
Plots predicted values and 95% confidence intervals computed after regressing
fairness beliefs over the occupational ranking/social distance measure. See notes
accompanying Figure 4.1 and Table 4.2 for information on scores. The vertical line
marks the first percentile of the occupational ranking variable within the subsam-
ple of university-educated respondents. As one might expect, few highly educated
individuals end up in the "lowest" occupations.
Source: BSAS 2003–2004 pooled.

Among people with a college degree, there is no relationship between proportionality beliefs and occupational ranking, suggesting that the positive correlation between the two documented in Appendix A4.2 is itself an artifact of
more educated individuals holding more anti-redistribution proportionality beliefs. In contrast, even *among* people with a tertiary degree, the extent to which
individuals end up in occupations socially proximate to the poor predicts how
unsympathetic they are toward beneficiaries of *redistribution to* policies. However, as the left panel shows, we still cannot reject the null that this finding is an
artifact of the correlation between reciprocity beliefs and LAVs: Even among
people with a tertiary degree, being socially more proximate to the bottom of
the social ladder is associated with more authoritarian values.

    To sum up, the overlap between reciprocity beliefs and measures of second
dimension attitudes cannot be easily dismissed. Off-the-shelf interpretations of
this pattern have limited empirical leverage. First, these theories have little to

say about the correlation between reciprocity beliefs and LAVs. Furthermore, as I have shown, these arguments hinge on empirical patterns that are themselves an artifact of this robust correlation.

Summary and Next Steps

Proportionality beliefs are, to a large extent, self-serving. Individuals who benefit more from the economic status quo, as proxied by income and occupational prestige, are also more likely to find it fair and thus more likely to oppose *redistribution from* policies as unfair. In this case, fairness reasoning and material self-interest lead to similar outcomes. Reciprocity beliefs follow a very different logic: A large portion of the poor believe free riding to be ubiquitous, are concerned about moral hazard and will consequently find it fair to punish free riders through spending cuts and intrusive monitoring of recipients. In contrast, a large portion of the rich hold the opposite fairness beliefs and policy preferences.

Part of the reason is the strong correlation between reciprocity beliefs and people's position on what political scientists call the liberal–authoritarian value scale, itself constitutive of the second dimension of political conflict. Why are answers to questions about sentencing and discipline in school informative of answers to questions about the deservingness of able-bodied beneficiaries of social solidarity? Does this suggest a blurring of the boundaries between economic and noneconomic attitudes? In Part II, I will propose and test an argument in which this correlation is to be expected.

But before we get there, I still need to examine one additional way in which people can form self-interested policy preferences. In Chapter 5, I examine the conditions under which people disregard what fairness reasoning prescribes and settle on a self-serving policy position instead.

Appendix

A4.1 Probing the Structure of Beliefs Beyond Great Britain

In Great Britain, income correlates with proportionality beliefs but does not correlate with reciprocity beliefs. Furthermore, more education implies more anti-redistribution proportionality beliefs alongside more pro-redistribution reciprocity beliefs. Is this true beyond Great Britain? To measure fairness beliefs in other countries, I use the cross-national measures of proportionality beliefs (ISSP, 2009) and reciprocity beliefs (ESS, 2008) introduced in Chapter 3. In contrast to the ESS, the ISSP dataset has many missing values on the income variable. I consequently limit my analysis to countries for which missing values represent less than 20% of the overall sample. To measure educational attainment, I recode education variables such that individuals belong to one of three categories: individuals who only hold a high school degree or less, individuals with a four-year tertiary degree or more and individuals who fall somewhere in between. To probe the correlations between fairness beliefs, on the one hand and education and income on the other, I use predicted values derived from an ordinary least squares (OLS) regression that includes both income and education. Table A4.1 presents the difference between predicted values for people with high income/education and people with low income/education. Note that, in the case of the ISSP, the income variables, and consequently the quantities of interest, are not comparable across countries.

Table A4.1 *Difference in fairness beliefs by income and education levels*

	Reciprocity beliefs (from pro-RT to anti-RT)				Proportionality beliefs (from pro-RF to anti-RF)	
	M1		M2		M1	
	Income (p10–p90)	Univ. (ref: HS)	Cultural values	Univ. (ref: HS)	Income (norm.)	Univ. (ref: HS)
Matches expectations						
FR	−0.03	−0.66	−0.71	−0.26	0.43	0.09
DK	−0.19	−0.71	−0.53	−0.33	0.60	0.49
BE	−0.08	−0.40	−0.59	−0.13	0.23	0.62
SE	−0.11	−0.32	−0.73	0.07	0.70	0.47
DE	0.11	−0.17	−0.54	0.08	0.34	0.53
AT	0.15	−0.25	−0.76	0.12		
FI	−0.02	−0.48	−0.56	−0.23		
NO	0.04	−0.26	−0.57	−0.01	3.99	0.56
GB	−0.10	−0.22	−0.57	−0.04		
SI	−0.18	−0.29	−0.56	0.02		
IE	0.07	−0.23	−0.48	−0.01		
ES	0.05	−0.40	−0.32	−0.22		
HR	−0.33	−0.30	−0.31	−0.41		
CH	−0.00	−0.56	−0.38	−0.39		
NL	−0.12	−0.39	−0.35	−0.27		
JP					0.22	0.46
Flag on education						
GR	−0.36	−0.00	−0.40	0.16		
RO	−0.06	−0.06	−0.44	0.07		
HU	−0.06	−0.00	−0.43	0.15		
US					0.41	−0.17
AU					0.76	0.04

(*continued*)

Table A4.1 *(cont.)*

	Reciprocity beliefs (from pro-RT to anti-RT)				Proportionality beliefs (from pro-RF to anti-RF)	
	M1		M2		M1	
	Income (p10–p90)	Univ. (ref: HS)	Cultural values	Univ. (ref: HS)	Income (norm.)	Univ. (ref: HS)
Does not match expectations						
PL	0.02	0.21	−0.18	0.28	0.07	0.59
EE	0.17	−0.29	−0.25	−0.24		
CZ	0.10	0.74	−0.27	0.79		
LV	−0.17	0.06	−0.19	0.11		
PT	−0.32	−0.23	−0.12	−0.18		

Reports differences in predicted fairness beliefs between high-income/education respondents and low-income/education respondents. Predicted values are computed by regressing fairness beliefs on income and education (M1) and adding LAV scores (M2). Fairness belief variables are standardized (country-specific mean and SD). Higher values indicate more anti-redistribution fairness beliefs. High education and low education are equal to a university degree and high school degree, respectively. For the ISSP, high and low income levels are equal to the highest and lowest income categories, respectively. These categories differ across countries, meaning that the estimates reported in the table cannot be compared across countries. For the ESS, high and low income levels are equal to the 90th and 10th percentiles, respectively. In the case of LAV scores, I compute the difference between predicted fairness beliefs for someone 1 SD above the mean (authoritarian) and someone 1 SD below the mean (liberal). *Source:* ESS 2008, ISSP 2009.

In the first cluster of countries, the patterns found for Great Britain seem to hold pretty well. In Sweden, for example, income correlates with proportionality beliefs but not reciprocity beliefs. In addition, more education means more conservative beliefs with regard to the former and more liberal beliefs with regard to the latter. Not all countries, however, show the same patterns. Note, for example, the weak income gradient on proportionality beliefs in the United States, something I will explore in more detail in Chapter 8. Similarly, in Norway, proportionality beliefs do not appear to be correlated with either income or education. Still, overall, the results indicate that correlations documented using British data are not unique to this country.

In the second part of this chapter, I discussed the correlation between reciprocity beliefs and LAVs. Model 2 (M2) in Table A4.1 adds LAVs to the analysis. Once LAVS are controlled for, the size of the coefficient on education decreases. This suggests that educational differences in authoritarian orientation help explain why more educated individuals have more pro-*redistribution to* fairness beliefs when it comes to the reciprocity norm, despite having more anti-*redistribution from* fairness beliefs when it comes to the proportionality norm.

A4.2 Occupational Ranking and Fairness Beliefs

Figure A4.1 plots average fairness beliefs by social occupational ranking bins. Notice how, as occupational ranking increases, fairness beliefs become more anti-redistribution and reciprocity beliefs more pro-redistribution.

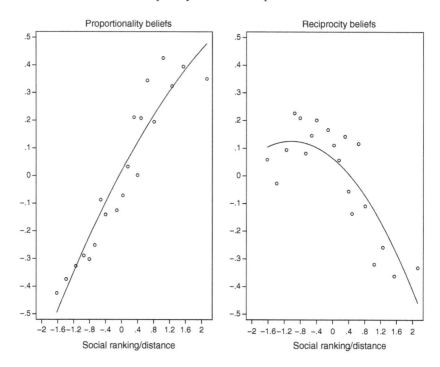

Figure A4.1 Occupational ranking and fairness beliefs: Full sample
Binned scatter plots (individual-level analysis). Variables are standardized. Higher values indicate more anti-redistribution fairness beliefs. Each bin corresponds to a occupational-ranking/social-distance score.
Source: BSAS 2003 and 2004.

5

When Material Self-interest Trumps
Fairness Reasoning

Pocketbook reasoning is difficult. It is both easier and more rewarding to do (in this case to say) the fair thing, that is, express support for a redistributive policy that would positively affect the fairness of the status quo or oppose one that would make the status quo less fair. Still, while reasoning in line with one's pocketbook is difficult for most people most of the time, there are important differences both across individuals and across different types of redistributive policies. Some policy proposals are more transparent about costs and benefits than others. Furthermore, for high-stakes policies, people will invest the necessary time to understand how a policy works and how it can be changed to best serve their own interest (Roth, Settele and Wohlfart, 2022). When stakes are transparent and high, people will disregard their fairness concerns and take the self-interested position instead.

This mechanism has the most consequences for policy attitudes shaped by reciprocity beliefs. Indeed, as discussed in Chapter 4, on *redistribution to* issues, many people are cross-pressured, meaning they are inclined, against their "objective" material interest, to support or oppose a given policy out of fairness concerns. For these individuals, reasoning as an income maximizer can result in a dramatic departure from what fairness reasoning would prescribe. In contrast, given that proportionality beliefs lead people to reason "as if" self-interested on *redistribution from* issues, whether one is doing the fair thing or the self-interested thing has smaller implications for policy attitudes.

In this chapter, I examine how this simple argument helps explain variations in the income gradient, namely differences in the extent to which the rich and the poor disagree on redistributive issues. The evidence presented in this chapter focuses on the *structure* of mass redistributive preferences. The implications for understanding the *dynamics* of mass redistributive preferences in times of rising inequality will be examined in Part II.

101

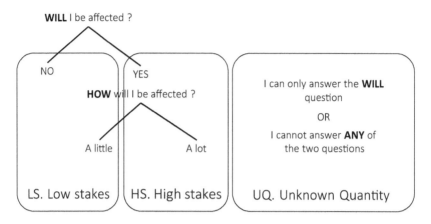

Figure 5.1 The three worlds of counterfactual reasoning

Combining the Two Motives: A Two-Step Approach

In the case of *redistribution from* policies, what counts as a fairness maximizing policy depends on how one answers the following question: "To what extent is market income proportional to merit?" In the case of *redistribution to* policies, what counts as a fairness maximizing policy depends on how one answers the following question: "Is the modal beneficiary free riding and undeserving?" Reasoning in a self-interested fashion about a given policy calls to mind a very different set of questions, namely, "Will my income be affected?" and "How much will my income be affected?" Policies for which one can assign a high probability of being affected, and also infer that the effect will be substantive, are high-stakes policies. Policies for which one can assign a low probability of being affected, or infer that the effect will be minimal, are low-stakes policies. In some situations, voters cannot assign any probability of being affected (Knight, 2012). Even those who can might still not know the extent of the impact, which could be small or large. In this case, the material implications of a change in the status quo are an unknown quantity. These differences are sketched in Figure 5.1.

The assumption that individuals behave selfishly and rationally (e.g., seeking additional information even when the issue is complex) in ways that maximize their income is most useful when stakes are high. Because many voters experience redistributive issues as either low stakes or an unknown quantity, reasoning according to one's material self-interest is the exception, not the norm.

To understand why redistributive issues are rarely experienced as high-stakes, it is worth contrasting the institutional environment of redistributive politics in representative democracies with the "highly structured and competitive environment" of "open markets" (Ostrom and Walker, 2003, p. 25). Actors participating in open markets face a high-stakes environment where information is provided at a manageable cost,[1] feedback is continuous and learning is strongly incentivized.[2] Such institutional setup rewards self-interested economic reasoning, decreases the latter's cognitive costs and penalizes competing non–self-interested and non-economic modes of reasoning. As a result, in the majority of cases, the behavior of individuals interacting through market institutions can be usefully approximated using the homo economicus theoretical tool box.[3]

Yet the *same* individuals, when engaged in "producing" redistributive social policies through the institutions of representative democracies, are unlikely to behave as self-interested, materially inclined and well-informed actors. This is partly due to the nature of redistributive politics in countries with mature welfare states. Indeed, self-interested politicians seeking to compromise between conflicting interests and to minimize the risk of a backlash will often propose and implement policies with diffuse redistributive implications. Strategic avoidance of policies with large redistributive implications is especially likely in countries with large welfare states and high levels of taxation (Pierson, 2001). Additionally, in these countries, low stakes often go hand in hand with high uncertainty. Indeed, states' capacity to generate cheap sovereign debt not only helps diffuse the costs of redistributive reforms by passing them on to future generations but also increases uncertainty by blurring the relationship between social spending and taxation. Finally, as highlighted by Downs (1957), politicians seeking to win elections will remain equivocal and ambiguous about the redistributive implications of their policy proposals. Alternative information-aggregating actors such as unions have often stepped in to close the information gap, but recent studies have shown that their contribution to public discourse has decreased dramatically in the past few decades (Farber et al., 2021; Wallerstein and Western, 2000).

---

[1] Price signals provide feedback at no cost and less accessible information can be supplied for a fee by specialized industries (e.g., tax lawyers and consulting firms).

[2] This is especially true for new market entrants as those who fail to behave in a self-interested fashion are quickly pushed out of the market.

[3] There are, of course, differences across types of market actors and market behaviors. Stakes are higher for consumers choosing which car to buy than for those choosing which snack to indulging in. Similarly, the disciplining effect of market institutions is especially large for market entrants.

Faced with a complex combination of taxes and transfers and only limited guidance from the political context, voters could still form self-interested preferences through "learning-by-doing," by which I mean the process of acting on one's preferences and then facing the consequences of these actions. Yet, as highlighted by Schumpeter more than half a century ago, in representative democracies, this specific form of learning is limited as voters rarely get to connect a political outcome to their own individual action, let alone policy preference (Schumpeter, 1950).

For most people, redistributive politics, as it plays out in representative democracies, is a low-stakes and/or an unknown quantity. But this general statement hides important variations across individuals and across policies: For some people, on some issues, fairness reasoning can be crowded out by a credible and sizable "threat" of material loss or "promise" of material gain.

Combining Fairness Reasoning and Material Self-interest

For a given individual, whether a policy proposal is low stakes, high stakes or an unknown quantity is determined by her own individual characteristics, the amount of information available regarding how these characteristics interact with existing policies and proposed policy changes, and the extent to which one faces incentives to acquire new information to turn uncertainty into a known risk. Take, for example, a 60-year-old American man, with adult children and aging high-income parents. Some policies will be high-stakes (e.g., a decrease in the inheritance tax to be paid when his parents die), others low-stakes (e.g., an increase in spending on Medicaid that he will only need if he falls into poverty) and some will be an unknown quantity (e.g., Obamacare, whose implications for already insured individuals are mediated by long-term adjustments in the healthcare market).

To account for this variation in uncertainty and stakes, I conceptualize preference formation as a two-step process. First, individuals rely on fairness reasoning to anchor their preferences following the "if fair then support," "if unfair then oppose" heuristic. Second, depending on information and material stakes, individuals will adjust their preferences in line with their material self-interest, something I call *self-serving adjustment* for short. The size of this adjustment will vary with the stakes: The higher the material stakes, the more extensive self-serving adjustment will be.

Assuming that people follow this two-step process generates testable predictions regarding the structure of mass attitudes, namely predictions regarding who will be particularly likely to self-servingly adjust, and how this varies across policy issues and institutional contexts.[4] One set of predictions pertains to ideological consistency and the other to the size of the income gradient. I examine each in turn.

Predicting Ideological Consistency: Not Always the Usual Suspects

From this two-step process, one can derive a simple but intriguing empirical prediction regarding ideological consistency. In the context of this book, ideological consistency describes the extent to which fairness beliefs align with policy preferences. Previous research has tied ideological consistency to "cognitive abilities," education level or one's level of engagement with politics and policy debates (Goren, 2001; Jacoby, 1991; Johnston, Lavine and Federico, 2017). I argue that another important factor is the interplay between fairness beliefs and material self-interest, as mediated by uncertainty over a policy's material consequences.

To understand why this is the case, let's first focus on *redistribution to* policies. When forming an opinion on these issues, individuals first ask themselves what is the fair thing to do (step 1 in Figure 5.2). People who believe that these policies benefit and encourage free riding will start from a baseline of low support. People who believe recipients are deserving cooperators who need to be treated in kind will start from a baseline of high support. This reliance on fairness reasoning is captured by the dashed lines connecting the lower-left corner to the upper-right corner. In contrast, the horizontal lines capture what support would look like if it was only self-interested. In a second step, people ask themselves how much this policy affects them, that is, how much income they gain if they are net beneficiaries or how much they lose if they are net contributors (step 2 in Figure 5.2). For net beneficiaries, the answer to this question is straightforward: They benefit a lot in the form of a monthly transfer they rely on to make ends meet. A change in the status quo would consequently have large and visible implications in the form of more or less disposable income. As a result, net beneficiaries who might find it unfair to reward free riding still support more generous *redistribution to* policies out of self-interest. Among

---

[4] This two-step process is a stylized representation of reality. Nevertheless, existing studies suggest that this two-step process is a decent approximation of people's thought process. Take, for example, the finding by Margalit (2013) that job loss triggers an increase in support for unemployment insurance, though only temporarily and mostly among Republicans. In "normal times," Republicans tend to oppose unemployment insurance because it rewards free riding. Job loss triggers self-serving adjustment among those affected. Over time, as their situation improves, and unemployment insurance is no longer experienced as a high stakes issue, individuals will revert to their original position, as defined by their beliefs about the fairness of the status quo.

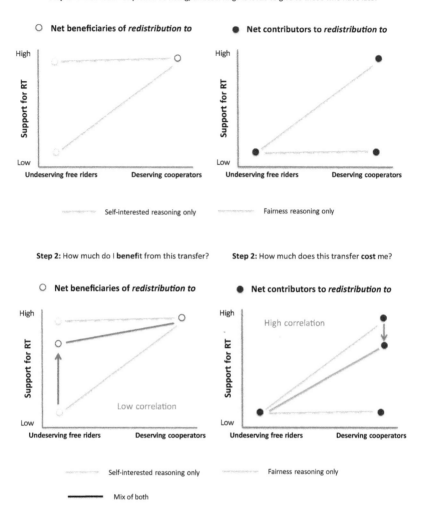

Figure 5.2   A two-step approach
RT: *redistribution to*.

net beneficiaries, because most people support *redistribution to* policies out of self-interest, there is only a small correlation between reciprocity beliefs and attitudes: Ideological consistency is low.

Net contributors know that they do not benefit from the transfer; for them, it is a cost. Yet in their case, the implications for their pocketbook are obscured by fiscal policy and the sheer complexity of the welfare state's funding structure. To understand if they will benefit from a change in the status quo, they need to know whether their taxes will be directly affected and if so, how much. Even if someone believes that a cut in social spending will come alongside a tax cut, the latter is unlikely to be large. In other words, for net contributors, *redistribution to* is either uncertain, low stakes or both, making self-serving counterfactual reasoning difficult. As a result, net contributors who think that these policies are fair stick to that position and do not update in a self-serving fashion (contrast the small downward arrow on the right, with the large upward arrow on the left). This implies that, among net contributors, reciprocity beliefs are predictive of policy preferences: ideological consistency is high.

Assuming most high-income people are net contributors and most low-income individuals are net beneficiaries, I consequently expect the correlation between reciprocity beliefs and support for *redistribution to* policies to be higher among high-income than low-income individuals. Again, as sketched in Figure 5.2, this difference in ideological consistency follows from higher rates of self-serving adjustment among low-income individuals.

Now let's shift the focus to *redistribution from* policies. Because they interfere with high earners' ability to accumulate income and wealth, these policies have more direct implications for high-income than for low-income individuals. As a result, high-income individuals are more likely to experience these policies (or at least a subset of them) as high stakes: Those who believe that more *redistribution from* is the fair thing to do might nevertheless oppose such policy change if it means, for example, an increase in their own tax bill. For low-income individuals, in contrast, *redistribution from* policies often affect others (e.g., progressive taxes) or only have indirect and hard-to-grasp implications (e.g., antitrust law). As a result, given that self-serving adjustment is more common among high-income than low-income individuals, I expect the latter to look ideologically more consistent than the former. This implies a higher correlation between proportionality beliefs and support for *redistribution from* policies among low-income than among high-income individuals.

To sum up, someone living around the poverty line is more likely to have informed and self-interested policy preferences when asked about changes to the earned income tax credit (EITC) than when asked about changes to the top marginal tax rate. Her opinion on the latter policy will be shaped instead by her beliefs about the deservingness of the rich, that is, her proportionality beliefs. Conversely, a millionnaire is likely to have informed and self-interested policy preferences with regard to changes in the top marginal tax rate, less so in the case of the EITC. Instead, when deciding what to do about the EITC, she will rely on her beliefs about the deservingness of the poor, that is, her reciprocity beliefs. I consequently expect high-income individuals to be more ideologically consistent than low-income individuals on *redistribution to* policy issues. In contrast, I expect low-income individuals to be more ideologically consistent than high-income individuals on *redistribution from* policy issues. When testing this prediction, I focus on the extent to which material self-interest affects the size of the *correlation* between fairness belief and policy attitudes.[5]

Evidence

I start by examining whether the correlation between reciprocity beliefs and *redistribution to* attitudes *increases* with income. In contrast, I expect the correlation between proportionality beliefs and *redistribution from* attitudes to *decrease* with income.

For this analysis, I return to the 2004 wave of the BSAS described in Chapters 3 and 4. To measure support for *redistribution to* policies, I use an item that asks about government spending on social benefits, namely: "The government should spend more money on welfare benefits for the poor, even if it means higher taxes." To measure support for *redistribution from* policies, I use a version of the traditional redistribution item that is explicitly designed to capture respondents' attitudes toward *existing* levels of redistribution, namely: "Do you think government does too much or too little to redistribute income from the better off to those who are less well off, or have they got it about right?" The main assumption is that people who answer "too much" to this question want less *redistribution from*. To measure fairness beliefs, I follow the same measurement strategy used in Chapters 3 and 4. The variable used to measure respondents' income level is described in Appendix A1.1.

I regress the *redistribution from* and *redistribution to* items on the one hand, on the fairness belief scores and the income measure on the other. I then include an interaction term between fairness beliefs and income, focusing first on reciprocity beliefs and second on proportionality beliefs.[6] Figure 5.3 presents predicted values for three income groups: bottom quintile, top quintile and the middle quintile.

In line with expectations, the correlation between reciprocity beliefs and opposition to welfare spending is lower among individuals whose income level indicates that they would likely be hurt by cuts to welfare benefits (Figure 5.3, left panel). This result suggests, in line with expectations, that low-income in-

---

[5] As discussed earlier, with regard to *levels* of support, whether one is doing the fair thing or the self-interested thing will have larger implications for *redistribution to* policies than *redistribution from* policies.

[6] When I examine the interaction between one type of fairness belief (e.g., reciprocity) and income, the second type of fairness beliefs (e.g., proportionality) is included as a control. However, note that the results are virtually the same irrespective of whether the omitted beliefs are included or not.

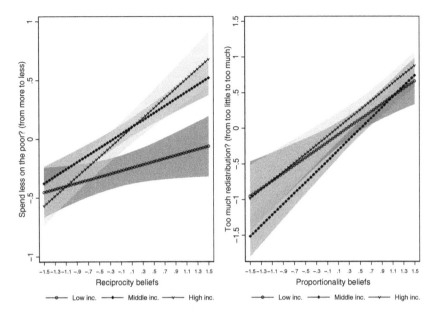

Figure 5.3   Income and ideological consistency in the BSAS
Plots predicted values and 95% confidence intervals computed after regressing
policy attitudes on fairness beliefs interacted with income. The income measure is
a categorical variable identifying people in the top quintile (high income), middle
quintile (middle income) and bottom quintile (low income).
Source: BSAS 2004.

dividuals who might support cuts because they punish free riders still oppose
them out of self-interest. If differences in ability to be ideologically constant
explain these results, then we should see a similar pattern when examining the
correlation between proportionality beliefs and opposition to more income redistribution. We do not; the correlation is the same across all income groups
(Figure 5.3, right panel).

Still, against my own expectations, I do not observe the reverse pattern,
namely, lower consistency among high-income individuals. One possibility is
that this latter result is an artifact of item wording. Indeed, the item used to
measure support for more *redistribution from* is very general and might fail
to trigger a reversal to self-interest among high-income individuals. To further
probe this issue, I turn to the original survey mentioned in Chapter 3 and described in Appendix A3.1. In the first part of the survey, respondents were asked
questions similar to the ones used in the BSAS to measure proportionality and
reciprocity beliefs. I use these items to compute fairness belief scores similar
to the one used in the previous analysis. Later in this survey, I asked respon-

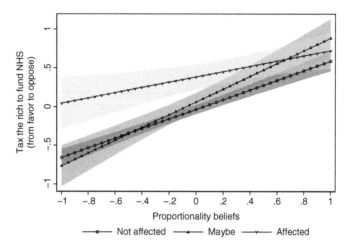

Figure 5.4   Income and ideological consistency: Opposition to taxing the rich
Plots predicted values and 95% confidence intervals computed after regressing
support for NHS tax over proportionality beliefs and interacted with exposure
dummies. Item wording: "One way the UK government can raise more revenue
for the NHS is to increase taxes on households with income over £100,000. To
what extent do you favor or oppose the following policy proposal: Increase taxes
on households with income over £100,000." Answers were collected in the form
of a 1 (strongly favor) to 7 (strongly oppose) Likert scale. They are standardized
for ease of interpretation.
Source: Dynata 2019. See Appendix A3.1 for more information.

dents their support for taxing the top 20% of the income distribution as a way
to fund the British National Health Service. Finally, at the end of the survey,
respondents were asked the likelihood that they would be affected by such tax:
"(N)ow imagine that the government decides to increase taxes on households
with income over £100,000. Would you expect your own taxes to go up?" Respondents had three response options: Yes, Maybe and No.[7]

I find that proportionality beliefs are highly correlated with opposition to
this proposed tax, while reciprocity beliefs are not (see Appendix A3.1). I interact proportionality beliefs with the dummied-out version of the exposure variable. Predicted values are presented in Figure 5.4. In line with expectations, the
correlation between proportionality beliefs and support for taxing high incomes
is higher among individuals who are not affected by the policy or are uncertain

---

[7]   I chose this question in light of the difficulties encountered when trying to measure income in
online surveys. I did not ask this question before the taxation question to avoid priming
individuals about their own material self-interest. This measurement strategy plausibly
assumes that people who oppose taxing the rich are not more likely to misrepresent their
income by declaring themselves rich even if they are not.

about the policy's effect on their own income. In contrast, this correlation is much lower among individuals who believe that they will be affected. In other words, individuals whose proportionality beliefs make them more likely to support the tax out of fairness concerns express higher than expected opposition to this proposed tax increase because they are aware of its adverse effect on their income. Because the question on exposure comes at the end of the survey, this awareness is not the result of being directly asked about exposure. Instead, it follows from item wording, with the explicit mention of an income threshold.

The reasoning and evidence presented in this section echoes an argument made by Rueda and Stegmueller (2019). They argue that, in a democracy, citizens wear two hats: a selfish hat (influence policy for one's own interest) and a social hat (influence policy in a way that is good for the public interest). In many cases, what is good for the self (what is income maximizing) is not in the interest of the collective. Because of a declining marginal return to consumption, "the relative importance of receiving benefits is greater for the poor than the relative importance of paying taxes is for the rich" (Rueda and Stegmueller, 2015, p. 3). This means that, on *redistribution to* issues, only people with enough income can indulge in wearing the social hat, explaining why support for *redistribution to* is more "ideological" and less self-interest among the rich than among the poor. Still, an emphasis on declining returns to consumption cannot explain why the converse is true for *redistribution from* issues, something the argument presented in this chapter can. Furthermore, by providing a more precise definition of the social hat, in the form of fairness reasoning, I am able to explain why, for some people, what is in the common interest is less redistribution, not more.

Jointly, this evidence shows that, against arguments emphasizing cognitive abilities, ideological consistency varies in predictable ways across income groups and policies. Next, I turn to my argument's implications for how we understand variations in the income gradient, that is, differences in the extent to which the rich and the poor disagree on redistributive issues.

Income and Social Policy Preferences

From the perspective of the benchmark model discussed in Chapter 1, the expectation is that the rich will support less redistribution than the poor, whether in the form of explicit opposition to income redistribution as measured using the traditional redistribution question, or in terms of higher support for tax and social spending cuts (and/or higher opposition to tax and spending increases). Figure 5.5 examines this expectation. It plots income differences in answers

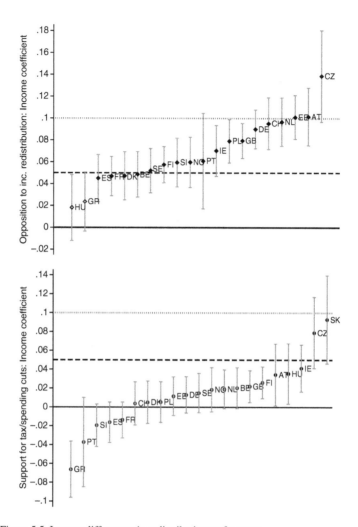

Figure 5.5 Income differences in redistributive preferences
Plots country-specific regression coefficients recovered after regressing outcome
variables on income (categorical, first-tenth decile) interacted with country dummies (no controls). Outcome variables are standardized (using country-specific
mean and SD), with higher values indicating opposition to redistribution/more
taxes and spending. Top panel: "The government should take measures to reduce
differences in income levels." Answer recorded using a 1 (agree) to 5 (disagree)
scale. Bottom panel: "If the government had to choose between increasing taxes
and spending more on social benefits and services, or decreasing taxes and spending less on social benefits and services, which should they do?" Answer recorded
using a 0 to 10 response scale. The scale is reversed so that higher values indicate
more support for tax and spending cuts. Interpretation: In CZ, the predicted difference between the first and the 10th decile is equal to 1.4 SD (top panel) and 0.75
SD (bottom panel).
Source: ESS 2008, weighted

to the traditional redistribution question as well as answers to a questions asking about taxes and social spending. The picture is mixed. On the one hand, answers to the traditional redistribution question differ across income levels, with most countries exhibiting at least a 0.5 SD attitudinal difference between bottom and top decile respondents. On the other hand, answers to the tax and spending item do not differ across income levels: Only a handful of countries exhibit a difference that is equal to 0.5 SD or more. In Greece, support for cuts in taxes and social spending is *higher* among low-income than high-income respondents. The Czech Republic is among the few countries with a substantive income gap on both items. In Great Britain, like in most other countries, support for redistribution – as traditionally measured – differs with respondents' income level, but support for tax and spending cuts does not. What explains these differences both across items and across countries?

Explaining Cross-Item and Cross-National Variations in the Income Gradient

In Chapter 4, I showed that proportionality beliefs correlate with income, while reciprocity beliefs do not. I also found that answers to the traditional redistribution item correlate with the former, not the latter. As a result, the existence of income differences in answers to the traditional redistribution item is to be expected: It reflects prior income differences in beliefs about the fairness of income inequality as defined by the proportionality norm. This, however, does not explain cross-national differences in the size of the income gradient. I will return to this question at the end of this chapter. First, I focus on explaining the low income gradient on the tax-spend item.

One possible reason for the absence of income differences is the comparatively larger weight given to reciprocity concerns when answering a question about tax and spending levels than when answering the traditional redistribution question. As Appendix A5.1 shows, this is indeed the case. The tax-spend item measures support for two types of changes to the status quo. One is a cut to existing levels of spending and taxation (6/10 response categories on the 0–10 scale). The other is an increase in existing levels of spending and taxation (0/4). A small income gradient has at least two causes. One is higher-than-expected support for cuts (over support for increases) among cross-pressured low-income individuals saying the fair thing (cut spending that goes to free riders) instead of the self-interested thing (do not cut spending). Another is higher-than-expected opposition to cuts (over opposition to increases) among cross-pressured high-income individuals saying the fair thing (do not cut spending that goes to deserving recipients) instead of the self-interested thing (cut spending, so you can cut my taxes). If my argument is correct, high-income individuals should "contribute" more than low-income ones to the flattening of the income gradient.

The reasoning is similar to the one put forward in our earlier discussion of welfare spending. While spending cuts represent a credible and large income loss for the poor, tax cuts represent an uncertain and small income gain for the rich. This means that low-income individuals who believe free riding is high prevalence weigh the punishment of undeserving free riders against the effects of benefits cuts on their own income. In contrast, high-income individuals who have the opposite reciprocity beliefs weigh the unfair punishment of deserving recipients against the benefits of tax cuts to their own pocketbook. If spending cuts' first-order effects on the poor are indeed larger and more credible than tax cuts' second-order effects on the rich, then we can expect asymmetry between the rich and the poor: Self-serving adjustment is larger for the former than the latter. High opposition to cuts within high-income respondents thus follows from the high proportion who hold pro-redistribution reciprocity beliefs. Empirically, this means that, among people with pro-redistribution reciprocity beliefs, there are limited attitudinal differences across income levels. Given self-serving adjustment among low-income individuals, this also implies that any evidence of an attitudinal income gap should be limited to the subset of voters with anti-redistribution reciprocity beliefs. This reasoning is sketched in Figure 5.6.

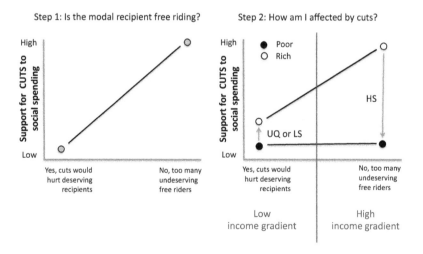

Figure 5.6 Support for cuts, reciprocity beliefs and self-serving adjustment
HS: high stakes, LS: low stakes, UQ: unknown quantity.

The existence of a large proportion of high-income respondents who trust that social spending is done fairly helps explain why the income gradient on the tax-spend item is small "on average." It does not explain why it varies across countries. Explaining why income is a better predictor in some countries than others amounts to explaining why the income gradient among people with pessimistic reciprocity beliefs is lower in some countries than others. Such differences might be due to low-income individuals failing to self-servingly adjust and support cuts instead. This would suggest that, in some countries, low-income individuals do not perceive that they benefit from the welfare state (see Holland (2018) for this argument applied to Latin America). Alternatively, high-income individuals might, despite their pessimistic free riding beliefs, oppose cuts for self-interested reasons. This suggests, more plausibly, that in some countries, social spending benefits all income groups: Even high-income individuals fear the consequences of spending cuts more than the (uncertain) benefits of tax cuts.

If this reasoning is correct, then cross-national differences in the size of the income gradient should be, at least partially, explained by cross-national differences in the distribution of social transfers. Where the probability of relying on publicly funded transfers is disproportionately higher for the poor, self-serving opposition to cuts among those concerned about free riding will be limited to low-income individuals. Where the probability of becoming a recipient is more evenly distributed among income groups, self-serving opposition to cuts will extend to those higher up the income ladder, explaining why support for cuts differs less by income.

What, in turn, explains cross-national differences in how social benefits are distributed in the population? Labor market conditions play an important role: The more unemployment risks are concentrated on the poor, the less high-income workers expect to rely on social transfers aimed at protecting against income shocks (Rehm, Hacker and Schlesinger, 2012). Policy design matters in two ways. First, it can exclude middle- and high-income groups *a priori*. By definition, means-tested public transfers are limited to the worse off (Korpi and Palme, 1998). Second, policy design affects middle- and high-income individuals' expectations of one day relying on social benefits, especially benefits targeted to those facing temporary job loss. A key factor is replacement rates, defined as the average share of past income replaced by social transfers on average. If replacement rates are low, social transfers have income-smoothing properties only for the poor. Middle- and high-income individuals who want to insure against the risk of catastrophic income loss (Moene and Wallerstein, 2001) will more likely self-insure through the private market or private savings. In contrast, in countries with high replacement rates, high-income individuals will positively value the income-smoothing properties of public unemployment insurance and social programs.[8] In other words, because of differences in labor market conditions and policy design, reliance on publicly funded transfers will be more or less concentrated on the bottom of the income ladder.

To sum up, based on my argument, the small income gradient documented in Figure 5.5 for the tax-spend item (bottom panel) has at least two sources: (1) a large proportion of high-income respondents who trust that social spending is done fairly and consequently oppose cuts out of fairness concerns and (2) self-interested opposition to cuts among people with pessimistic beliefs about the prevalence of free riding. Cross-national differences in the size of this income gradient can be, at least partially, explained by differences in benefit concentration. Benefit concentration has the most implications for the attitudes of high-income individuals who hold anti-redistribution reciprocity beliefs: As benefit concentration decreases, so does their support for cuts and so does the income gradient.

Evidence

To test these predictions, I rely on the 2008 wave of the ESS. My main outcome of interest is the tax-spend item used in Figure 5.5, bottom panel. To measure reciprocity beliefs, I used the same ESS survey items and measurement strategy introduced in Chapter 3. First, I examine whether reliance on fairness reasoning, namely, the extent to which tax-spend attitudes correlate with reciprocity beliefs, increases with income. Specifically, I regress the tax-spend variable on reciprocity beliefs interacted with income. I run this analysis on the pooled data using a hierarchical linear model with individuals nested in countries. When analyzing the pooled data, I model the coefficients on individual-level predictors as random effects.

Column (1) in Table 5.1 reproduces the basic pattern observed in Figure 5.5: On average, income does not predict attitudinal differences in terms of support for tax and spending cuts. Column (2) shows that individuals who differ in their free riding beliefs by 2 SD also disagree substantively in terms of tax-spend attitudes: The average difference between the two is 0.43 SD. As shown in the online appendix, the coefficient on free riding beliefs is barely affected by the introduction of socio-economic controls, confirming the prior finding that free riding beliefs are orthogonal to the likelihood of being a recipient of benefit transfers. The model reported in Column (3) interacts reciprocity beliefs with

---

[8] In addition, overall benefit generosity – which includes benefit duration in addition to replacement rates – directly affects the likelihood of *becoming* a recipient, with more generous unemployment transfers being associated with more time spent by unemployed (Borghans, Gielen and Luttmer, 2014; Chetty, 2005).

Table 5.1 *Predicting support for tax and spending cuts*

	(1)	(2)	(3)
Income [1–10]	0.10	0.02*	0.02*
	(0.01)	(0.01)	(0.01)
Reciprocity beliefs		0.43***	0.22**
		(0.04)	(0.07)
Reciprocity beliefs * income			0.04**
			(0.01)
Constant	− 0.08*	− 0.11**	− 0.10**
	(0.04)	(0.04)	(0.04)
N	30,142	29,908	29,908

Outcome variable is standardized using the country-specific mean and SD. Reciprocity belief scores are demeaned and divided by 2 standard deviations using country-specific mean and SD. Coefficients can be interpreted as a β SD change in support for cuts following a 2 SD change in reciprocity beliefs. Income variable ranges from 1 (first decile) to 10 (tenth decile). Significance levels: * p<.05, ** p<.01 *** p<.001. *Source*: ESS 2008.

income levels. The coefficient on the interaction term indicates that the correlation between reciprocity beliefs and support for spending and tax cuts is more than twice as large among top decile respondents ($0.22 + 10 \times 0.04 = 0.62$) than among bottom decile respondents ($0.22 + 1 \times 0.04 = 0.26$). Among people with anti-redistribution reciprocity beliefs (1 SD above country mean), the difference in tax-spend attitudes between top and bottom decile respondents is equal to 0.36 SD ($[0.02 + 0.5 \times 0.04][10 − 1]$). Among people with pro-redistribution reciprocity beliefs (1 SD below country mean), there are no attitudinal differences between the rich and the poor ($[0.02 − 0.5 \times 0.04][10 − 1] = 0$).

Figure 5.7 presents predicted attitudinal differences by reciprocity beliefs and income group, focusing on the case of Great Britain.[9] In this case, I recode the income measure to distinguish between people in the top income quintile, people in the bottom income quintile and people in the quintiles in between.[10] In the analysis, the resulting trichotomous variable is dummied out. In practice, this enables me to drop the assumption that income's effect on policy attitudes

[9] Results are similar for all countries in the sample. See online appendix for the same analysis using Danish data.

[10] To identify income cut-offs – the P20 and the P80 – I use estimates from the Luxembourg Income Study (LIS) Database available at www.lisdatacenter.org (multiple countries; March 2016, Luxembourg: LIS). See online appendix for more detail on this variable.

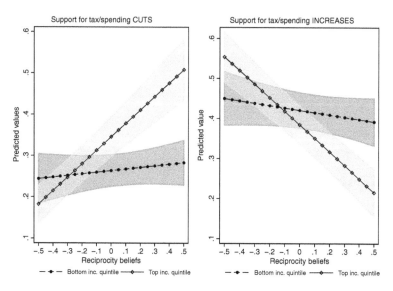

Figure 5.7 Predicting tax-spend preferences in Great Britain
Plots predicted values and 95% confidence intervals computed after regressing outcome variables on free riding beliefs and interacted with income quintile dummies.
Predicted values are generated using free riding scores running from 1 SD below
to 1 SD above the mean. See notes in Figure 5.5 for outcome wording. Left panel:
probability of choosing cuts over increases. Right panel: probability of choosing
increases over cuts.
Source: ESS 2008, weighted.

is linear.[11] To facilitate interpretation, I switch to two dichotomous measures of
tax-spend preferences. The first one (left panel) identifies individuals who explicitly support tax and spending cuts over increases (they pick the 0/4 answers
on the 0/10 scale; see notes in Figure 5.5 for wording). The other measure (right
panel) identifies individuals who explicitly support tax and spending increases
over cuts (they pick the 6/10 answers on the 0/10 scale).

Irrespective of the outcome used, reciprocity beliefs correlate with tax-spend
attitudes more so among the rich than among the poor. This means that income
differences align with economic expectations (i.e., more anti-spending and anti-
taxes attitudes among high-income than low-income respondents) only among
people who find the status quo unfair because it benefits free riders. Among
people who find the system fair (i.e., moral hazard is not a concern and recipients are deserving), there are no income differences. This is due to higher-
than-expected – based on their "objective" material self-interest – opposition to

---

[11] Note, however, that predicted attitudes plotted in Figure 5.7 still rely on the assumption of a
linear relationship between policy preferences and free riding beliefs. This assumption seems
plausible in light of empirical patterns plotted in Appendix A5.1.

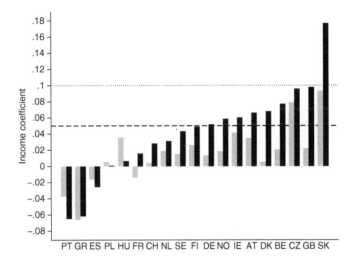

Figure 5.8 Cross-country differences in the income gradient: Sub-group analysis
Gray bars reproduce the income coefficients plotted in Figure 5.5. The dark bars
represent the same coefficients but limiting the sample to individuals in the top
quartile of their country's reciprocity score distribution.
Source: ESS 2008.

tax and spending cuts (and support for tax and spending increases) on the part
of high-income individuals who find the system fair. In other words, it is this
group that exerts a downward pressure on the income gradient, explaining the
weak correlation documented in Figure 5.5.

Figure 5.8 examines how this pattern varies by country. Specifically, it plots
the relationship between income and answers to the tax-spend item, limiting
the sample to individuals whose reciprocity belief scores place them in their
country's top quartile (i.e., the subset most likely to find recipients undeserving and be concerned about free riding). For reference, I also plot the original
income coefficients computed using the full sample and plotted in Figure 5.5.
If my framework has any explanatory power, then the income gradient for this
specific subset of individuals should be larger than the income gradient for the
full country sample. This is the case for 14 of the countries under study. For 10
countries, attitudinal differences in this subgroup reach or surpass the 0.5 SD
benchmark, that is, attitudinal differences between the top and bottom deciles
differing by at least half a standard deviation.

Still, for a little over a third of the countries in this sample, even within the
subset of people with the most anti-redistribution reciprocity beliefs, the income gradient remains small or negative. A possible reason, I argued, is that
social transfers reach higher up the income ladder in some countries than in

Table 5.2 *Benefit concentration and the size of the income gradient*

Sample used depending on recip. beliefs	(1) Full sample	(2) Score ≤20th p.	(3) Score ≤country av.	(4) Score >country av.	(5) Score ≥80th p.
Income	0.03***	0.01	0.02**	0.05***	0.07***
	(0.00)	(0.01)	(0.01)	(0.01)	(0.01)
Benef. conc.	0.20***	0.14	0.27**	0.22*	0.34**
	(0.05)	(0.14)	(0.09)	(0.09)	(0.13)
Income * benef. conc.	−0.04***	−0.01	−0.04**	−0.06***	−0.09***
	(0.01)	(0.02)	(0.01)	(0.01)	(0.02)
Constant	−0.18***	−0.40***	−0.34***	−0.09*	−0.09
	(0.02)	(0.06)	(0.04)	(0.04)	(0.06)
N	27,885	7,158	13,958	13,707	6,946

Outcome variable is the tax-spend item standardized using the country-specific mean and SD. Income variable categorizes respondents by income deciles. Coefficient on income can be interpreted as a $\beta_I * 10$ SD change in in tax-spend attitudes following a change from the bottom- to the top-income decile. Benefit concentration variable is normalized, higher values indicate lower concentration. Significance levels: *p<.05, ** p<.01 *** p<.001.
Source: ESS 2008.

others. This would suggest that, in countries on the left in Figure 5.8, income remains a poor predictor because even high-income individuals who are concerned about free riding benefit from social spending and adjust their preferences self-servingly.

To test this argument, I rely on data provided by the OECD (2008) on benefit concentration. The OECD's research team has computed a measure similar to a Gini coefficient, which captures the differences between a group's share of the population and its share of all the cash transfers going to individuals of working age in a given year. A value of 0 indicates that all income groups (ranked according to their disposable income) receive an equal share of all cash transfers. A negative coefficient indicates that lower income groups receive a higher share of transfers than their share of disposable income.[12] I normalize this variable such that 0 captures the smallest possible value (high concentration) and 1 the highest possible value (low concentration).

I examine whether the income gradient among individuals most concerned about free riding decreases as benefit concentration decreases. Table 5.2 reports regression results from a hierarchical linear model with a two-level in-

[12] In the online appendix, I detail a set of checks run to assess the quality of this measure for capturing cross-national differences in benefit concentration.

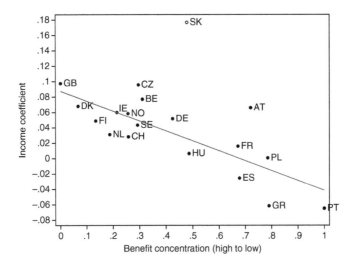

Figure 5.9 Income gradient and benefit concentration
Plots income coefficients (dark bars in Figure 5.8) against benefit concentration
measures.
Source: ESS 2008, OECD (2008).

teraction between income (individual level) and benefit concentration (country level). Columns (1) reports results for the full sample. Columns (2)–(5) report results for different subsamples of the data, starting with people who hold the most pro-redistribution reciprocity beliefs (with scores below the 20th percentile in their country) and ending with people who hold the most anti-redistribution reciprocity beliefs (with scores above the 80th percentile in their country).

Notice how the absolute value of the interaction term between income and benefit concentration increases from left (column (2)) to right (column (5)). This suggests that changes in the income gradient tied to cross-national differences in benefit concentration are mostly due to changes in the tax-spend preferences of people with the most pessimistic reciprocity beliefs. Figure 5.9 presents this evidence visually. First, for each country, I compute the income gradient for people with a reciprocity belief score equal or above the 80th percentile in their country. Specifically, I regress attitudes toward cuts in taxes and social spending on income and use the regression coefficient to proxy for the correlation between the two (see dark bars in Figure 5.8). I then plot these estimates against the benefit concentration measures. As Figure 5.9 shows, when benefit concentration decreases, so does the size of the income gradient, with Slovakia being a notable outlier. This aligns with results in column (5).

The argument presented in this chapter helps identify in which groups and countries one can expect income to be a good predictor of different levels of support for cuts in taxes and social spending. In line with expectations, I found that the income gradient is the largest among people with anti-redistribution reciprocity beliefs, especially so in countries where social benefits are most concentrated on the worse off.

I now return to the traditional redistribution question: Can my argument also explain why income is a good predictor of answers to this item in some countries but not others? This issue was examined in detail by Beramendi and Rehm (2016). They find that cross-national variation in the income gradient for this survey item has to do with differences in fiscal systems: The more progressive the system, the larger the income gradient. Reinterpreted in light of my argument, I would expect these differences to originate from differences in the attitudes of high-income individuals who tend to support income redistribution because they think that it is the fair thing to do in light of their proportionality beliefs. Those who live in countries with a progressive tax system are more likely to take the self-interested positions on this issue, explaining the larger income gradient. Unfortunately, given the absence of a dataset that includes cross-national measures of proportionality beliefs and high-quality income data, I cannot test this prediction.

There are many other insights one can glean from this simple two-step setup. In Chapter 7, for example, I will discuss the role of fiscal adjustment, which, under the right conditions, can make it easier for high-income respondents to connect generous *redistribution to* policies to their own tax bill. In this case, I expect high-income respondents with pro-redistribution reciprocity beliefs to be the ones who self-servingly adjust and decrease their support for generous *redistribution to* policies.

Summary and Next Steps

Jointly, Chapters 4 and 5 show that, when it comes to redistributive preferences, material self-interest plays an important, if indirect, role. To understand what this role is, fairness reasoning is key. First, reliance on proportionality beliefs mean more people reason as if self-interested on *redistribution from* issues than on *redistribution to* issues. Second, fairness reasoning and material self-interest combine in predictable ways. Most of the time, redistributive social policies' implications for one's own bottom line are unclear, making fairness reasoning the default (and anchoring) mode of reasoning. Yet, there are exceptions depending on policy design and how it interacts with one's own socioeconomic conditions. Using this simple framework, I was able to unpack systematic differences in ideological consistency across income groups as well as the low correlation between income and support for cuts in taxes and social spending.

This chapter concludes Part I of the book, in which I presented and tested the argument's micro-foundations. In Part II, I build on these foundations to examine the book's core issue, namely, the *dynamics* of mass redistributive preferences in times of rising inequality.

Appendix

A5.1 Reciprocity Beliefs and Attitudes toward Tax and Spending Cuts

Figure A5.1 uses data from the 2008 wave of the ESS to plot the country- and individual-level correlations between reciprocity beliefs and attitudes toward tax and social spending cuts. Reciprocity beliefs were computed using the ESS items described in Chapters 3 and 4. While answers to the traditional redistribution item do not correlate with reciprocity beliefs (see Chapter 3), answers to the tax-spend item do.

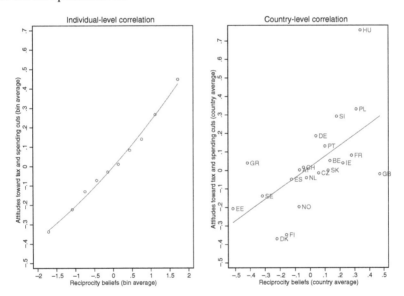

Figure A5.1 Tax-spend preferences and free riding beliefs
Left panel: binned scatter plot of tax-spend attitudes against reciprocity beliefs (individual-level analysis, pooled data). Variables are standardized using country-specific mean and SD. Right panel: plots average support for tax and spending cuts against average reciprocity beliefs (country-level analysis). Reciprocity beliefs are measured by combining answer to the items listed in Table 3.6 using weights recovered from an EFA on the pooled data. Variables are standardized using the mean and the SD from the pooled data. Higher values indicate more concern for free riding and more support for tax and spending cuts.
Source: ESS 2008.

PART II

Changes in Demand for Redistribution

6

Explaining Stability and Change

Let's summarize what we have achieved so far. I have described a moral system constituted of at least two "spheres" of fairness, each with their own social good and shared distributive principle (Walzer, 1983). The market economy produces one type of good – market income – whose allocation is, at least partly, regulated through the proportionality principle. The collective, through the welfare state, pools resources to produce a second type of good – social insurance in the form of social benefits – whose allocation to those who receive more than they contribute is, at least partly, regulated through the reciprocity principle. Jointly, these two allocation principles form the bases of a moral system that helps mitigate envy, monitor opportunistic behavior and foster cooperation. In practice, this means that people seek to behave in ways that move the status quo closer to a fair allocation, as defined by the proportionality and reciprocity norms. In the context of this book, to behave fairly implies expressing policy preferences that align with one's empirical beliefs about the fairness of the status quo. Empirically, this means that proportionality beliefs covary with attitudes toward policies that shape the distribution of market income (*redistribution from* policies), while reciprocity beliefs covary with support for policies that redistribute resources to those who cannot provide for themselves (*redistribution to* policies). While people's policy preferences are often better predicted by their long-term beliefs about the fairness of the status quo than by a policy's implications for their own pocketbook, this does not imply that material self-interest plays no role. First, the correlation patterns between proportionality beliefs on the one hand, and economic earning capacity on the other, suggest that people form proportionality beliefs in a self-serving fashion (more on this in Chapter 9). Second, while material self-interest does not explain how reciprocity beliefs form, it helps understand when reciprocity beliefs matter: The larger a policy's implications for their own pocketbook, the more people are likely to deviate from what is fair according to their reciprocity beliefs in favor of what is economically self-serving.

In this chapter, I take stock of several insights that follow from this interpretative framework. One set of insights concerns the benchmark model's main blind spots: It overlooks the filtering role of fairness beliefs and fails to account for the *redistribution to* facet of redistributive policy preferences. Once these blind spots are accounted for, there are few reasons to expect a systematic relationship between an increase in income inequality and demand for redistribution. Another set of insights draws attention to important yet overlooked factors driving mass attitudinal change. These factors include fiscal stress, survey design and long-term partisan dynamics. As I will show in the remaining chapters, they help explain the puzzling empirical patterns described in Chapter 1.

One factor, immigration-induced ethnic diversity, is conspicuous by its absence. In many countries, the rise in income inequality has gone alongside a rise in ethnic diversity. Part of the disconnect between inequality and support for redistribution could be due to hostility to immigrants. Specifically, in a context in which the poor and the unemployed are stereotyped as racially "other," such hostility might erode the majority's support for redistributive policies. Building on the argument presented in Part I, I conclude this chapter by proposing several amendments to this line of reasoning, which, jointly, explain why, in Part II, immigration-induced diversity ultimately takes a back seat.

Identifying the Benchmark Model's Blind Spots

As noted in Chapter 1, pundits and researchers have puzzled over the missing left turn: In light of dramatic increases in income inequality, voters should be asking for more income redistribution, not less free trade and immigration. In their contribution, Meltzer and Richard (1981) helpfully laid out the institutional and behavioral assumptions underpinning this expectation, namely a tax and transfer system designed to be redistributive and voters that are fully informed rational income maximizers. If these assumptions hold, then all voters need is information about the income distribution and how it has changed over time (Cruces, Perez-Truglia and Tetaz, 2013; Kuziemko et al., 2013; Sands and de Kadt, 2020; Trump, 2018). Building on the argument made in Part I, I am now in a better position to assess the limits of this line of reasoning.

Income Inequality as Seen Through the Lenses of Fairness

Because of the importance of fairness reasoning, focusing on changes in the income distribution and voters' knowledge of such changes – as suggested by the benchmark model – is unlikely to tell us much about attitudinal trends in Great Britain, the United States and beyond. For most people, income inequality is an abstract reality, meaningful only when interpreted through the lenses of fairness reasoning, that is, in light of their existing proportionality beliefs. As a result, fairness reasoning introduces a wedge between changes in the market income distribution and support for redistribution, specifically *redistribution from*. Studies that focus on information about inequality as the missing link in the causal chain assume a very specific distribution of fairness beliefs, one in which the median voter finds the status quo unfair, as defined by the proportionality norm. Only then can we expect a rise in income inequality to translate into growing demand for more egalitarian policies. However, whether or not a majority perceives income inequality as a violation of the proportionality norm is something to be explained, not assumed.

There might still be a bare-bones version of the benchmark model to salvage, namely, one that does not focus on income inequality per se but on the myriad of personal experiences (e.g., job loss, job insecurity or wage stagnation) that underpin a change in the income distribution. In line with the two-step model of preference formation discussed in Chapter 5, one might expect individuals faced with an economic shock – a high-stakes situation – to disregard what is fair and express economically self-serving preferences instead. In support of this bare-bones version, there is good evidence that "[N]egative economic shocks tend to increase support for more expansive social policy" (Margalit, 2013).

Yet, even then, the argument presented in Part I provides few reasons to expect individuals experiences with material hardship to affect *aggregate*-level trends in redistributive preferences. Indeed, the role of fairness beliefs means that the effect of an economic shock will likely be transient. In line with this expectation, Margalit (2013) finds that job loss increases support for unemployment insurance among Republicans but only temporarily so. In other words, job loss triggers a short-term reversion to self-interest among those affected who might usually oppose these policies out of reciprocity concerns. Over time, as their situation improves, and unemployment insurance is no longer experienced as a high-stakes issue, individuals will revert to their original position, as defined by their beliefs about the fairness of the status quo. A more permanent change would require either a "permanent" state of hardship or a change in underlying fairness beliefs. As I discuss in Part II, the experience of hardship is not enough on its own for belief change to take place.

In Search of *Redistribution To*

As discussed in the previous section, the benchmark model overlooks the filtering role of proportionality beliefs. It is also blind to attitudinal change affecting support for more or less inclusive and redistributive social insurance, that is, support for *redistribution to* policies. The benchmark model conceptualizes redistributive politics as the decision by the median voter – backed by the bottom 50% of the income distribution – to take from the other richer half in order to increase her own disposable income. In doing so, it implicitly focuses on policies that take market income from those who have more of it, that is, *redistribution from* policies. This conceptualization of redistributive politics is very different from one in which the median voter has to decide whether (and how much) to contribute to a public insurance fund to insure against the risk of not being able to provide for oneself, something famously pointed out by Moene and Wallerstein (2001). Social insurance is most redistributive when it provides a generous income floor for all, meaning that benefits access and benefit levels are not conditional on past contributions. Attitudes toward benefit generosity and inclusivity, policy design features that I have called *redistribution to* policies, are the benchmark model's other major blind spots. As discussed in Chapter 4, support for *redistribution to* policies is rarely self-interested: instead, reciprocity beliefs do most of the heavy lifting. These beliefs are orthogonal to proportionality beliefs that prop up attitudes toward *redistribution from* policies. As I will show in Part II when discussing the British and American cases, most of the action appears to be in the realm of reciprocity beliefs and *redistribution to* policies. In other words, the benchmark model also fails because it looks under the wrong lamppost.

Based on the interpretative framework developed in Part I, there are few reasons to expect an increase in income inequality to affect demand for redistribution in systematic ways. So what should researchers expect instead? What factors should they be focusing their attention on? Answering these questions occupies the remaining chapters of this book.

Explaining the Dynamics of Demand for Redistribution

What are the mechanisms of change implied by the argument presented in Part I? By definition, changes in attitudes toward redistributive social policies follow from changes in how people reason about these policies. Based on the framework presented in Part I, there are at least three causal pathways for change. The first pathway is a change in the relative mix of motives voters rely on when reasoning about a given redistributive issue (the *motive mix* pathway). For cross-pressured voters (i.e., voters whose fairness beliefs do not align with their objective material interest), a reversion to pocketbook reasoning at the expense of fairness reasoning (or vice versa) will have important attitudinal consequences. Holding the motive mix constant, the second pathway, most relevant for policy proposals that combine both proportionality and reciprocity concerns, is the fairness norm people rely on to interpret a policy proposal. Because fairness beliefs differ across the two norms, the same individuals will come to different conclusions depending on which norm of fairness is most salient. This pathway has been extensively studied under the umbrella term of "priming" or "framing effect" (the *framing* pathway).[1] The third causal pathway is a change in fairness beliefs. As beliefs about the fairness of the status quo change so do preferences over fairness maximizing policies (the *belief change* pathway).

To theorize attitudinal change, researchers consequently need to understand how each individual pathway can be activated by contextual factors. Absent activating factors, one has no reason to expect attitudes toward redistributive social policies to change.

Given this book's emphasis on *aggregate* and *long-term* trends in support for redistribution, in Part II, I focus on contextual factors that activate one or more pathways at the *same* time among a *large* share of people. Furthermore, I disregard factors with only short-term implications. Indeed, contextual factors that affect small groups of people for short periods of time and/or in uncoordinated ways will not generate a consistent signal that can be picked up in aggregate data. With that in mind, what are the combinations of pathways and activating contextual factors to focus on? Below, and in the remaining chapters, I discuss the role of fiscal stress, survey design and partisan dynamics.

Fiscal Stress and Motive Mix

It is comparatively easier for net beneficiaries to understand how they would be hurt by less *redistribution to* policies than it is for net contributors to understand how they would benefit from such retrenchment. As a result, when reasoning

---

[1] The literature in political psychology explicitly distinguishes between framing and priming effects, as each implies a different type of cognitive process. For example, Chong and Druckman (2007) point out that priming describes the ways in which the salience of a given issue automatically affects which considerations are on people's mind, while framing is a more deliberate process through which people weigh the relative importance of competing considerations suggested by available frames. To the extent that both mechanisms affect which considerations shape how people answering a survey question, I choose to overlook these nuances and discuss them jointly.

about retrenchment, low-income individuals take the income-maximizing position and high-income individuals the fairness-maximizing one, explaining why many high-income voters who do not benefit from *redistribution to* policies generally support it because it is the "fair thing to do." Doing the fair thing, I argue, is most prevalent when the opportunity costs of *redistribution to* policies are hidden by deficits and complicated budget arbitrations. This changes when closing the deficit becomes a policy goal. In such a context, tax increases help net contributors put a price tag on "doing the fair thing." This comes at the expense of support for social programs that transfer resources to the worse off.

This causal pathway is discussed in Chapter 7, focusing on the case of France. In France, tax increases are a credible threat: Since the 1990s, they have occurred at regular intervals, always to deal with fiscal imbalances tied to social insurance. Contrast this to the United States, where the threat of tax increases has remained elusive due to legislative gridlock and the country's ability to borrow at very low interest rates.[2] Using French observational and experimental evidence, I show that fiscal stress and fiscal adjustment can weaken the coalitions underpinning the welfare state's most redistributive features by introducing a wedge between net beneficiaries of *redistribution to* policies on the one hand, and altruistic net contributors on the other.

Survey Design and Framing

It is well known that the survey structure and item wording affect the answers people provide to survey questions. When it comes to redistributive preferences, not paying attention to measurement and design can come at a cost. As shown in Chapter 3, the traditional redistribution item tends to capture one facet of support for redistribution, namely *redistribution from*. Attitudes on this dimension covary with beliefs about the extent to which, in Friedman's words, "payment is in accordance to product" (Friedman, 1962, p. 167). One reason is that, in its most common wording, this item focuses people's attention on the distribution of market income and the fairness of the individual economic race. Still, in many versions of this item, there is an explicit reference made to low-income individuals, which also primes people to think about social solidarity and the deservingness of welfare recipients.

---

[2] Unfortunately, Great Britain, which also experienced fiscal adjustment, lacks similarly fine-tuned items. In addition, austerity measures became a partisan issue pitting the Conservative party against the New Labour. This type of partisan polarization makes it harder to document the role of fiscal concerns among well-off New Labour voters. In France, in contrast, the Socialist Party implemented a large share of the tax hikes and spending cuts.

Given this ambivalence, interpreting overtime changes in answers to this item can be tricky. In Chapter 8, I show that the decline in agreement with the standard item on redistribution documented in Great Britain is partly an artifact of question ordering and framing effects. Correcting for the latter reveals that the decline in support for redistribution in Great Britain is lopsided: It affects only one facet of redistributive preferences, leaving a space open for some types of redistributive reforms (policies that *redistribute from* the wealthy) and narrowing the available space for others (policies that *redistributes to* to the poor and the unemployed).

While survey design is an important activating factor, its implications are somewhat mundane: Item wording and ordering do not directly affect what people want but only the empirical manifestation of what people want. Similarly, people's answers to surveys can be affected by changes in how elites frame a given policy issue, with often only short-lived effects. In Part II, I examine how elite competition can also have more durable implications. As I explain next, to make this point, I build on Zaller's seminal work on opinion formation and attitudinal change, adapted to explaining the formation of fairness beliefs.

Partisan Dynamics and Belief Change

In the process of building electoral coalitions, political elites competing for power change the nature and scope of perspectives and arguments available in voters' discursive context. More specifically, parties and candidates who actively compete over an issue will affect the salience of an issue area, the range of policy alternatives available within this issue area and how easy it is to distinguish these policy alternatives from one another (Sniderman and Bullock, 2004, p. 346). As documented by the literature on framing effects, changes in issue salience and exposure to competing policy frames temporarily affect people's answers to issue-related survey items. Specifically, they affect which type of fairness beliefs matter most for how people answer ambiguously worded survey item, including the traditional redistribution item.

By altering the range of policy considerations citizens are exposed to, political elites can also generate conditions conducive to more durable attitudinal change. For this to happen, elites' impact on the discursive context needs to be extensive and persistent, something akin to a cultural shift. A famous example, discussed in Part II, is Margaret Thatcher's move to challenge the Keynesian consensus in British politics. This strategic shift generated a level of ideological pluralism unmatched in the postwar period. Over time, pluralism dropped as the Labour Party embraced Thatcher's message of lower taxes, free trade, balanced budget and welfare reform. Ultimately, in the space of a decade,

Great Britain switched from a Keynesian consensus to what is often called a neoliberal consensus. This right-wing shift in the discursive context stands in sharp contrast with America's polarized landscape in which each party increasingly represents separate echo chambers. These long-term partisan dynamics are qualitatively different from the short-term changes in elite rhetoric mentioned earlier. They can directly impact people's fairness beliefs by affecting their discursive context. Only when exposed to new considerations about the fairness of the status quo can people incorporate these considerations into their own proto-ideological worldview and update their fairness beliefs accordingly. While a systemic change in people's discursive contexts is not sufficient for mass belief change, it is a necessary condition.

Beliefs about the fairness of the status quo are "assets" that people "invest in" to make sense of the world around them and feel good about themselves in the eyes of others who share similar fairness beliefs (Bénabou and Tirole, 2011, 2016). As a result, exposure to new considerations is not enough. Also important are the individual-level factors that explain how people selectively incorporate some considerations and selectively reject others. First, people resist considerations too distant from the ones they already hold. Second, people are more likely to incorporate consonant fairness considerations and resist dissonant ones. In the case of proportionality beliefs, people with limited earning capacity are more likely to incorporate pro-redistribution considerations that point to the status quo as unfair and resist anti-redistirbution claims that describe the status quo as fair. In the case of reciprocity beliefs, people who are more sensitive to free riding resist dissonant pro-redistribution considerations about the low prevalence of free riding and embrace consonant anti-redistribution ones about the deservingness of recipients. In other words, to document changes in fairness beliefs, researchers need to look for the perfect storm, that is, a situation in which contextual-pull and individual-push factors align to promote mass belief change. These conditions, I show, are met in the United States and Great Britain, though only in the case of reciprocity beliefs.

As argued in Part I, belief change only selectively affects policy preferences: The impact is smaller for people who, given high material stakes, are more likely to deviate from what fairness reasoning prescribes. For example, low-income Republicans might "follow the leader" (Lenz, 2009) when it comes to forming reciprocity beliefs: Their authoritarian values make them very receptive to claims about the high prevalence of free riding among (non-white) recipients. However, they are much less likely to translate these beliefs into opposition to *redistribution to* policies, even when partisan frames that should activate free riding concerns are present. The opposite is true for high-income Democrat. As a result, most of the decline in the US income gradient can be traced back to an increase in support for *redistribution to* within this latter group, not a decrease in support among low-income voters concerned that benefits are going to the undeserving.

Immigration and Redistribution: A Complicated Picture

Before diving in more detail into the role of fiscal stress, survey design and partisan dynamics, I briefly discuss the role of a fourth factor, prevalent in research on changing demand for redistribution in Europe, namely immigration-induced diversity.

The electoral success of far-right welfare chauvinist parties suggests an intimate connection between immigration and social policy preferences (De Koster, Achterberg and Van der Waal, 2013; Schumacher and Van Kersbergen, 2016). A long line of work has sought to unpack this connection. This literature starts from the assumption that people are parochial altruists, that is, they "care more about the well-being of other people, the more they are like (themselves)" (Kristov, Lindert and McClelland, 1992, p. 146). Mass low-skill immigration from developing countries means that, increasingly, the modal beneficiary of redistributive social policies is perceived to be non-white and non-Christian, thus potentially eroding mass support for redistribution in West European countries. The argument presented in Part I highlights some of the limits of this line of reasoning.

First, not all aspects of redistribution will be affected by parochial concerns, and researchers need to choose their empirical strategy accordingly. Indeed, one can reasonably expect ethnic diversity to have limited implications for support for *redistribution from* policies (e.g., pre-distribution and progressive taxation policies). Instead, most of the effect should be concentrated on *redistribution to* policies, that is, policies that benefit the worse off either by increasing benefit generosity or extending benefit coverage to a larger group of individuals.[3]

The distinction between two types of redistributive policies rooted in two types of fairness norms also helps clarify confusing claims regarding the "deservingness" of immigrants. The American literature on deservingness finds

---

[3] Appendix A6.1 illustrates this point. I show that individuals with more negative attitudes toward immigrants and immigration are also more likely to disagree that it is the government's job to provide a decent standard of living for the unemployed. In contrast, there is no correlation between anti-immigrant sentiment and support for income redistribution measured using the traditional redistribution item. This point is worth emphasizing: Previous studies on the impact of immigration on attitudes toward redistribution tend to pick survey items indiscriminately, unhelpfully combining *redistribution from* and *redistribution to* items into a unique index (e.g., Alesina, Miano and Stantcheva, 2018).

that, in the American context, race is used by white respondents as a cue to infer low effort (Fong and Luttmer, 2009; Gilens, 1999). Extrapolating, one might expect immigrants to also be stereotyped as lazy. Yet, on this metric, given that immigrants are perceived as willing to work harder than native citizens, they are usually perceived as *more* deserving. These results are only contradictory if one overlooks the existence of at least two fairness principles: one relevant for assessing how deserving one is of policies that affect the distribution of market income (*redistribution from*) and the other for assessing how deserving one is of social solidarity (*redistribution to*). Because immigrants are hardworking, they are deserving of policies such as a fair wage, bargaining rights against employers or lower taxes (as defined by the proportionality norm). This does not imply that their access to social benefits is perceived as fair according to the reciprocity norm, something I examine in more detail in Chapter 10.

When studying the relationship between immigration and demand for redistribution broadly defined, researchers also tend to overlook the interplay between other-regarding concerns (such as parochial altruism) and material self-interest. This is especially important in the European context, where immigration-induced ethnic diversity became politically visible at least two decades after welfare states had matured into generous and all encompassing institutions sustained by specific combinations of fairness beliefs and self-interest. In contrast, in the United States, the politicization of racial boundaries and prejudice hindered the *creation* of a generous welfare state. These differences in historical sequencing have implications for the claim that, in Europe, immigration is eroding support for redistribution.

Let's start with attitudes toward generous transfers targeted to the worse-off. As previously discussed, it is mostly high-income individuals who have the "luxury" to express their parochial inclinations when asked about such *redistribution to* policies (see also Rueda, 2018). Low-income individuals, in contrast, are cross-pressured: They might oppose generous social transfers as a baseline because it benefits minority groups; yet for pocketbook reasons, they will self-servingly adjust their level of support for more generous spending. In other words, in Europe, immigration's eroding effect is mitigated by the existence of a group of voters whose potential support for retrenchment – out of a desire to punish the undeserving immigrant – conflicts with their position as beneficiaries of social transfers. This insight sheds a new light on the robust yet rarely discussed finding that the presence of low-skill immigration has the largest effect on the preferences of high-income individuals (Dahlberg, Edmark and Lundqvist, 2012; Rueda, 2018; Runst, 2018).

One implication is that political entrepreneurs seeking to leverage parochial altruism to cut social spending will downplay spending cuts and emphasize instead "closing" the welfare state, specifically, challenge legal norms that give social rights to immigrants (Cavaillé and Ferwerda, 2023; Scheve and Stasavage, 2006). This aligns with the evolution of the Far Right in Europe. Breaking with their previous emphasis on the need to "starve the beast," far-right leaders in countries like France or Austria have now embraced the welfare state and put welfare chauvinism – in which social transfers are generous but limited to citizens – at the center of their platforms (Betz, 2016). Countries like Denmark have recently sought to establish a strong differentiation of social rights according to nationality and length of presence on the territory (Martinsen, 2020).

Support for such efforts to "close" the welfare state can be interpreted as expressing a form of lower demand for income redistribution, as selectively excluding populations who stand to benefit more from redistributive social policies mechanically decreases redistribution. Yet people's support for "closing" the welfare state comes with many caveats. In the 2016 wave of the ESS, respondents were asked at what point people migrating from other countries "should obtain the same rights to social benefits and services as citizens already living here." Very few respondents thought that immigrants should never get equal social rights (with a maximum of 15% in Austria, see Cavaillé and Van der Straeten, 2023). The stance that newcomers should immediately be granted full access to benefits and services was endorsed by an equally small minority (with the exception of Portugal and Sweden, with around 20% choosing to grant immediate access). Instead, in most countries, the modal position was to condition social rights on residence and payment of taxes for at least a year. In other words, with the exception of Finland, the Netherlands and Austria, topline results point to an implicit "good-faith-effort" criterion. Results from 2008 produce very similar results (Mewes and Mau, 2012), suggesting that, contra a simple version of the parochial altruism thesis, the 2014 refugee crisis did not trigger a wave of welfare chauvinist sentiments across Europe.

If immigration-induced diversity is having an effect on mass redistributive preferences, it is a complicated one, moderated by material self-interest and an understanding of the welfare state's boundaries as relatively porous. As I discuss next, even more worrying for this line of reasoning is the absence of evidence to support the argument's micro-foundations: Altruism, while conditional, is not narrowly parochial.

Moving Beyond Parochial Altruism

A central assumption in the parochial altruism line of reasoning is that the relationship between diversity and redistributive preferences is mediated by the belief that immigrants are "more represented among the beneficiaries of redistribution." Yet evidence in favor of such assumption is limited: Correcting people's beliefs about the size of the immigrant population and its reliance on social benefits does not seem to affect support for redistributive social policies (Alesina, Miano and Stantcheva, 2018).[4]

One reason is that the perception that the modal recipient is an immigrant (shared by many people) does not imply the belief that immigrants do not deserve to benefit from *redistribution to* policies (shared by a smaller subset of the population).[5] Again, the evidence suggests a key role for the reciprocity norm, that is, the norm according to which cooperative and uncooperative (i.e., free riding) behavior should be met in kind.[6] Perceived "good faith effort" by immigrants to avoid free riding promotes inclusion into the "Nation" and thus positive altruism. Moral outrage and negative altruism (here by denying access to social benefits) are targeted at "welfare shoppers" or "economic migrants" who try to "pass" as refugees.

Racist or xenophobic motives very likely explain why a subset of people come to the conclusion that immigrants' access to social benefits violates the norm of reciprocity. For these individuals, rhetoric of deservingness provides a fig leaf for less socially acceptable opinions. Still, from a theoretical perspective, parochial altruism is of limited help: It cannot explain individual differences beyond the tautological claim that some people are more parochial than others.

Starting from fairness reasoning in general – and the reciprocity norm in particular – can offer some analytical leverage. First, as discussed in Chapter 4, people who find immigrants' undeserving of *redistribution to* policies tend to think the same of all recipients, irrespective of the latter's ethnic background. This suggests individual differences in terms of how people reason about moral hazard and free riding in general, a hypothesis I explore in more detail in Chapter 10. Second, perceived violations of the reciprocity norm are not limited to

---

[4] Similarly, correcting white American respondents' perceptions of the racial composition of welfare recipients does not significantly influence their support for welfare (Akesson et al., 2022).

[5] This disconnect is best demonstrated by Larsen's comparison of Great Britain, Denmark and Sweden (Larsen and Dejgaard, 2013). In Great Britain, where a casual observer of British politics might assume immigrants to be undeserving beneficiaries of social solidarity, the poor and welfare recipients portrayed in the media as "scroungers" are white. In Denmark and Sweden, with more recent immigration and lower levels of diversity, "the poor and welfare recipients increasingly have come to be perceived as non-white" (Larsen and Dejgaard, 2013), *without* undermining the beliefs that the modal recipient is deserving of social solidarity.

[6] For example, vignette experiments on the willingness to transfer resources to a low-income recipient routinely find that a few years of living and working in a country are often enough for a non-white Muslim immigrant to be treated in a hypothetical experimental context as if a native recipient with a similar job history (see Haderup Larsen and Schaeffer (2020) and Kootstra (2016) for recent examples).

immigrants unfairly receiving benefits they do not deserve. Fairness grievances also include the perception that deserving natives unfairly receive less bene-fits than immigrants.[7] This suggests that grievances over immigrants' access to social benefits are part of a larger set of grievances targeted at the polity as whole. Understanding how such grievances form will require moving beyond parochial altruism.

A third avenue for research builds on the argument presented in Chapter 2, which emphasizes the tight relationship between group membership, resource pooling and the reciprocity norm. In Europe, citizenship gives unconditional access to the welfare state and the welfare state is what gives citizenship its economic and symbolic value.[8] Put differently, and as argued in Chapter 2, meaning and status derived from being a "productive" member of society have at least two distinct sources. One source is an individual's market value made visible to all through one's income. The other is an individual's membership in a resource-pooling endeavor of an unprecedented scope. Relatively easy access to social benefits can threaten the status-boosting properties of this club good and generate hostility toward people who can "easily join." Yet, this does not preclude granting benefits to the hardworking type of immigrant on the other. If anything, it contributes to marking insiders as themselves hardworking "high status" individuals. Not all individuals need this status boost, and identifying those who do could shed new light on who is most likely to experience immi-grants' access as unfair (see Shayo (2009) for a related an example).

Summary and Next Steps

In this transition chapter, I have discussed several insights that follow from the argument presented in Part I, especially when it comes to unpacking the dynamics of demand for redistribution. I have identified three contextual factors hypothesized to affect attitudes through three causal pathways. These are fiscal stress and a reversal to material self-interest, survey design and framing effects, partisan dynamics and belief change. Fiscal stress, survey design and partisan dynamics do not constitute an exhaustive list of activating factors. They were

---

[7] For example, in the 2014 wave of the ESS, respondents were asked if they think the government treats them better, the same, or worse than it treats immigrants. In Great Britain, the share of people who thought that immigrants were better treated than they themselves were was 46%, in France 34% and in Austria 38%. In Sweden, the share was much lower at 12%.

[8] This latter point is worth emphasizing: As described by Castel (1995), in the postwar era, having social rights, namely, access to social insurance derived from stable employment, was central to individuals' self-worth (usually white male breadwinners).

selected for their explanatory power with regard to the puzzling cases discussed in the introduction.[9] Chapters 7–10 puts this explanatory power to the test.

I also used the framework presented in Part I to critically examine a fourth factor, immigration-induced diversity. First, its eroding power on mass support for redistribution is not as extensive as often argued, especially in the European context where this argument is routinely mobilized. Second, researchers' understanding of the micro-foundations underpinning this hypothesized erosion is incomplete at best. I have proposed several lines of inquiry, all focused on explaining why people come to very different conclusions regarding the fairness of immigrants' access to the welfare state. Still, it is beyond the scope of this book to explore them in detail. I consequently limit my inquiry to discussing immigration only when necessary, for example, when immigration shocks or other immigration-induced factors provide a plausible alternative interpretation of my results.

Appendix

A6.1 Social Policy Preferences and Anti-Immigrant Sentiment

The importance of carefully conceptualizing (and correctly measuring) the types of attitudes affected by anti-immigrant sentiment is illustrated in Figure A6.1. I use survey data from the ESS to plot the correlation between anti-immigrant sentiments (a binned index) and two policy items. The item on the right measures agreement/disagreement with the claim that "the government should take measures to reduce differences in income levels" (support for redistribution as traditionally measured in existing research), while the item on the left measures agreement/disagreement with the claim that it is the government's responsibility to ensure a reasonable standard of living for the unemployed.

As Figure A6.1 shows, individuals with more negative attitudes toward immigrants and immigration are also more likely to disagree that it is the government's job to provide a decent standard of living for the unemployed.

---

[9] As a reminder, in Great Britain and in the United States, any evidence of attitudinal change goes against common expectation: a decline in aggregate support in Great Britain and a decline in the attitudinal income gradient in the United States. Also noteworthy is the difference between Great Britain and Germany, two countries with similar increases in income inequality but with opposite attitudinal trends. A final case is France, one of the few countries to have experienced a nation-wide year-long social movement –*Les Gilets Jaunes* – focusing on economic issues and asking for more income redistribution, despite no increase in income inequality.

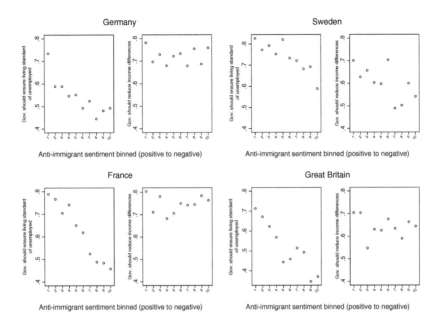

Figure A6.1 Social policy preferences and anti-immigrant sentiment
Binned scatter plots (individual-level analysis). The anti-immigrant sentiment variable on the X-axis is split into 10 bins of equal size. This variable is measured by combining six survey items (additive scale) asking about immigration's economic and cultural "cost" and about preferences for increasing or decreasing migration inflows. See Chapter 4 for item wording. For each country, the left figure plots the share who agrees that "the government should ensure a decent standard of living for the unemployed." The right figure plots the share who agrees that the government should redistribute income (traditional measure).
Source: ESS 2016, weighted.

Notice, in contrast, the absence of a correlation between anti-immigrant sentiment and support for income redistribution. This pattern suggests (with some exceptions, see Sweden in Figure A6.1), a connection between hostility to immigrants and a *subset* of social policy preferences, namely preferences toward policies that explicitly redistribute to the worse off.

7

Fiscal Stress and the Erosion of Social Solidarity

Two groups display the highest support for generous *redistribution to* policies: (1) low-income beneficiaries, irrespective of their reciprocity beliefs and (2) high-income contributors who trust that these policies benefit deserving recipients. This coalition is held together thanks to *redistribution to* policies' asymmetric economic implications. For low-income beneficiaries, *redistribution to* policies are high stakes, explaining high baseline support irrespective of reciprocity beliefs. In contrast, the uncertainty over the costs to high-income contributors of more generous *redistribution to* policies favors fairness reasoning, explaining higher-than-expected support within this group. In this chapter, I argue that fiscal stress, in the form of fiscal adjustment, can introduce a wedge in this pro-*redistribution to* coalition. The intuition is simple: When the tax implications of generous social spending are no longer a hypothetical, it becomes much easier for people to reason from the perspective of their own pocketbook. In such a context, high-income respondents will react by choosing to concentrate financial efforts on social programs they directly benefit from. This comes at the expense of support for *redistribution to* policies.

When Altruism Gets a Price Tag

The welfare state is a bundle of social programs that transfer resources from people in the good state of the world (the employed, rich, healthy and young) to people in the bad state (the unemployed, poor, sick and elderly). A key parameter for fiscal stress is the dependency ratio, that is, the share of recipients (people in the bad state of the world) over the share of contributors (people in the good state). A deterioration in the dependency ratio increases the price of altruistic support for *redistribution to* policies in the form of tax increases needed to maintain generous social transfers to the worse off. Such tax increases are hard for voters to anticipate: Budget deficits and growing sovereign debt amidst declining borrowing costs (Blanchard, 2019) mean fiscal adjustments happen in haphazard ways depending on who wins elections and on international constraints. Furthermore, due to a complicated tax code and funding system, fiscal adjustment's implications are far from straightforward, and politicians, fearing a backlash from affected populations, have only limited incentives to provide clarifying cues. In such a context, high-income individuals' reliance on fairness reasoning is to be expected.

Uncertainty is resolved when the government commits to, and ultimately implements, fiscal adjustment. Not only do people realize that the government faces a budget constraint, they also experience the personal cost of a worsening dependency ratio. Once altruism gets a price tag, in the form of tax increases to maintain generous social transfers to the worse off, net contributors will revert to a more self-interested position, disregarding what fairness reasoning prescribes. Net beneficiaries, on the other hand, will always oppose the erosion of generous *redistribution to* policies. In other words, when fiscal adjustment becomes a credible threat, the attitudes of net beneficiaries and net contributors will diverge, generating an income gap where previously there had been none.

Figure 7.1 sketches how this plays out empirically. When the pocketbook consequences of generous *redistribution to* policies are uncertain, some among the economically secure will support *redistribution to* policies because it benefits deserving recipients and is consequently the fair thing to do. Others, concerned about the prevalence of free riding, oppose it because it would be unfair to let free riders go unpunished. Self-interested reasoning triggered by the lifting of the tax veil decreases support for *redistribution to* among the former, while the latter, partly due to a ceiling effect, are much less affected. Self-serving adjustment among net contributors, thus, implies increasingly diverging attitudes between net contributors and net beneficiaries. Notice how in Figure 7.1, baseline support is higher on the left-hand side than on the right-hand side.

This argument also has implications for the dynamics of mass attitudes toward *redistribution to* policies in recessionary times. Recessions triggered by financial crises or a global pandemic temporarily increase the number of deserving recipients (they are poor or unemployed for reasons they cannot control). As a result, in time of economic hardship and absent a credible threat of fiscal adjustment, support for *redistribution to* policies among the economically secure should go up – or at least not erode – because helping deserving recipients is the fair thing to do. When recessions are associated with austerity measures, as happened after the Great Recession, this support will go down, especially among net contributors who usually believe that generous *redistribution to* policies is the fair thing to do.

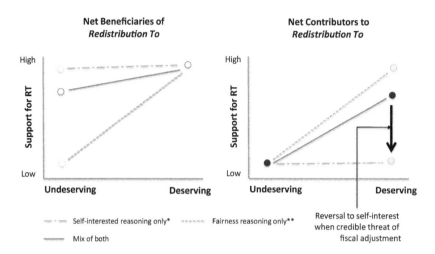

Figure 7.1 Fiscal stress and support for *redistribution to* policies
Support for *redistribution to* policies as predicted by reciprocity beliefs under three scenarios: self-interested reasoning, fairness reasoning and a mix of both.
* Do I benefit from this transfer? How much does it cost me? Would I benefit (be hurt) from seeing it cut (expanded)? ** What is the fair thing to do, given how deserving the modal recipient is?

To test these implications, I focus on the case of France. Why France? One reason is the availability of a unique decades-long longitudinal survey, the DREES barometer, that includes a set of questions particularly well suited for testing this causal pathway. Unlike other surveys, which often ask vague questions about social and welfare spending, question wording in the DREES barometer directly captures two important aspects of support for *redistribution to* policies. One is the willingness to personally contribute, through payroll taxes, to limiting the erosion of social benefits targeted to the poor and the unemployed. The other is support for making access to benefits such as healthcare or unemployment benefits universal, irrespective of past payroll contributions.

As I explain next, another reason for choosing France is that this country provides the ideal setting for testing the argument presented in this chapter. No evidence for my argument in the French context would be damaging.

France: A Most-Likely Case

France has dealt with a mismatch between revenue and spending for several decades now. During the 1980s, fiscal adjustment was repeatedly delayed. Starting in the mid-1990s, governments (usually on the left) started introducing

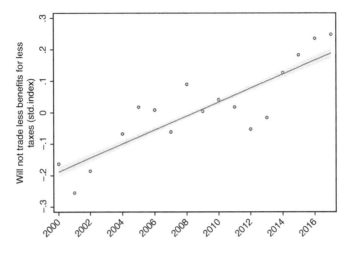

Figure 7.2 Opposition to benefit cuts in France
Plots overtime change in opposition to benefit cuts, even if it means lower taxes.
Item wording (author translation): "Would you accept a cut in pension/health benefits in exchange for a cut in income and payroll taxes?" (Definitely yes, maybe yes, maybe no, definitely no). Answers to the pension and health benefits items are correlated with each other and can be combined into a simple additive index, which is then standardized for ease of interpretation.
Source: Baromètre d'opinion DREES 2000–2016, weighted.

new taxes, one of them explicitly targeted at reimbursing past debt generated by the welfare state and the other aimed at raising new revenue for public health care. These taxes have increased regularly over time, though not fast enough to match the growth in spending. During that period, people have expressed growing concerns that fiscal adjustment might mean a decline in pension and healthcare benefits.

Figure 7.2 captures this trend. It plots changes in the extent to which respondents favor less benefits (in this case, healthcare and retirement benefits) if it means less taxes. Since 2000, the index combining answers to questions about health care and pensions has shifted by nearly half a SD, indicating a declining share of respondents willing to trade less benefits against less taxes. Growing opposition to benefit cuts provides a reasonable proxy of growing concerns that benefits might be significantly cut. Notice the sharp increase between 2012 and 2017. This increase reflects the country's economic and political contexts. Following the Great Recession in 2009, French bonds were downgraded, raising concerns of a debt crisis. At the same time, Greece was in the midst of its own debt crisis, demonstrating to French voters that failure to

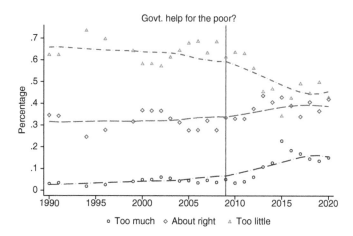

Figure 7.3 Attitudes toward *redistribution to* policies in France
Plots answers to the following question (author translation): "Thinking about what
the government does to help the poor: Do you think what it does is too little, about
right, too much?" The vertical line marks the onset of the Great Recession.
Source: Conditions de vie et aspirations, 1979–2020, weighted.

balance the books could have dire consequences. Furthermore, between 2010
and 2014, both the Sarkozy and Hollande governments implemented significant
fiscal adjustment in the form of tax increases and targeted benefit cuts. In 2017,
Emmanuel Macron was elected after announcing his goal of reforming public
pensions and introduced a bill to that effect in 2019. In other words, in France,
fiscal adjustment was and is far from a hypothetical distant threat, making this
country an ideal case to test my argument.

Another reason for focusing on France is the puzzling decline in support
for welfare spending in the aftermath of the Great Recession. Figure 7.3 plots
the share of respondents who say that the government's financial effort in helping the worse off is either too little, about right or too generous. Up until the
Great Recession, the overall pattern is that of stability with roughly 65% of respondents answering that the government is doing too little. There is a peak at
73% during the 1993–1994 recession. The pattern post-2009 is strikingly different: Despite an increase in unemployment and paltry growth rates, the share
of individuals who believe that the government is doing too little decreases
steadily to 45%. In the meantime, as one might expect following a recession,
the share of people who attribute poverty to labor market conditions has gone
up (Baromètre d'opinion DREES 2000–2016, not shown). In other words, despite no evidence that perceptions of the poor have changed, and despite an

economic recession, there is no increase in support for spending targeted to the poor and the unemployed. Relative to the 1993–1994 recession, support is down by 30 percentage points.

If the argument presented earlier is correct, trends post-2009 look different from trends in the early 1990s because French citizens, exposed to austerity measures to address fiscal imbalances, have become increasingly aware of the cost to their pocketbook of maintaining generous *redistribution to* policies. In such a context, I expect people to revert to a more self-interested position and abandon altruistic support for programs they do not benefit from. Support for *redistribution to* policies will erode *despite* the perception that recipients are more deserving. This erosion should be larger among net contributors to *redistribution to* policies. Empirically, this implies a growing attitudinal gap between net contributors and net beneficiaries of *redistribution to* policies.

To test these expectations, I first turn to the DREES barometer and examine how attitudinal trends vary by income category. The longitudinal survey data are only suggestive of a possible relationship between fiscal stress and diverging preferences between net beneficiaries of, and net contributors to, *redistribution to* policies. As a follow-up, I also use a survey experiment designed to probe the impact of fiscal stress on *redistribution to* preferences and test the hypothesized self-serving adjustment sketched in Figure 7.1.

The Return of the Income Gradient

To measure attitudes toward *redistribution to* policies, I rely on the two sets of items briefly described earlier. One set of items asks respondents about their willingness to pay more payroll taxes to minimize a decline in the generosity of benefits targeted to the poor (in this case, child benefits) and the unemployed.[1] The same question is asked with regard to pensions and health care. The second set of items used to measure attitudes toward *redistribution to* policies asks respondents whether they believe that access to social benefits should be limited to those who have paid into the system (versus guaranteeing unconditional access for all).[2] Respondents are asked their opinion about conditional versus unconditional access with regard to health care, pensions, unemployment insurance and child benefits.

---

[1] "Depending on your ability to pay, would you be willing to pay more payroll taxes to maintain current benefit levels? Yes certainly, maybe, not really, definitely not." (author's translation).

[2] "In your opinion, [benefit type] should (1) only be accessible to those who pay payroll taxes, (2) only be accessible to those who cannot make ends meet or (3) be accessible to all irrespective of social background and job type." (author's translation). Very few people choose option 2.

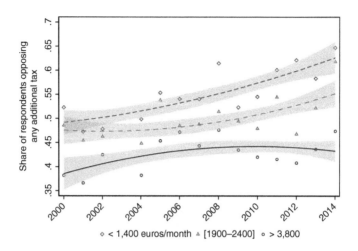

Figure 7.4 Taxation fatigue in France by income
Plots share of each income category unwilling to pay more payroll taxes irrespective of the benefit being asked about (e.g., unemployment, child benefit, health care
or pension). An income-specific quadratic fit using the underlying data is over-
layed on the binned data. Item wording (author's translation): "In the future and in
line with your ability to pay, would you be willing to pay more payroll contributions to maintain benefit levels for the following social programs: child benefits,
unemployment insurance, health care and pensions?" (Yes absolutely, yes, no, no
absolutely not). Individuals who answer "no" or "no, absolutely not" are coded
as 1.
Source: Baromètre d'opinion DREES 2000–2018, weighted.

A quick note on the first set of items asking about willingness to pay. Opposition to paying more taxes to finance transfers to the poor and the unemployed
could be interpreted as a decline in support for *redistribution to* policies, it
could also merely capture the unwillingness to pay any taxes, irrespective of
the social program under consideration. As Figure 7.4 shows, there is indeed
evidence of growing taxation fatigue. The figure plots the share of individuals who say that they are unwilling to pay more taxes irrespective of the social
benefit mentioned (child benefits, unemployment, pensions or health care). This
share is also broken down according to income level. The increase in opposition to any tax is the largest among low-income respondents, with a stable 40%
of high-income respondents opposing any tax increases.

To account for taxation fatigue, I focus on measuring the extent to which
people choose to target their taxation effort (assuming that they are not experiencing taxation fatigue) on programs they are themselves most likely to
benefit form. Specifically, I examine whether a respondent is *more* willing to

fund health care and pensions than to fund unemployment and childcare using four paired comparisons (i.e., health care versus unemployment, pensions versus unemployment, healthcare versus child benefits and pensions versus child benefits). A positive value indicates that a respondent prioritizes universal programs she can expect to rely on (health care and pensions) over more targeted programs (unemployment and child benefits). A negative value indicates the opposite priority. A value of zero applies to someone willing to pay for both or unwilling to pay for either.[3] This means that an increase in any of the four indicators is either due to a decline in the share of people prioritizing funding for unemployment and childcare or an increase in the share prioritizing healthcare and pension benefits, not to taxation fatigue. Because all four paired indicators are highly correlated (Cronbach's $\alpha = 0.79$), I combine them into one summary score that I then standardize.

For expository purposes, I also combine answers to the four questions asking about conditional access to health care, pensions, unemployment insurance and child benefits. The answers across the four items are highly correlated (Cronbach's $\alpha = 0.80$). The maximum score identifies individuals who support excluding noncontributors for all four programs; the minimum score identifies those who oppose exclusion for all four programs. To facilitate interpretation, the final index score is also standardized.

I proxy one's position as a net contributor or net beneficiary of *redistribution to* policies using household income. Because of a stable income distribution, as well as limited inflation, the income variable available in the DREES longitudinal survey has barely changed since 2000, enabling the overtime comparison of attitudinal trends across income levels. This descriptive approach, plotted in Figures 7.5 and 7.6, has the benefit of simplicity and transparency.

The top panel in Figure 7.5 documents an increase in the share of individuals who prioritize universal programs they can expect to rely on over more targeted programs. The bottom panel documents a growing income gap, with stable attitudes among low-income respondents and an anti-solidarity turn among high-income respondents. These diverging trends are mostly limited to the post-2008 period. In other words, while high-income individuals are not turning against taxation "en masse" (see Figure 7.4), they are increasingly choosing to focus revenue on maintaining the generosity of social programs they are more likely to themselves rely on. In contrast, after correcting for taxation fatigue, there is no such decline among low-income respondents.

---

[3] On average, 50% of respondents are willing to contribute to both and 30% refuse to contribute to either. In other words, the analysis relies on the 30% of respondents who favor either targeted programs (10%) or universal programs (20%).

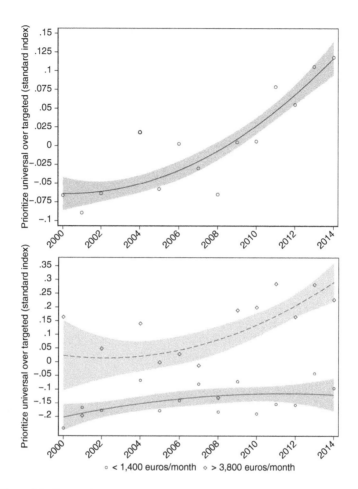

Figure 7.5 Changes in support for *redistribution to* policies (measure 1)
Plots mean prioritization scores by year (top panel) and by year and income level
(bottom panel). Higher values indicate that more people favor universal programs
(i.e., pensions or health care) over targeted ones (childcare and unemployment
insurance). In contrast to Figure 7.6., because of fewer observations, the quadratic
fit does not includes a break for 2009. See the text for a detailed overview of how
the scores were computed.
Source: Baromètre d'opinion DREES 2000–2018, weighted.

Figure 7.6 plots changes in support for conditional access. Note that the response options changed in 2016 and the subsequent years. Starting from 2016,
respondents could pick a fourth option, one that mentioned making access conditional on past contributions while guaranteeing a minimal safety net for others who did not qualify. The mentioning of the safety net resulted in a jump in

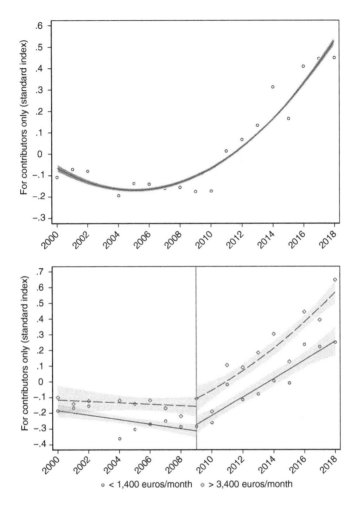

Figure 7.6 Changes in support for *redistribution to* policies (measure 2)
Plots mean conditionality scores by year (top panel) and by year and income level (bottom panel). Higher values indicate that more people favor limiting access to social benefits to people who already paid into the system. In the bottom panel, the quadratic fit includes a break for 2009. Note that the response options changed in 2016. The figure is corrected to account for this change, though caution is required when comparing pre- and post-2015 values. See the text for more detail.
Source: Baromètre d'opinion DREES 2000–2018, weighted.

support for conditional access. To correct for this jump, I compute the average support for conditional access in the three years before and the three years after the change and take the difference between the two averages. I then substract this difference (0.23) from the year average starting from 2016. Nevertheless, data collected after 2015 should be interpreted with caution.

As shown in Figure 7.6, support for making benefit access conditional on past contributions has increased across the board, even among the poor. One possible explanation is that the income measure is too coarse to identify one's position as a net beneficiary of *redistribution to* policies. Among low-income individuals, some have secured social rights through past contributions and likely do not believe that they would be affected by such conditional access. Still, in line with expectations, the increase is larger among high-income respondents: While the income gap is virtually nonexistent in 2000, it is equal to nearly half a SD in 2014.

Evidence presented in Figures 7.5 and 7.6 show that, during the Great Recession, support for *redistribution to* policies has gone down, especially among high-income respondents. This, alongside evidence of a growing awareness of the government's budget constraint (Figure 7.2), aligns with the hypothesized self-serving adjustment among a subset of economically secure individuals.

What About Immigration?

What else might explain these trends? As discussed in Chapter 6, a common way to interpret a decline in support for *redistribution to* policies is to tie it to growing hostility to immigrants, an argument popularized by Alesina and Glaeser (2006). This suggest a possible competing interpretation, namely that these trends could be the result of the 2014 refugee crisis.

One issue with this interpretation is timing: The refugee crisis became salient in late 2015, three years after the beginning of the Hollande presidency and five years after the onset of the Great Recession in France. As visible in Figures 7.5 and 7.6, attitudinal change predates 2015 and appears mostly tied to the Great Recession and its aftermath. To further probe this competing interpretation, in Appendix A7.1, I use survey questions capturing hostility to immigrants to examine whether xenophobia might be driving trends among high-income individuals. Against this interpretation, I find no evidence that this overtime pattern is mostly driven by high-income individual who think that there are "too many immigrant workers in France."

More importantly, the empirical expectation examined here (a growing income gap) cannot be easily accounted for by a parochial altruism-type argument. Remember that the economically secure who find the poor and the unemployed deserving are much more likely to be cosmopolitans and less likely to be ethnocentric. According to the parochial altruism argument, they should be the least likely to decrease their support for redistribution to the poor and the unemployed for parochial reasons. In the following section, I use a survey experiment to show that, contra such expectation, in the face of fiscal stress, support for *redistribution to* policies within this group goes down.

Micro-foundations: A Survey Experiment

I have argued that net contributors, who support *redistribution to* because it is the fair thing to do, revert to a more self-interested position when they are aware of *redistribution to* policies' implications for their own pocketbook in the form of higher taxes. To test this mechanism, I collect original survey data from a nonrepresentative sample of French respondents. I examine whether being primed to think about fiscal stress changes how people reason about *redistribution to* policies, as a function of both one's likelihood of benefiting from these policies and one's beliefs about their fairness as predicted by one's perceptions of the prevalence of free riding.

Design Overview

I posted the survey on a French crowdsourcing platform.[4] Respondents were randomly assigned to two treatment conditions: the control condition and the fiscal stress condition.[5] Individuals in the control condition were exposed to a visual sketch of the structure of the French welfare state. The audio emphasized the insurance properties of the welfare state, explaining that social transfers are designed to help people who can no longer provide for themselves. The audio concluded with a reminder that social transfers are paid for by social contributions and taxes. Individuals in the fiscal stress condition were exposed to the same information, followed by an additional section presented on a separate web page. The visual and the associated audio for this second section described the mismatch between spending generated by social benefits and revenue from taxes and social contributions. The audio also explained that this mismatch had generated debt, which was equal to 27 billion euros in 1996 and had increased to 227 billion euros in 2014. The visual was a simple bar chart plotting this increase.[6]

---

[4] The survey was completed in the Fall of 2016. See www.foulefactory.com.

[5] For more information on the sample, randomization, attrition and the overall design of the survey and different treatment conditions, see the online appendix.

[6] These amounts come from the annual accounts of the CADES, a separate accounting structure set up to tackle the share of the public debt generated by the welfare state.

This treatment was designed with the French public debate in mind. Political elites have emphasized the structural roots of the welfare state's deficit and reform is presented as an accounting necessity. In addition, the financial situation of the French welfare state is explicitly distinguished from the overall sovereign debt. Tax increases have always been justified to make the welfare state financially sustainable. The treatment primes people to think about the fiscal unsustainability of the welfare state and the related threat of a fiscal adjustment.[7]

Based on the argument presented in this chapter, whether or not one stands to benefit from *redistribution to* policies should be a better predictor of support for *redistribution to* policies in the treatment group than in the control group. If the reversal mechanism described in Figure 7.1 is at play, then I expect economically secure individuals who hold pro-redistribution reciprocity beliefs to be the most affected by the treatment in the form of lower support for *redistribution to* policies.

Outcomes of Interest

To measure attitudes toward *redistribution to* policies, I use versions of the questions available in the DREES barometer. First, I measure respondents' willingness to pay more taxes to maintain the benefit generosity of unemployment benefits and welfare.[8] I also collect the same information with regard to pensions and health care. In line with the previous analysis, I use programs that cover universal risks as the reference policies. Below, I present results using public health care as the main reference (results are similar when using pensions as the reference category). I also ask respondents whether they support making access to health care and public pensions conditional on prior contributions.

I expect the fiscal stress treatment to have different consequences whether one is a net contributor to *redistribution to* or a net beneficiary. With the observational data, I have used income measures to proxy for membership in these two groups. Good income measures are notoriously hard to recover in

---

[7] As a manipulation check, I asked respondents their perceptions of the welfare state's sustainability, focusing on unemployment insurance, health care and pensions. I combine respondents' option into an index and find that the treatment decreased the (already small) number of individuals who, for at least one of the social programs, chose a response category implying that a given social program was fiscally sustainable. This suggest that the treatment was correctly interpreted.

[8] The child benefit item available in the DREES barometer is ambiguous as many benefits are conditional on the number of children, not on household income. I thus prefer to ask about welfare.

online surveys, especially in France where talking about one's income can be taboo. I consequently rely on a work-around designed to distinguish people who are economically secure, and likely to be net contributors, from people who are economically insecure, and likely to be net beneficiaries. Specifically, I combine answers to two survey questions: one asking respondents about their perceptions of their current income/lifestyle relative to their perception of the average French income/lifestyle and another asking respondents about their perceived likelihood of becoming poor in the next five years. Note that, given this measurement strategy, and to avoid complications around retirees, I focus on individuals of working age only. In Appendix A7.2, I describe how I combine answers to these questions to distinguish the economically secure from the insecure. Through this classification process, I drop 130 respondents who consider themselves of average income/lifestyle and do not know about their future risk of being poor. I end up with 52% of respondents classified as economically insecure, something one might expect from a micro-tasking platform (as different from a more traditional online panel).

I measure reciprocity beliefs using three survey items that I combine into individual scores using weights recovered from a factor analysis. One item asks about moral hazard (i.e., benefits make people lazy), another asks about the work ethic of the unemployed and a third item measures support for denying benefits to unemployed workers who refuse the job offered to them. The resulting factor scores are coded such that higher values indicate more conservative responses, namely higher concerns over free riding. These items were asked after the treatment to avoid having respondents in the treatment condition interpret the deficit as a result of free riding. I find no evidence that beliefs were affected by the treatment: This is true whether looking at the full sample or breaking the analysis down by economic status (insecure or secure).

Results

Table 7.1 plots the share of respondents in each treatment condition that expresses (1) willingness to contribute to funding unemployment benefits or welfare, irrespective of their position on health care, (2) willingness to fund health care only and (3) taxation fatigue (unwilling to fund both targeted programs and health care). The results are further broken down by economic status.[9]

---

[9] Results are similar when using pensions as the reference category.

Table 7.1 *Mean outcome by treatment condition and economic hardship*

	Unemployment		Welfare	
	Control	Fiscal stress	Control	Fiscal stress
WTP† for targeted benefits (%)				
Economically secure	38	28	40	33
Economically insecure	32	38	33	41
Delta	6	−10*	7	−8
Absolute effect size (% points)		16*		15**
WTP for health care only (%)				
Economically secure	25	32	23	25
Economically insecure	22	16	18	11
Delta	3	16*	5	14
Absolute effect size (% points)		13*		9
Unwilling to pay for either (%)				
Economically secure	36	39	37	38
Economically insecure	45	45	48	47
Delta	−9	−6	−11	−10
Absolute effect size (% points)		3		1

* 90% confidence level, ** 95% confidence level.
† WTP: Willingness to pay.
Source: Foule Factory 2016.

As Table 7.1 shows, all of the action is in the *difference* between economically secure individuals and economically insecure individuals. In the control group, the former are more willing to fund transfers targeted to the unemployed and families with children than the latter, in line with what one might expect given differences in ability to pay. In the treatment conditions, and in line with expectations, these differences flip and the economically insecure become more willing to contribute, despite lower ability to pay, while the economically secure become less willing.

Figure 7.7 presents differences between treatment and control in terms of attitudes toward conditional benefit access. The baseline answer is support for universal access; individuals who want to make access conditional are coded as 1. While the gap between the economically secure and insecure is indistinguishable from zero in the control condition, it is negative in the fiscal stress condition: The economically insecure are more likely to support universal access relative to the economically secure. Results are stronger for health care than for pensions. As is the case for the previous items, this difference across

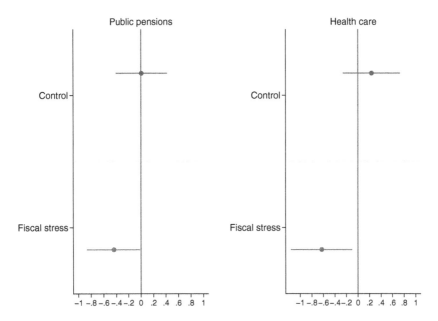

Figure 7.7 Effect of economic situation on support for conditional access
Plots regression coefficients from a logit regression predicting support for conditional access (ref: support for universal access). The independent variable is a dummy variable with 1 indicating that a respondent is classified as economically insecure and 0 if classified as economically secure.
Source: Foule Factory 2016.

treatment conditions is due to both the economically secure decreasing their support for universal access and the economically secure increasing it.[10]

To check for self-serving adjustment among the economically secure, I regress willingness to contribute on reciprocity beliefs interacted with a dummy variable capturing treatment conditions. This analysis shows that the coefficient on reciprocity beliefs is smaller for the fiscal stress condition than for the control condition.[11] Next, I examine whether this difference is due to economically secure respondents in the fiscal stress condition updating their policy preferences in a self-interested fashion.

To test this, I further interact reciprocity beliefs with the economic hardship variable. Figure 7.8 plots the economically secure's predicted willingness to pay for targeted transfers, as a function of their reciprocity beliefs. In the fiscal

---

[10] See the online appendix for results broken down according to economic hardship categories.
[11] These results are available in the online appendix.

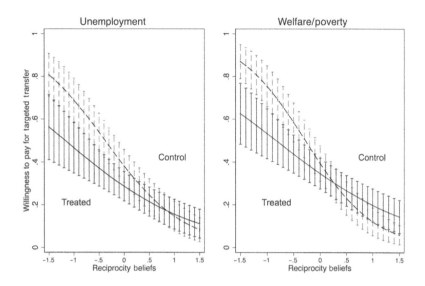

Figure 7.8 Effect sizes and reciprocity beliefs among the economically secure
Plots the economically secure's predicted willingness to pay more taxes for targeted programs in treatment and control as a function of reciprocity beliefs. Predictions are derived from a logit regression ran on the economically secure only and regressing willingness to pay as a function of reciprocity beliefs interacted with the treatment dummy.
Source: Foule Factory 2016.

stress condition, people with more pro-redistribution reciprocity beliefs are, relative to the control group, less willing to pay for targeted benefits. For people who are 1 SD to the left of the score average, the difference between treatment and control is twice as much as that found in the sample as a whole. Individuals concerned about free riding (1 SD to the right of the score average) are not affected: They already oppose paying for the poor and the unemployed. There is no such interaction between free riding beliefs and treatment conditions among the economically insecure (see Appendix A7.3). Overall, these findings align with the hypothesis of a self-serving adjustment among altruistic economically secure individuals in conditions of fiscal stress.

The experimental data suggest economically secure respondents maximize their disposable incomes by decreasing their willingness to contribute to policies they do not benefit from. For policies that benefit all, including themselves, the economically secure maximize their own net transfers by excluding net beneficiaries who contribute less than they receive. Economically insecure individuals react in the opposite direction. As a result, respondents' financial situation becomes a much better predictor of social policy preferences in the fiscal stress condition than in the control condition. In line with expectations, results are partly driven by those who believe that *redistribution to* policies do not reward free riding and are thus fair.

Summary and Next Steps

From the perspective of the benchmark model, France is a puzzling case: how to explain *Les Gilets Jaunes* when income inequality has remained so stable? Evidence discussed in Part I offers some answers: France stands out as a country extremely critical of markets and much more likely to perceive income inequality as unfair. Following the Great Recession, these beliefs helped sustain a social movement like *Les Gilets Jaunes*, asking for more *redistribution from* the rich to the rest of the population.

Still, as I showed in this chapter, and in line with my argument, pro-redistribution proportionality beliefs do not protect against the eroding effects of fiscal stress on support for *redistribution to* policies. In a country where fiscal stress is salient and translates into growing anxiety over future fiscal adjustment, the economically secure's altruistic commitment to social solidarity can erode, even in time of growing need such as in the aftermath of the Great Recession. These cracks can remain dormant unless attempts to balance the budget, especially in hard times, activate them. In France, while the share of the labor force with weak labor market attachment continues to grow (Emmenerger et al., 2012), the political coalition underpinning the policies targeted to this group is showing signs of weakness.

The French case provides an example of a change in the motive mix among the altruistic rich. In the remaining chapters, I turn to the two other pathways, namely framing effects and belief change.

Appendix

A7.1 Hostility to Immigrants and Changes in Support for *Redistribution to*

To measure anti-immigrant sentiment, I use a survey question that asks respondents' agreement with the claim that there are too many "immigrant workers" in

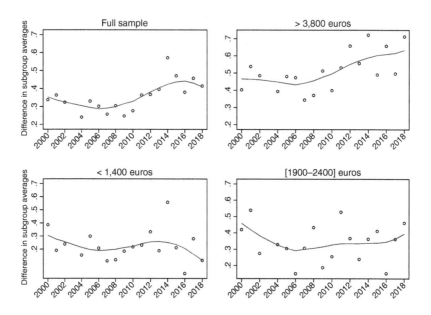

Figure A7.1 Anti-immigrant sentiment and support for conditional access
Plots differences in mean conditionality scores between people who agree that
there are too many immigrant workers and people who disagree, by year. Given the
change in item wording (see page 152), data collected after 2015 is only indicative.
Source: Baromètre d'opinion DREES 2000–2018.

France. People who agree with this claim are coded as 1. Note that the "neither–
nor" response category is not an option in this survey; people can only express
disagreement or agreement.

First, I compute the average conditionality score (plotted in Figure 7.6), broken down by year and by level of anti-immigrant sentiment. I then take the difference between the two. An increase in the absolute value of this difference
indicates that people who agree that there are too many immigrants workers are
turning against universal access at a faster pace than people who disagree.

Figure A7.1 plots this difference for the full sample and for specific income groups. In the full sample, there is no evidence of attitudinal polarization
between the two groups. There is a small increase for high-income individuals, but this increase is substantively limited at 0.15 SD, especially when compared with the overall increase in the index (0.7 SD). If people hostile to immigrants are leading the way, then people who express no hostility are right
behind them.

Table A7.1 *Items used to measure economic security: Cross-tabulation*

	Yes	No	Already poor	DNK	Total
Well above average	0	*12*	0	*2*	14
Above average	**22**	*135*	1	*47*	205
Average	**84**	*151*	27	123	385
Below average	67	39	63	46	215
Well below average	26	3	41	2	72
DNK	3	3	3	7	16
Total	202	343	135	227	907

The left column lists answers to the income/lifestyle item. The top row lists answers to the item on the subjective probability of being poor in the next five years. Respondents in nonitalic **bold** are classified as economically insecure and those in *italic bold* are classified as economically secure.
Source: Foule Factory 2016.

A7.2 Distinguishing the Economically Insecure from the Secure

I define the economically secure as those with a strong labor market attachment and with an earning capacity that places them among the net contributors to policies targeted to the poor. Economic insecurity, on the other hand, is most often tied to job insecurity and a low earning capacity. Note that, given this measurement strategy, I focus on individuals of working age only.

I use a combination of two survey items. One asks individuals about their perception of their current income/lifestyle relative to their perception of the average French income/lifestyle (*niveau de vie*). I also asked respondents about their perceived likelihood of becoming poor in the next five years. Table A7.1 presents a cross-tabulation of these two items. Individuals who believed that they were or would become poor in the next five years were classified as economically insecure. Individuals who thought that they would not become poor were classified as economically secure. For individuals who did not have formed beliefs about their future exposure to poverty, I relied on additional information about their subjective income/lifestyle. Individuals who believed that they were below average were classified as economically insecure. Individuals who believed that they were above average were classified as economically secure.

As you can see from Table A7.1, only 23 out of the 219 individuals who think their lifestyle is above average also think that they are at risk of becoming

Table A7.2 *Labor market status of the economically secure/insecure*

	Economically secure	Economically insecure
Working full time	**55.1**	32.6
Working part time	8	9.6
Working but only on and off	4.3	5.44
Unemployed and looking for work	5.6	**21.5**
Permanently unemployed	0.7	**6.7**
Student	14.5	8.8
Apprenticeship	2	2.3
Homemaker	5.6	7.2
Retired	4.6	5.7
Total	100	100

Respondents in non-italic **bold** are classified as economically insecure and respondents in *italic bold* are classified as economically secure.
Source: Foule Factory 2016.

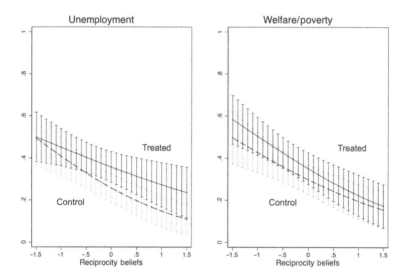

Figure A7.2 Effect sizes and reciprocity beliefs among the economically insecure
Plots the economically insecure's predicted willingness to pay more taxes for targeted programs in treatment and control as a function of reciprocity beliefs. Predictions are derived from a logit regression ran on the economically secure only and regressing willingness to pay as a function of reciprocity beliefs interacted with the treatment dummy.
Source: Foule Factory 2016.

poor. Only 42 out of 297 who think that their lifestyle is below average think that they do not face any risk of becoming poor. Table A7.2 presents the labor situation of the economically secure compared to that of the economically insecure. The great majority of the unemployed workers are in the economically insecure category.

A7.3 Effect Sizes among the Economically Insecure

Figure A7.2 replicates the analysis in Figure 7.8, focusing on the economically insecure. In this group, being told about the financial situation of the welfare state does not affect willingness to contribute.

8

Partisan Dynamics and Mass Attitudinal Change

Despite a sharp rise in income inequality, support for redistribution – as traditionally measured – has *decreased* in Great Britain, not increased. In the United States, I found that overall stability in mass support for redistribution hides a *decrease* in the attitudinal gap between high- and low-income respondents, not the expected increase. This chapter traces these surprising patterns to belief change and framing effects, themselves triggered by changes in how elites compete over redistributive issues. In line with the argument presented in Part I, I also show that belief change plays out differently depending on (1) which type of fairness beliefs is affected by partisan dynamics (proportionality or reciprocity) and (2) people's position as net beneficiaries of (or net contributors to) *redistribution to* policies, as proxied by their income level. In Great Britain in particular, I find that framing effects tied to survey design further explain how belief change affects answers to the traditional redistribution question.

I start by discussing how partisan competition contributes to attitudinal change through both framing effects and belief change. Next, I describe partisan dynamics in Great Britain and the United States and flesh out expectations for attitudinal change. I then revisit attitudinal trends discussed in Chapter 1 in light of these expectations.

Partisan Dynamics, Fairness Beliefs and Survey Answers: A Framework

Zaller's "simple theory of the survey response" offers a good starting point for understanding the role of partisan dynamics (Zaller, 1992; Zaller and Feldman, 1992). According to Zaller, "Most citizens do not possess preformed attitudes at the level of specificity demanded in surveys." Rather, they carry around in their heads "a mix of only partially consistent ideas and considerations." When answering a survey question, people reach into their own "basket" of existing considerations: Which considerations end up being sampled affect how people answer the survey question. This framework succinctly capture two possible sources of attitudinal change: a change in the considerations people sample from and – holding these considerations fixed – a change in the types of considerations that are easier to retrieve.

One can easily transpose this framework to attitudes toward redistributive social policies as conceived in this book. I am particularly interested in people's basket of *fairness* considerations, that is, all the considerations relevant to assessing the fairness of the status quo as prescribed by a given fairness norm. The running tallies of these norm-specific thoughts and considerations are what I have called proportionality and reciprocity beliefs. For survey questions that ask about *redistribution from* issues, people sample from considerations relevant to assessing the fairness of the status quo, as defined by the proportionality norm. For *redistribution to* questions, they sample from considerations relevant to assessing the fairness of the status quo, as defined by the reciprocity norm. Answers provided as a result of sampling from "mostly fair" considerations will differ from answers provided as a result of sampling from "mostly unfair" considerations. For ambiguously worded questions, answers provided as a result of sampling proportionality considerations will differ from answers provided as a result of sampling reciprocity considerations. This framework succinctly captures the two hypothesized pathways for attitudinal change: framing effects, which affect the types of considerations that are easier to retrieve when answering a survey question, and belief change, which describes a significant change in the fairness considerations people sample from.

According to Zaller, partisan competition contributes to attitudinal change by exposing people to competing fairness frames and by creating conditions favorable to belief change. Political elites rely on fairness frames and considerations to build partisan identities, identify political friends and foes, and shape policy debates. In doing so, they affect the type of fairness considerations easier for people to retrieve when answering a survey question. They also expose people to new fairness considerations, some of which will be incorporated into people's own basket of fairness considerations. Without new considerations to incorporate into one's own basket, people's fairness beliefs are unlikely to change. In other words, partisan dynamics, by shaping the type of fairness considerations people are exposed to, also shape the fairness beliefs people hold.[1]

---

[1] Needless to say, people can be exposed to competing frames and new fairness considerations in other ways, by developing new friendships, moving to a new country or switching professions. As previously mentioned, I focus on partisan competition because of its system-wide effect on the discursive context.

In this model, belief change results from the interaction between changes in people's discursive context (itself shaped by long-term partisan dynamics) and people's reaction to these changes. Some people are less exposed than others to discursive changes: They do not read the newspaper and they never talk about politics with friends and family. As a result, they are not exposed to any new considerations to incorporate into their own proto-ideological worldview about the fairness of the status quo. Conditional on exposure, people are more likely to incorporate considerations that echo what they already believe about the fairness of the status quo. In the short run, belief change is slow and incremental: The apple never falls far from the tree.

Another important factor is partisanship: For people with a strong partisan identity, whether or not a given set of frames and claims originate from their preferred party will affect the likelihood of incorporating this claim into their own basket of considerations. In Chapters 9 and 10, I move beyond the existing literature's emphasis on partisanship and identify additional individual-level factors that predict who will incorporate new fairness claims and who will resist doing so. Starting with proportionality beliefs, I argue that individual economic factors help explain who is most likely to incorporate changes in elite messaging pertaining to the fairness of market institutions and income inequality. Simply put, people experiencing economic hardship will be more likely to resist dissonant claims about the fairness of the economic status quo and more likely to accept consonant ones about how unfair it is. With regard to reciprocity beliefs, I expect people with liberal values, relative to people with authoritarian values, to resist dissonant anti-redistribution considerations about the prevalence of free riding and embrace consonant pro-redistribution ones about the deservingness of recipients.

This simple model suggests several reasons for *stable* fairness beliefs, especially when measured using survey data and when studied in the aggregate.[2] First, belief stability often follows from *benign neglect*: If the fairness of the status quo is no longer something elites actively disagree and compete over, belief change is less likely. Conversely, belief change is more likely following major and sustained changes in the discursive context. Second, when the discursive context is changing, stability can also mean active *resistance* among a large group of individuals to the incorporation of new fairness claims. Note that, with

---

[2] This latter point is worth emphasizing one more time. I am interested in patterns of change that can be observed using longitudinal surveys (usually yearly repeated cross sections of a population). This requires that enough people change their survey answers in the same direction, in response, for example, to a change in their discursive context as shaped by supply-side dynamics.

observational data, attitudinal stability due to benign neglect and stability due to active resistance are empirically equivalent and can only be distinguished by carefully parsing out the evidence.

In line with the argument made in Chapter 5, belief change, when it happens, should only selectively affect policy preferences: The impact will be smaller for people who, given high material stakes, are more likely to deviate from what fairness reasoning prescribes. For example, low-income authoritarian voters, while receptive to claims about the high prevalence of free riding among recipients, will nevertheless be less likely to translate these beliefs into opposition to *redistribution to* policies.

In the remaining parts of this chapter, I build on these insights to revisit attitudinal trends in Great Britain and the United States, focusing on aggregate and group-specific trends. In Chapters 9 and 10, I turn my attention to belief change specifically and use panel data to document the push and pull between elite discourse on the one hand, and economic conditions and liberal–authoritarian values on the other.

Declining Support for Redistribution in Great Britain: Revisiting the Evidence

In Great Britain, redistributive issues have always been at the center of political competition. However, the ways in which the two main parties compete and disagree over redistributive issues have changed dramatically over time. Note that in this chapter, and the remainder of the book, when discussing different types of discursive and attitudinal change, I will use the words anti-redistribution/pro-redistribution and right-wing/left-wing interchangeably.

Partisan Dynamics in Great Britain: An Overview

In the late 1970s, in response to economic pressures, British parties became sharply divided over redistributive issues. The turning point was Margaret Thatcher's election as the leader of the Conservative Party in February 1975, followed by her successful electoral bid in May 1979. Thatcher's platform was a direct challenge to the neo-Keynesian postwar consensus (Hall, 1993; Kalyvas, 1994; Matthijs, 2012). Economic prosperity, Thatcher argued, required rebalancing the British economy in favor of market forces and at the expense of the state. Privatization of state-owned companies was one of Thatcher's flagship policies. In making her case to voters, Thatcher emphasized market efficiency in the service of economic growth and an ownership society (housing and "capitalism of the masses") in line with conservative values. The Labour opposition responded in kind with a very radical 1983 manifesto calling for more, not less, nationalization of industries. Each party defended its platform with references to the (un)fairness of the status quo. Thacher presented her policies as designed to build a society "within which each makes the best of his talent" and where rent-extracting unions did not run the show. For the left wing of the Labour Party, more nationalization would bring "a fundamental and irreversible shift in the distribution of wealth and power in favor of the working people and their families" (Tony Benn, cited by Kalyvas (1994), p. 321). Progressive income taxation also made a notable appearance, with Thatcher offering to cut corporate taxes and Labour seeking to address social injustice by going after tax evasion and introducing "an annual wealth tax on the small minority of rich people whose total net personal wealth exceeds £150,000" (cited by Matthijs, 2012). She also framed strikes and unions as symptomatic of a bloated state system overcome by rent seeking at the expense of hardworking citizens (Hay, 2018; Matthijs, 2012).

In other words, Thatcher denounced the state's extensive intervention in the economic realm as producing unfair outcomes. She disrupted the discursive context by infusing anti-redistribution right-wing proportionality concerns, which until then had been relatively absent from political discourse. This shift from consensus to dissensus provided ideal conditions for attitudinal change. First, with two clear competing frames, each activating very different conceptions of the fairness of the status quo, voters could more efficiently align their policy preferences with their own fairness beliefs. Second, exposure to new anti-redistribution fairness considerations increased the likelihood of an anti-redistribution shift in fairness beliefs among people most likely to incorporate such fairness considerations, whether due to their partisan identity or their own economic conditions.

One common interpretation of this period is that Thatcher was echoing and leveraging growing dissatisfaction with the scope of government intervention and the size of the public sector. In contrast, I argue that, in a context where few elites questioned the status quo, it was Thatcher's portrayal of an alternative world with more markets and free enterprise that facilitated aggregate attitudinal change, not the other way around.

Survey data collected by Kalyvas (1994), and reproduced in Figure 8.1, support this interpretation. In 1964, 10 years before Thatcher's successful leadership bid, 21% of respondents supported the privatization of publicly owned industries. According to a poll that ran in October 1974, support for priva-

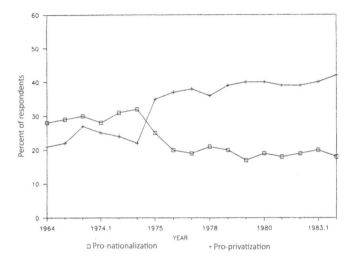

Figure 8.1 Attitudes toward the privatization of government-owned industries in
Great Britain
Reproduced with permission from (Kalyvas, 1994, p. 325).

tization was still around 20%. A year later, in the Fall of 1975, this support
had increased to 35%. The trend continued until it stabilized four years later
at around 40%. In other words, privatization, after having been supported by
a minority for more than a decade, became, in the space of a few years, the
favored policy of a large plurality. The turning point occurred between October
1974 and the fall of 1975. In February 1975, Margaret Thatcher was elected as
head of the Conservative Party.[3]

In other words, a change in elite discourse helps explain both the *timing*
and *direction* of mass attitudinal change. In a context in which partisan dynamics increased the salience of right-wing fairness cues, people with right-wing
proportionality beliefs were better able to align their answer to a question on
nationalization with their proportionality beliefs, explaining the sharp decline
in support for nationalization after Thatcher's election. By exposing people to
right-wing fairness considerations, Thatcher also created conditions favorable

---

[3] Kalyvas also collected data around a similar swing in leadership discourse in France,
specifically, before and after Francois Mitterand's famous 1983 "pause" in the nationalization
of key industries and banks, which started after he took power in 1981. In March 1983, the
month Mitterand announced the policy change, 46% of respondents supported nationalization,
the same share recorded a decade earlier in 1976. Seven months later, support had dropped to
34%, stabilizing to 30% in 1985.

to a more long-term right-wing shift in fairness beliefs, something I will discuss in more detail in Chapter 9.

During Thatcher's decade in power, the British economy underwent a fundamental restructuring. Manufacturing and union membership sharply declined, affecting the Labour Party's capacity to mobilize its core electorate. The scale of change during the 1980s, as well as the internal divisions between radical and revisionist members of the Labour Party (Rodden, 2019), profoundly transformed the Labour Party's economic platform, resulting in a gradual convergence toward the Conservative Party on economic issues. Ultimately, the party's leadership settled on a policy platform described by Stephanie Mudge as "neoliberalized leftism" (Mudge, 2018).

Convergence can take place through *omission* or *co-optation*. Convergence by omission happens when a party drops an issue from its own platform. Convergence can also occur through co-optation akin to a "steal the thunder" strategy. In this case, a party will be the first mover in co-opting a policy position usually associated with its opponent. When convergence occurs, be it by omission or by co-optation, the discursive context's degree of ideological pluralism shifts dramatically. In the British case, it shifted in favor of a markedly right-wing consensus. Still, there are important differences between the two types of convergence: Convergence by omission decreases the salience of an issue, while convergence by co-optation increases it. Great Britain stands out as having experienced both types of convergence. Convergence by omission characterizes changes in elite competition on *redistribution from* policies, convergence by co-optation characterizes changes in elite competition on *redistribution to* policies. I discuss each in turn.

Redistribution From: Convergence by Omission

There are many important symbolic milestones marking the Labour party's convergence by omission on *redistribution from* issues. One is Callaghan's official renunciation of Keynesianism in 1976. Others include Kinnock's victory over the hard left in the latter part of the 1980s and Tony Blair's revision of Clause IV in 1995, which erased any reference to "common ownership of the means of production" in the party's Constitution. In a 1999 document,[4] Tony Blair gave a succinct overview of the ideological underpinnings of this shift away from "old" to "new" Labour. According to this document, social justice, a core goal for social democratic parties, is to be achieved through public investments in human capital formation and technical innovation, investment

---

[4] This document was a joint statement with Gerard Schroeder.

friendly tax cuts[5] and a more flexible labor market with decreased labor costs[6] aimed at promoting "go-ahead mentality and a new entrepreneurial spirit at all levels of society" (Blair and Schroeder, 2000). In other words, the role of social democratic parties is to promote equity, not equality. In this perspective, the ability of market institutions to translate effort into rewards is assumed, and the role of the government is to make sure that government regulation does not interfere with such mechanism and ensure everyone can acquire the skills most rewarded on the labor market. Ultimately, the goal is not to compensate for economic institutions' inherent fairness as defined by the proportionality norm; it is rather to ensure that these institutions truly live up to their promise of a fair world where rewards are proportional to effort and income differences are fair.

In other words, over a period of a decade, the Labour Party went from vocally arguing that markets were inherently unable to provide a fair distribution of resources to a party promoting itself as most able to enhance markets' natural ability to reward effort and merit. As a result, disagreement over the fundamental causes of inequality and progressive taxation virtually disappeared from political discourse in Great Britain. In a telling analysis of House of Parliament speeches, Tom O'Grady documents the steady decline in the utterance of the word "redistribution," with "the lowest use recorded on the eve of the financial crisis" (O'Grady, 2021).

Redistribution To: Convergence by Co-optation

While the word "redistribution" was on the decline, references to "work, reform and fraud" were, starting in the early 1990s, on the rise. According to O'Grady's analysis, this language "remained popular up to the end of the 2000s, its occurrence further increasing in the early 2010s" (O'Grady, 2021). Until the late 1990s, this language had been mostly used by Conservative Members of Parliament (MPs). O'Grady demonstrates that the increase in salience is tied to changes in the discourse of Labour MPs. He also finds that while positive and negative rhetoric coexisted in the late 1980s, starting in the mid-1990s, the language became almost exclusively negative in tone.

These trends can be traced back to Tony Blair's decision to explicitly co-opt the conservative agenda on *redistribution to* issues. Blair's signature reforms included (1) an increase in transfers targeted to the "working poor," especially

---

[5] The text embraced supply-side economics : "For instance, corporate tax cuts raise profitability and strengthen the incentives to invest. Higher investment expands economic activity and increases productive potential. It helps create a virtuous circle of growth increasing the resources available for public spending on social purposes."

[6] "The reduction of non-wage labour costs through structural reform of social security systems and a more employment friendly tax and contribution structure that looks to the future is of particular importance."

families with children, through the expansion of progressive income tax credit and (2) reform of transfer programs targeted to the nonworking poor, especially unemployment insurance and disability benefits. The goal was to create "a social security system that opens up new opportunities and encourages initiative, creativity and readiness to take on new challenges" and to transform "the safety net of entitlements into a springboard to personal responsibility" (Blair and Schroeder, 2000).

On the issue of unemployment benefits, Blair and Brown mostly pursued a policy shift that started under Thatcher. In the 1980s, replacement rates were sharply cut and entitlement conditions hardened, culminating in the introduction of the restrictive Jobseekers Allowance in 1996 (Clasen et al., 2001). The launching of the so-called "New Deal" programs by the first Blair administration in 1999 (Torfing, 1999) further transformed unemployment insurance into a program of means-tested transfers targeted to those most likely to be in and out of stable unemployment (i.e., long-term unemployed, the young and the disabled). The contribution-based insurance scheme was slowly retrenched and then merged with existing programs of social transfers to other nonworking individuals. The New Labour accompanied this policy move "with a 'get-tough' style, [using] the language of 'welfare crackdowns' and 'targeting benefit thieves'" (Horton, 2010, p. 39). Throughout the 2000s, the New Labour leadership further reformed the unemployment system, repeatedly emphasizing conditionality and the need for recipients to engage in work-related activities or risk seeing their benefits reduced.[7] Other flagship social policies, such as ending child poverty and making work pay, were targeted to the most vulnerable groups. While policy statements around children and their mothers were on average positive, rapidly, the debate shifted to abuse of these targeted transfers.[8]

This attempt at outbidding the Conservative Party on *redistribution to* policies had lofty goals. Simply put, the New Labour's solution to poverty was to court people with authoritarian values by minimizing "moral hazard," punishing free riding and getting people back to work, while still addressing poverty by targeting transfers to deserving recipients, in the form of earned income tax credits to low-wage workers and families with young children. These reforms had a visible positive impact on the bottom of the income distribution. Yet, from the perspective of inequality reduction, the redistributive transfers happening

---

[7] Disability benefits have also been at the center of much attention, most famously when the attempt to stop disability transfers from going to "able-bodied disabled" was outsourced to private-for-profit organizations who applied extremely stringent criteria for distinguishing the "legitimately" disabled from others.

[8] Articles on the (white) single mother "popping out" children to avoid having to work became a staple of British tabloids (Larsen and Dejgaard, 2013).

Table 8.1 *Subjective placements of the Labour and Conservative parties (1987–2001)*

Policy		1987	1991	1997	2001
Social services	Labour	3.03	2.83	**3.59**	4.17
	Conservative	7.16	7.06	6.94	**6.21**
	Difference	4.13	4.23	3.35	2.04
Nationalization	Labour	2.92	3.59	**4.66**	5.45
	Conservative	9.14	8.38	8.00	7.50
	Difference	6.22	4.79	3.34	2.05
Inflation/unemployment	Labour	2.33	**2.98**	3.14	3.73
	Conservative	6.38	6.44	6.16	5.88
	Difference	4.05	3.46	3.02	2.15
Redistribution	Labour	2.95	3.08	**3.49**	4.65
	Conservative	8.43	7.90	8.21	**7.47**
	Difference	5.48	4.82	4.72	2.82
Average Lab–Con gap		4.97	4.33	3.61	2.27

The numbers reported in the table are the mean positions that British Election Study respondents ascribed to the Labour and Conservative parties along the issue scales, computed, for each scale in each year, over all respondents who gave a valid party placement on the scale. The rows labeled "Difference" report the difference between the mean placements of the Conservative Party and the mean placement of the Labour Party. All four scales range from 1 to 11, with higher numbers denoting that positions are perceived as more right wing.
Source: British Election Survey; reproduced from Milazzo, Adams and Green (2012).

through the tax system were outpaced by exponential income growth at the top of the income distribution, which were rarely discussed. Instead, public discourse was saturated with references to the undeserving poor. British tabloids, which originally supported Tony Blair, efficiently amplified this rhetoric.

A De-polarized Party System

Convergence by omission and co-optation under Blair meant fewer ideological differences between the two main British parties, at least on economic and redistributive issues. This general convergence between the two parties was noticed by voters. Table 8.1 reports the mean positions that British Election Survey respondents assigned to the Labour and Conservative parties along four policy scales relating to preferences for providing social services versus cutting taxes, support for income redistribution, preferences for fighting inflation versus lowering unemployment and support for nationalization of industry.[9]

[9] Unfortunately, the items are only comparable across four waves between 1987 and 2001 (Milazzo, Adams and Green, 2012, p. 266).

Notice how, on all items, except for the one on privatization (a topic that mostly occupied the late 1970s, not the 1990s), the biggest changes in perceived differences are around the time of the 1997 and 2001 elections, following Blair's successful bid.

In the words of Evans and Tilley (2012), "The Labour party's move to the centre" under Blair "weakened the ideological distinctiveness of the signals sent to the electorate by the two main parties." The consequences of this convergence between the two mainstream parties include a decline in the number of voters who identify with a party, and among those who do identify with a party, a decline in the number of strong partisans (Dalton, 2013).[10] As I will discuss later, the opposite process has taken place in the United States.

The salience of *redistribution to* issues remained high throughout the 2010s, with one major difference compared with previous years: In response to drastic cuts to welfare spending by the Cameron government, Labour "took the side of benefits recipients and defended the welfare system" (O'Grady, 2021). In the 2010s, the discursive context increasingly included both negative and positive statements about welfare, moral hazard and free riding. Negative claims mostly came from Conservative leaders who presented cuts in social benefits as the way out of the Great Recession: With lower benefits, unemployed workers would be incentivized to work, and with lower spending, Great Britain would control its deficits, which would be beneficial to economic growth by restoring "market trust." The Conservatives justified austerity measures through repeated references to moral hazard, "strivers" being burdened by "shirkers," and the need to end the "something-for-nothing society." The Labour Party pushed back against this rhetoric, presenting beneficiaries as victims of the worst recession since the 1920s: Without any jobs to fill, benefits cuts would have a large human cost and would not help spur growth.

In 2015, thanks to grassroots mobilization, Jeremy Corbyn won control of the party. The Corbyn leadership represented an opportunity to not only shift to the left on *redistribution to* issues but also re-politicize *redistribution from* issues, that is, challenge the "neoliberal consensus" of the 1990s and 2000s the same way Thatcher had challenged the Keynesian consensus of the 1950s and 1960s. In practice, this agenda was hijacked by the Brexit referendum that divided the Labour Party.[11] Corbyn, confronted with internal dissent over Brexit and accusations of antisemitism, struggled to convey the type of clear and disrupting fairness message required to foster belief change.

---

[10] Relatedly, a growing share of voters appear to be indifferent to which party will ultimately win elections (Dassonneville and Hooghe, 2018).

[11] The resulting partisan realignment has further contributed to the weakening of partisan identities in Great Britain.

Attitudinal change is more likely following major and sustained changes in the discursive context. Based on the partisan dynamics described above, two periods are of particular interest: 1976–1979, the period during which Thatcher came to power; and 1995–1997, the period during which Tony Blair came to power. Both periods mark a disruption in how elites compete over redistributive issues. Earlier, I discussed tentative evidence for the 1976–1979 period. In the following sections, I focus on the 1995–1997 period, for which extensive survey data are available. I also speculate on what might have happened had Brexit not disrupted the nascent polarization over redistributive issues.

Implications for Attitudinal Stability and Change

Figure 8.2 summarizes long-term partisan dynamics in Great Britain. The late 1990s and early 2000s stand out as inhospitable to any increase in support for redistribution, especially *redistribution to*. Indeed, shifts in elite competition at the beginning of the period meant that, over two decades, people were routinely exposed to claims about the prevalence of free riding and concerns about moral hazard. I expect beliefs about the prevalence of free riding to reflect this conservative shift in the discursive context. Given that this messaging was common to both parties, partisan identity should not help predict who is most likely to resist right-wing elite messaging.

As discussed in Chapter 4, income is a poor predictor of reciprocity beliefs: People who are most likely to benefit from *redistribution to* policies are not more likely to resist negative rhetoric about free riding welfare recipients. Instead, the best predictor of resistance is whether or not someone holds liberal

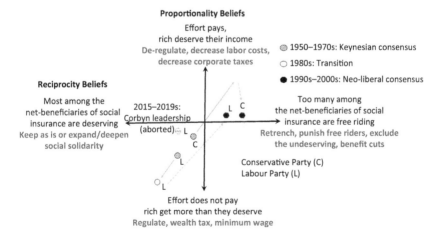

Figure 8.2 The evolution of partisan dynamics in Great Britain

or authoritarian values, which is itself uncorrelated with income. I consequently expect belief change to affect all income groups.

Yet, in line with findings discussed in Chapter 5, income, while it does not predict differences in reciprocity beliefs, should help predict the extent to which a conservative shift in reciprocity beliefs affects support for *redistribution to* policies. Particularly, I expect low-income individuals to maintain high self-interested opposition to cuts in social benefits, this *despite* a conservative shift in reciprocity beliefs. In contrast, among high-income individuals, support for cuts to social benefits should increase in line with changing reciprocity beliefs. The result should be a growing divergence between the attitudes of the rich and the poor on the issue of cuts to social benefits.

Expectations for proportionality beliefs and support for *redistribution from* policies are less straightforward. On the one hand, the omission of proportionality concerns from national debate approximates what I have called "benign neglect," which suggests a discursive context favorable to attitudinal stability, not attitudinal change. On the other hand, convergence by omission also implies a right-wing shift in the discursive context, especially for people who traditionally vote for the Labour Party. Whether such changes are enough to affect aggregate proportionality beliefs is an empirical question. Given that reciprocity concerns were much more salient than proportionality concerns, if we do observe a right-wing shift in proportionality beliefs, it should not be as large as the right-wing shift in reciprocity beliefs.

Jointly, these expectations suggest that the decline in the share of individuals who agree with income redistribution, as traditionally worded, is specifically due to people who increasingly oppose *redistribution to* the poor out of reciprocity concerns, not people who increasingly oppose *redistribution from* the rich out of proportionality concerns. Note that this prediction is in tension with evidence presented in Chapter 3 showing that reciprocity beliefs do not shape answers to the traditional redistribution item, only proportionality beliefs do. This means that a conservative shift in reciprocity beliefs should not affect the share of respondents who express support for redistribution. As I will show, the evidence is not as contradictory as it seems and can be easily explained by looking at the framing effects resulting from the design of the BSAS.

The Dynamics of Demand for Redistribution in Great Britain

To unpack how support for income redistribution has changed in Great Britain, I start by examining trends in mass fairness beliefs. Have people become more likely to find differences in market rewards fair? Does a growing share of

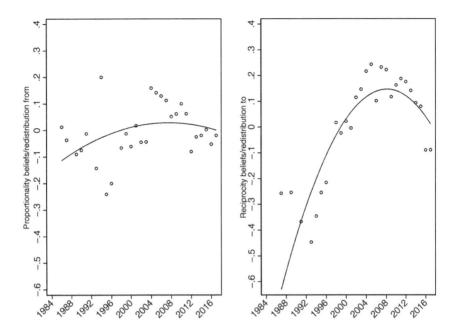

Figure 8.3 Fairness beliefs in Great Britain: Longitudinal trends
Plots changes in proportionality (top panel) and reciprocity (bottom panel) beliefs:
values derived following an EFA (see Chapter 3 for more information). Higher
values indicate more anti-redistribution fairness beliefs.
Source: BSAS longitudinal dataset, weighted.

respondents find it unfair that some receive more in social benefits than they
pay in taxes? To answer these questions, I examine trends in reciprocity and
proportionality beliefs. Using factor analysis, I combine the items identified
in Chapters 3 and 4 into individual scores and plot yearly averages for both
scores.[12] As shown in the left-hand panel of Figure 8.3, proportionality beliefs
are mostly stable over this period, fluctuating around the sample mean. The
picture for reciprocity beliefs is dramatically different: From the late 1980s
to the late 2000s, the average score has undergone a right-wing shift equal to
roughly 0.6 SD of the overall sample distribution. After a stable period in the
2000s, there has been a left-wing shift starting around the Great Recession.

---

[12] As a reminder, the proportionality beliefs index includes items such as "There is one law for
the rich and one for the poor" or "Working people do not get their fair share of the nation's
wealth." The reciprocity beliefs index includes items such as "Many people who get welfare
don't really deserve any help" or "Without welfare people would learn to stand on their own
two feet." Note that, in this case, I do not include items that specifically ask about redistribution
or spending on the poor and the unemployed, though the results are virtually the same if I do.

Nevertheless, reciprocity beliefs are still 0.4 SD more right-wing today than they were in the late 1980s.

Figure 8.4 breaks the analysis down by partisanship and income level. As expected, partisanship and income do not predict who is most likely to experience this right-wing shift. Notice how, in line with the results from Chapter 3, there is a large income gap with regard to proportionality beliefs but not reciprocity beliefs. In contrast, low-income individuals are more right wing than high-income individuals when it comes to expressing concerns that *redistribution to* policies unfairly reward free riders.

The anti-redistribution shift in reciprocity beliefs roughly mirrors partisan dynamics with the biggest change occurring among people who identify with the Labour Party. As shown in Figure 8.5, there is a large break before and after the 1997 elections, when most voters are exposed for the first time to Tony Blair's strategic repositioning of the party's platform. Notice the absence of a break in the most recent period: Labour's return to more left-wing rhetoric has had limited effects on Labour voters' reciprocity beliefs.[13] Despite a large increase in unemployment and underemployment, as well as dramatic cuts in welfare spending, and more favorable elite messaging, reciprocity beliefs are still more conservative today than they were in the late 1980s.

One reason is generational replacement. As shown in Figure 8.6 (left panel), between-cohort differences follow an inverted U-shape from right-wing to left-wing and back to right-wing. These trends suggest that people who came of age in the 1950s, 1960s and 1970s were exposed to a set of fairness considerations very different from those who came of age in the 1980s onward. In other words, despite specific period effects (e.g., the Great Recession), evidence points to a long-term conservative shift in reciprocity beliefs that mirrors the long-term shift from a Keynesian to a neoliberal elite consensus. This latter shift has also affected proportionality beliefs: While, in the aggregate, proportionality beliefs are mostly stable (Figure 8.6, right panel), there are notable cohort differences, which is unsurprising given differences in the discursive context across cohorts (see also Grasso et al., 2019).

Based on the argument in Part I, the sharp shift in reciprocity beliefs should have implications for mass support for policies that benefit the poor and the unemployed and for social solidarity more generally. However, this effect should

---

[13] Given that this is cross-sectional data, the 1997 break is likely due to a mix of attitudinal change and partisan sorting, that is, people with more right-wing reciprocity beliefs switching to the Labour Party. Unfortunately, I do not have access to panel data that could help identify the relative importance of each. In Chapter 9, I use panel data from the British Household Panel Survey, which includes a set of proportionality items. I find a similar (though less dramatic) right-wing shift around 1997 and show that it is largely the result of attitudinal change among people who voted for the Labour Party in the past.

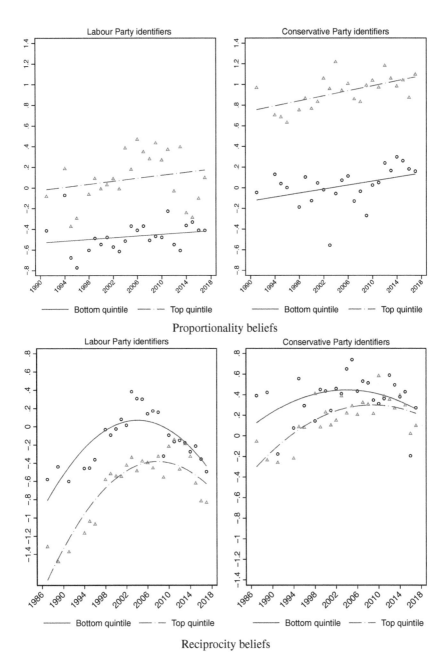

Figure 8.4 Fairness beliefs in Great Britain by partisanship and income
Plots changes in proportionality (top panel) and reciprocity (bottom panel) beliefs
by partisanship and income level. For information on the income variable, see
Appendix A1.1.
Source: BSAS longitudinal dataset, weighted.

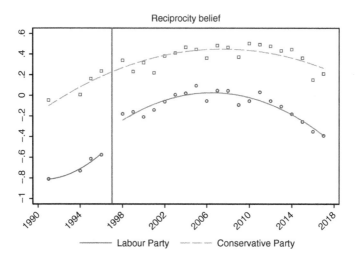

Figure 8.5 Reciprocity beliefs in Great Britain: 1997 break
Plots changes in proportionality beliefs by partisanship. The vertical line marks
Tony Blair's successful 1997 electoral bid.
Source: BSAS longitudinal dataset, weighted.

be limited to people who do not expect to rely on these programs. In Figure 8.7,
I plot disagreement with the claim that "the government should spend more
money on welfare benefits for the poor" (top panel, left figure).[14] To better compare with Figure 8.4, the bottom panel also breaks the analysis down according
to partisanship. In line with expectations, low-income individuals, despite an
anti-redistribution shift in reciprocity beliefs, do not increase their support for
welfare cuts. In contrast, the anti-redistribution shift in reciprocity beliefs is
fully reflected in the welfare attitudes of high-income individuals. One consequence is the emergence of an income gradient: While there were no income-
related differences in the late 1980s, today, the attitudinal gap is equal to 30
percentage points. In other words, material self-interest matters. In this case,
for low-income respondents, it takes the form of a deviation from what fairness
reasoning prescribes, in line with the two-step process documented in Chapter
5. The result is a significant income gap in support for *redistribution to* policies,
despite the absence of an income gap on reciprocity beliefs.

[14] The pattern holds when plotting agreement with this claim instead of disagreement.
   Specifically, while both income groups experience a decline in the share of respondents who
   agree with this claim, this decline is larger for high-income respondents. See Cavaillé (2022)
   for more detail.

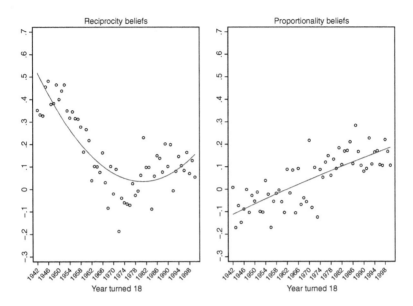

Figure 8.6 Fairness beliefs in Great Britain: Generational analysis
Plots average fairness beliefs by birth cohort. Cohort differences have been computed using only data from 2002 to 2006, thus minimizing the risk that generational differences are due to period effects. The general pattern replicates if I use data from 2010 to 2014.
Source: BSAS longitudinal dataset.

Now, let's cycle back to the original puzzle described in Chapter 1, namely the decline in the share of individuals who agree with income redistribution as traditionally measured. As shown in Chapter 3, the traditional redistribution item captures only half of the action, specifically, the *redistribution from* facet of demand for redistribution. Attitudes toward *redistribution from* policies covary with beliefs about the extent to which, in Friedman's words, "payment is in accordance to product" (Friedman, 1962, p. 167). If Great Britain has experienced a change in reciprocity beliefs, not proportionality beliefs, and if answers to the traditional redistribution item correlate with the latter and not the former, why such a decline?

A careful analysis indicates that this decline is an artifact of question ordering and the resulting framing effect. In the BSAS, the traditional redistribution item has been asked as part of a recurring segment of a self-completion supplement to fill in after the main in-person interview. Throughout the years, the order of the recurring items has been mostly fixed: First comes a block of items asking about welfare recipients, and the prevalence of free riding, and

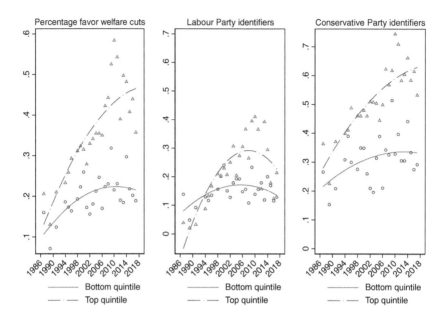

Figure 8.7 Support for welfare cuts in Great Britain by partisanship and income
Plots trends in support for cuts to welfare benefits by partisanship and income
level. Respondents who disagree that "the government should spend more money
on welfare benefits for the poor, even if it leads to higher taxes" are coded as 1.
For information on the income variable, see Appendix A1.1.
Source: BSAS longitudinal dataset, weighted.

then comes the traditional redistribution question as part of a block of items
originally designed to capture a respondent's attitudes toward inequality, and
big business. The traditional redistribution item is always asked right after the
block of items on welfare recipients and at the beginning of the block asking
about income inequality and big business.[15] Primed to think about welfare, the
poor and the unemployed respondents in the BSAS answer the item about redistribution from the better off to the worse off partly through the reciprocity lens.
In Zaller's words, reciprocity considerations are at the top of people's basket
of considerations. As a result, respondents, because they have in mind free riding among recipients, express lower support for redistribution than one would
expect, absent such framing effect. Furthermore, over time, their answers to
the traditional redistribution question reflect right-wing changes in reciprocity
beliefs, not stable proportionality beliefs.

[15] One exception is the 1993 wave. For this wave, two unrelated items separate the two blocks.

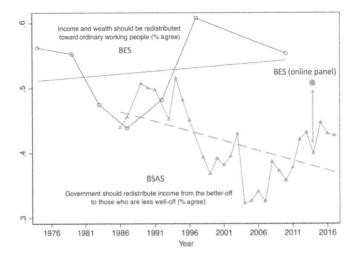

Figure 8.8 Overtime changes in support for redistribution in Great Britain: BSAS versus BES
Plots changes in support for redistribution measured using the traditional redistribution question. Y-axis: The percentage of respondents who chose "Agree strongly/Agree." Item wording in figure.
Source: BSAS longitudinal dataset (weighted), BES longitudinal dataset (weighted) and BES online panel wave 1 (weighted).

Data from alternative surveys support this interpretation. Figure 8.8 plots the BSAS item alongside average answers to a similar item asked in the British Elections Studies between 1972 and 1996 and repeated once in the BSAS in 2010. Notice the difference across items and surveys: Support for redistribution is higher by 10–20 percentage points on average in the BES and is, if anything, increasing over time. The 2014 wave of the BES online panel included the same item as the one asked in the BSAS: That year, support for redistribution was higher by more than 10 percentage points in the BES relative to the BSAS (see Figure 8.8). In the 2010 wave of the BSAS, a subset of 837 individuals were also asked to answer both the BSAS item (right after the welfare items block) and, in a different section of the survey, a very similar item worded as follows: "It is the responsibility of the government to reduce the differences in income between people with high incomes and those with low incomes." Support for redistribution was 17 percentage points higher when measured using this second item (not shown). Note that these differences occur within the *same* respondents. In other words, the bulk of the fluctuations in agreement with redistribution recorded using the BSAS data[16] can be accounted for by question ordering: Once the latter is corrected for, attitudes toward income redistribution are much more stable.[17]

Evidence from the BSAS and the BES shows that the decline in support for redistribution in Great Britain is lopsided: It affects only one facet of redistributive preferences, leaving a space open for some types of redistributive reforms (policies that *redistribute from* the wealthy) and narrowing the available space for others (policies that *redistributes to* those who cannot provide for themselves). This is confirmed using data from the Role of Government module of the ISSP. Based on this dataset, Great Britain has experienced a large decline (roughly 30 percentage points) in support for social policies that benefit the unemployed, reflecting the underlying change in reciprocity beliefs. In contrast, support for redistribution as traditionally measured is, in line with trends in proportionality beliefs, stable (not shown).

What If

Before moving to the American case, a few concluding thoughts regarding the future of demand for more *redistribution from* policies in Great Britain: What if someone within the Labour Party learns from Thatcher's playbook and succeeds in turning the party to the left on *redistribution from* issues? Based on my argument, such change in elite rhetoric is a necessary, if not sufficient, condition for observing large shifts in attitudes toward redistributive policies. It provides a discursive context more hospital to a left-wing shift in support for *redistribution from* policies, one in which belief change and framing effects increase the share of individuals who express support for such policies.

A comparison with Germany is here instructive. In both Great Britain and Germany, disagreement over how to best foster economic growth generated important tensions between the traditional Left and the pro-market "Third Way" (Great Britain) or "Neue Mitte" (Germany). These tensions played out very differently in each country. In Great Britain, the first-past-the-post system meant that the traditional Left had to fight its own war *within* the New Labour Party. Overall, it took two decades for what Rodden (2019) calls the urban ideologues to (temporarily) regain control of the party. The German proportional electoral system, in contrast, enabled the traditional Left, backed by union opposition to

---

[16] Namely, a 10 to 20 % points decline in the share who "agree" between 1992 and 2006, followed by a recovery between 2006 and 2018.

[17] I regress average score on the redistribution item over average proportionality and reciprocity scores and find that the bulk of the variation (70%) is explained by changes in the reciprocity scores (N=29).

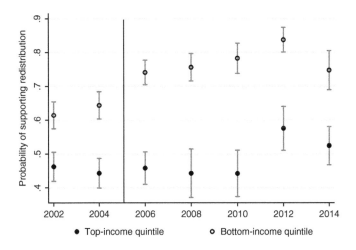

Figure 8.9 Change in support for redistribution in Germany: Top versus bottom quintile

Plots the percentage that agrees with the claim "(t)he government should take measures to reduce differences in income levels," by income quintile (see Chapter 5 for detail on income measure). Notice how a major attitudinal change happens between 2004 and 2006.

Source: ESS 2002–2014.

the Hartz IV reforms, to pursue its agenda outside of the SPD and consequently re-politicize redistributive issues following the break with the SPD in 2005.[18]

Remember from Chapter 1 that Germany was one of the few cases of an increase in support for redistribution as traditionally measured. Figure 8.9 uses data from the ESS to plot this increase among top- and bottom- income quintile German respondents. In 2002, the difference in support for redistribution between top- and bottom-quintile respondents was around 15 percentage points. By 2006, the difference had doubled to 29 percentage points. The increase is entirely due to a rise in support for redistribution among the bottom-quintile respondents. Support continues to rise in this group from 2006 to 2010. In 2010, the gap reaches 34 percentage points. In 2012 and 2014, top quintile individuals finally catch up, with a seven-year delay.

[18] Evidence on the nature and timing of partisan dynamics in Germany is provided in the online appendix. Using newspaper data collected by Kriesi et al. (2012), I also document a left-wing shift in the discursive context starting in 2005, the year when an SPD splinter group formed *Die Linke* following an electoral alliance with the German Communist Party, a minor party whose small electoral success was limited to regions in East Germany. In other words, elite competition in Germany promoted a discursive context more favorable to voters expressing growing support for *redistribution from* policies.

Attitudinal trends in Germany can be plausibly linked to post-convergence partisan dynamics very different from those previously described in Great Britain. As a baseline, low-income individuals have more left-wing proportionality beliefs. In a context in which partisan dynamics increase the salience of left-wing fairness cues, we can expect members of this group to better align their answers to the traditional redistribution question with their proportionality beliefs. Furthermore, because fairness considerations covered the ideological gamut, left-wing changes in proportionality beliefs were more likely (see Chapter 9 for more evidence on this mechanism). In contrast, in Great Britain, the depoliticization by omission characteristic of the New Labour years made it cognitively more difficult to express left-wing redistributive preferences and form more left-wing fairness beliefs. These differences in partisan dynamics help explain why in Germany, unlike in Great Britain, growing income inequality has occurred alongside growing support for redistribution (see Figure 1.4 in Chapter 9).

Extrapolating from the German case, if the Labour Party decides to challenge the previously described "neo-liberal" consensus, one can expect similar increases in support for redistribution. As I discuss in the concluding chapter, in the current institutional and economic context, the likelihood of this taking place is very low.

Great Britain: To Sum Up

Changes in mass fairness beliefs mirror the Labour Party's decision to co-opt the Conservatives' agenda on redistributive issues. Yet, people are not just empty shells passively reflecting short- and long-term changes in the discursive context. As shown above, people can resist aligning their policy preferences with their fairness beliefs. With regard to fairness beliefs, they can accept some fairness considerations or reject others. In the British case, resistance appears to have been especially weak on the reciprocity front and stronger on the proportionality front, something I will examine more closely in Chapters 8 and 9.

Overall, the evidence for Great Britain further supports the claim made in Chapter 2 and tested in Chapter 3, that support for *redistribution to* and support for *redistribution from* represent two separate facets of redistributive preferences rooted in two different norms of fairness, each with their own overtime dynamics. It is also informative of the power of contextual framing effects, from the most trivial (item ordering) to the least trivial (strategic repositioning by the main center-left party to capture centrist voters). Finally, it highlights the role partisan dynamics play in shaping the timing and direction of aggregate fairness belief change: Absent large discursive shocks resulting from strategic repositioning by mainstream parties, aggregate mass attitudes would have remained relatively stable.

Having demonstrated the value of the framework presented in this book for unpacking attitudinal change in Great Britain, I now turn to the Uniteds States.

Declining Income Gradient in the United States: Revisiting the Evidence

In the American case, agreement with the claim that the government ought to "reduce income differences between the rich and the poor" has remained relatively stable. In Chapter 1, I also found evidence that this stability hides some reshuffling as indicated by the decline in the attitudinal gap between high- and low-income respondents. Can my argument make sense of these trends? I start by briefly reviewing partisan dynamics in the United States. I then flesh out implications for attitudinal change and then revisit the data discussed in Chapter 1 in light of these expectations.

Partisan Dynamics in the United States: An Overview

The United States has the purest two-party system of any industrialized country. Classic theories suggest that two-party systems encourage the parties to adopt converging platforms. While this has indeed happened in Great Britain, this is not the case in the United States. Anyone who has ever read an English-speaking newspaper knows that America is polarized (McCarty, Poole and Rosenthal, 1997), but what does this mean in practice?

The best evidence comes from rising partisan differences in Congressional voting patterns: Party line voting is now the norm, replacing the bi-partisan legislative coalitions of the 1950s and 1960s. Assuming a data-generation process approximating a spatial model of politics, McCarty, Poole and Rosenthal (1997) used roll call data to position individual members of Congress in a multidimensional policy space. This quantitative exercise provides researchers with two important pieces of information. First, the number of dimensions needed to maximize goodness-of-fit has declined over time: Divisions based on social, cultural and religious issues have been absorbed into the primary partisan division on economic issues. Second, changes in members' positions point to important differences between the two parties: The Republican Party has experienced a marked shift to the right, while the Democratic Party's shift to the left appears mostly tied to a gradual disappearance of Southern Democrats following the 1964 Civil Rights Act.

The causes of polarization in congressional voting are still the topic of heated scholarly debates.[19] In contrast, the implications for mass behavior are well documented and mostly agreed upon. Over time, there is considerable evidence of a growing correlation between partisan identity, subjective ideology and policy preferences. Individuals who identify as conservatives have sorted themselves into the Republican Party, and those who identify as liberals now associate themselves with the Democratic Party (Rodden, 2021), a phenomenon known as partisan sorting (Levendusky, 2009). There is also evidence of voters shifting their policy positions to better align them with that of their preferred party (Johnston, Lavine and Federico, 2017; Lenz, 2009; Levendusky, 2009). Because each party increasingly represents very different and internally consistent clusters of policy positions, partisan cues now serve as reliable heuristics for voters to navigate politics. Concomitantly, voters develop strong affections (positive and negative) toward the main parties, becoming even more receptive to partisan cues (Druckman, Peterson and Slothuus, 2013).

Voters' attachment to (or distaste for) one party over the other often has little to do with the party's position on a subset of specific policies. Instead what matters is what these policies, taken together, convey about the fairness of the status quo and what to do about it. In other words, people side with the party that best speaks to their vision of the status quo as either fair or unfair. Republicans, compared with Democrats, hold more anti-redistribution proportionality beliefs: They are more likely to believe that effort pays, that market institutions are fair and that income differences are fair (Gross and Manrique-Vallier, 2012). They also have more anti-redistribution reciprocity beliefs: They are more likely to believe that government support generates moral hazard and to be concerned about the prevalence of free riding (Gilens, 1999).

Despite partisan differences in both proportionality and reciprocity beliefs, the main point of partisan contention, and increasingly so over time, is *redistribution to* policies, that is, the extent to which government should help those who cannot help themselves. Take, for example, the aftermaths of the Great Recession. Occupy Wall Street was a grassroots movement whose opposition to global finance was rooted in perceived violations of the proportionality norm. The Tea Party was a grassroots movement whose anger against government bailouts and universal health care was rooted in moral hazard concerns and perceived violations of the reciprocity norm. Occupy Wall Street had a limited impact on electoral politics. In contrast, Tea Party concerns were readily incorporated into legislative and national debates.

---

[19] See Barber et al. (2015) for a review.

One factor explaining this asymmetry is the fact that, unlike many European countries, the United States did not experience the type of politicized class conflict that pitted losers against winners of market capitalism (Piketty, 2020; Sombart, 1976). As a consequence, the argument that market mechanisms are inherently unfair and require extensive government intervention to correct them is rarely made by elected officials, except in the rare (if consequential) moment when antitrust legislation gets passed.

Another factor is the tight connection between race and reciprocity concerns on the one hand, and *redistribution to* policies on the other. In the United States, disagreement over *redistribution to* policies has always had strong racial undertones (Richardson, 2004; Schram, Soss and Fording, 2010; Skocpol and Williamson, 2011). As I pointed out in Chapter 6, in the United States, unlike in Europe, racial divisions were salient at the creation of the welfare state. Social insurance programs created in the aftermath of the Great Depression have always been popular: They address the insurance needs of the majority of the population, needs that cannot be met by markets, even well-functioning ones. What is less popular and more divisive is whether, and how, to ensure that these programs address the needs of the very poor, especially poor minorities. As the party system has itself become increasingly organized along racial lines and racial concerns, this has further contributed to the politicization of *redistribution to* issues, at the expense of *redistribution from* issues.

The overlap between race and reciprocity concerns in American culture is well documented both qualitatively (e.g., see Lamont and Molnar, 2002) and quantitatively, the latter in the form of the "racial resentment" scale (also called symbolic or modern racism scale). This scale was designed to better measure prejudice in the postwar period when, following the Holocaust, arguments regarding biological superiority had been expunged from public discourse (Henry and Sears, 2009; Kinder and Sears, 1981). Items used to measure racial resentment ask about Blacks' perceived work ethic and the extent to which they get more than they deserve. In the words of Sears et al. (1997), these items help identify individuals who believe that "racial discrimination is largely a thing of the past, that blacks should just work harder to overcome their disadvantages and that blacks are making excessive demands for special treatment and get too much attention from elites, so their (material) gains are often undeserved." Item wording does not make explicit reference to specific goods blacks are believed to get unfair access to, but qualitative work suggests that people interpret these items as implicitly referring to social benefits and public jobs (Cramer, 2016; Hochschild, 2018). That people in charge of mapping long-term attitudinal change in the United States settled on these items is itself revealing, and further conveys the intimate connection in the United States between racial animosity and fairness concerns over who benefits from government spending.

The process through which party lines and disagreement over *redistribution to* issues came to overlap started in the 1960s. Before the Civil Rights Act, racialized disagreement over *redistribution to* divided members of the same party and remained relatively low salience. Following the Southern Realignment, this disagreement no longer runs within but between the two main parties: In the words of McCarty et al., "The race issue has been absorbed into the main redistributive dimension" (McCarty, Poole and Rosenthal, 2008, p. 11). One result is that it has moved reciprocity concerns and *redistribution to* policies to the center of American redistributive politics. In contrast, since the 1980s, and at least up until the Biden administration, proportionality concerns and disagreement over *redistribution from* policies have been less salient, with Democrats moving closer to Republicans on these issues, especially so under Bill Clinton. Politicians supporting government activism have tried hard to take race out of redistributive politics, most famously Bill Clinton with welfare reform (Soss and Schram, 2007, p. 113) and Obama with healthcare reform. Because of the growing overlap between party lines and disagreement over the boundaries of social solidarity, they often failed.

Implications for Attitudinal Stability and Change

The growing ideological distinctiveness of the Democratic and Republican parties on *redistribution to* policies should help voters pick the party most aligned with their own reciprocity beliefs (partisan sorting). Voters who start somewhat ambivalent will update in line with partisan messaging regarding the fairness of the status quo (belief change). The result should be a growing correlation between (racialized) reciprocity beliefs and partisanship. In contrast, given the relative consensus on proportionality issues, the correlation between proportionality beliefs and partisanship should remain roughly stable over the period.

What then explains the decline in the income gradient documented in Chapter 1? Mechanically, such a decline can follow from an increase in support for redistribution among high-income respondents, a decrease among low-income respondents or both. Existing studies of social policy preferences in the United Sates suggest focusing on low-income individuals. According to this line of work, the decline in the income gradient is due to decreasing support for *redistribution to* policies among low-income respondents who believe that they unfairly benefits undeserving minorities (e.g., Gilens 1999).

In contrast, on the basis of the argument presented in Part I, I expect a decline in the income gradient to be the result of attitudinal change among *high-income* respondents. As discussed in Chapter 5, a weak income gradient is most often tied to higher-than-expected support for *redistribution to* among high-income individuals, not lower-than-expected support among low-income individuals. Indeed, wanting to say the "fair thing" instead of the "self-interested thing" is much more likely among high-income respondents than among low-income respondents, who support generous social transfers out of self-interest, irrespective of their beliefs about the prevalence of free riding. As a result, if reciprocity concerns are driving the decline in the income gradient, then it should have larger implications for high-income respondents than for low-income ones.

The Dynamics of Demand for Redistribution in the United States

I start by examining whether party polarization has had larger implications for mass reciprocity beliefs than for mass proportionality beliefs. To do so, I combine evidence from the American National Election Survey (ANES) and data collected by the Pew Research Center. To proxy for racialized reciprocity beliefs, I use the four racial resentment items available in the ANES. The Pew dataset includes a battery of items about the relationship between effort and rewards, as well as business power. These items are listed in Table 8.2.

I combine these items into individual scores, which are then standardized. Figure 8.10 plots average scores by partisanship. As you can see with the left

Table 8.2 *Measuring fairness beliefs using the ANES and the PEW data*

Racial resentment (Proxies for racialized reciprocity beliefs)	Proportionality beliefs
Over the past few years, blacks have gotten less than they deserve	Success in life is pretty much determined by forces outside our control
Irish, Italian, Jewish, and many other minorities overcame prejudice and worked their way up. Blacks should do the same without any special favors	Hard work offers little guarantee of success
It's really a matter of some people not trying hard enough; if blacks would only try harder, they could be just as well-off as whites	There is too much power concentrated in the hands of a few big companies
Generations of slavery and discrimination have created conditions that make it difficult for blacks to work their way out of the lower class	Business corporations make too much profit

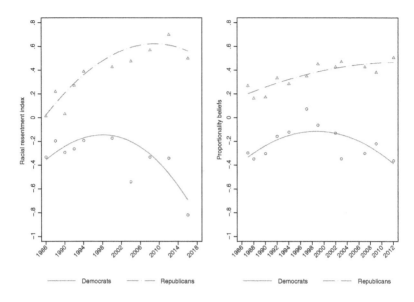

Figure 8.10 Fairness beliefs in the United States by partisanship
Plots changes in racial resentment (left panel) and proportionality beliefs (right panel) by partisanship. Higher values indicate more anti-redistribution response patterns, that is, "blacks are undeserving" and "effort pays."
Source: Pew Research Center longitudinal dataset (weighted) and ANES longitudinal dataset (weighted).

panel, over the past three decades, the gap between Republicans and Democrats on the racial resentment scale has grown from 0.2 SD to 1.2 SD, representing a sixfold increase. In contrast, partisan differences for proportionality beliefs have remained roughly stable, increasing by a mere 0.2 SD.

Overall, Figure 8.10 provides support for the claim that, while there are large differences between the two parties in terms of proportionality beliefs, the growing correlation between partisanship and fairness beliefs mostly concerns reciprocity beliefs. Put differently, alongside stable partisan differences with regard to support for *redistribution from* policies, there have been growing partisan differences in terms of support for *redistribution to* policies.

This suggests a friendly amendment to an important debate in American politics on the ideological content of partisan polarization. While studies that rely on roll call data conclude that competition in Congress is unidimensional and remains centered on economic issues, other research emphasizes the growing salience of cultural and noneconomic issues (Hetherington and Weiler, 2009).

One important empirical manifestation of these dynamics is the growing correlation between "authoritarian orientation" items and partisanship. If political polarization is mostly over economic issues (as found in the roll call data), how to make sense of the growing predictive power of authoritarian orientation (as found in mass survey data)? The framework presented in this book helps reconcile these contrasting claims. As shown in Chapter 4, noneconomic values, such as liberal–authoritarian values, correlate with *redistribution to* preferences through reciprocity beliefs. When partisan dynamics mostly center on *redistribution to* issues, the distinction between economic and noneconomic issues is in name only. In Chapter 10, I will explore this overlap in more detail.

Figure 8.11 (left panel) examines trends in support for redistribution by partisan identification. As expected, the stable trend found in Chapter 1 hides party-based polarization, with a marked shift against redistribution on the part of Republican voters and a more recent shift in favor of redistribution on the

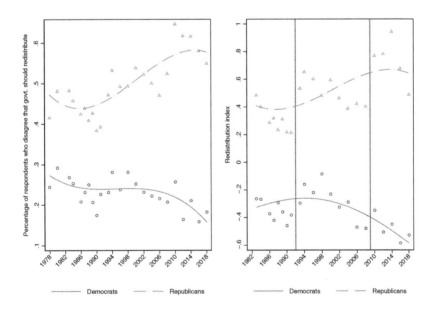

Figure 8.11 Support for redistribution in the United States by partisanship
Plots changes in support for redistribution as measured using the traditional redistribution item (left panel) and an index of items asking about redistributive policies (right panel). See the text for wording. The two vertical lines mark the 1993 and 2008 healthcare bills.
Source: GSS longitudinal dataset, weighted.

part of Democratic voters. This timing roughly matches changes in racialized reciprocity beliefs described in the previous section.

The right panel plots partisan differences on a redistributive index that includes not only the traditional redistribution item but also two items about the size of government[20] and one item about spending on welfare.[21] These items are highly correlated and jointly capture individuals' attitudes toward government-provided income support, a rough proxy of support for *redistribution to* policies. Note the significant jumps on the Republican side in 1992–1994 and 2008–2010. These periods correspond to bitter redistributive battles over healthcare reform during the Clinton and the Obama administrations, and over unemployment benefits and income support for those hurt by the Great Recession during the first Obama administration. These jumps are likely the result of both belief change and framing effects in response to strong anti-redistribution and anti-"big-government" partisan cues.

Figure 8.12 plots the racial resentment index by income level. There is no evidence that changes in racialized reciprocity beliefs differ along income lines. High- and low-income Republicans are shifting to the right at a similar pace, while high- and low-income Democrats are shifting to the left, also at a similar pace. Still, I expect the effect of belief change on support for redistribution to be mediated by income, with implications for changes in the income gradient.

Figure 8.13 plots trends in support for redistribution (GSS) and support for government provided income support (ANES) by partisanship and income levels. In both the GSS and the ANES, the evidence points to high-income Democrats as the group of voters responsible for the decline in the income gradient. The absence of a decrease in support for redistribution among high-income Republicans is mostly due to ceiling effects: In the GSS, less than 20% of this group (10% in the ANES) support income redistribution.

Anyone familiar with American public opinion might suggest a competing interpretation of these results, one that emphasizes the correlation between income and attention paid to politics. As shown by Johnston, Lavine and Federico (2017), engaged citizens who align with Democrats or Republicans for cultural and noneconomic reasons (i.e., abortion, gay right or multiculturalism) take

---

[20] The two items are worded as follows: "(S)ome people think that the government in Washington is trying to do too many things that should be left to individuals and private businesses. Others disagree and think that the government should do even more to solve our country's problems," "Washington should do everything possible to improve the standard of living of all poor Americans. Other people think it is not the government's responsibility, and that each person should take care of himself." Respondents are asked to place themselves in terms of which statements they find themselves closest to.

[21] Respondents were asked whether spending on welfare is "too little, about right or too much."

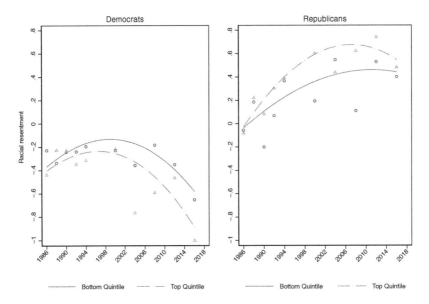

Figure 8.12 Racial resentment in the United States by income and partisanship
Plots changes in racial resentment scores by partisanship and income level. For information on the income variable, see Appendix A1.1.
Source: GSS longitudinal dataset, weighted.

their economic policy cues from trusted partisan elites and update their support for redistribution accordingly. In other words, the trends described in Figure 8.13 could be due to higher levels of attention to politics among high-income Democrats, especially relative to low-income Republicans: Because they are more exposed to party cues, they are also more likely to "follow their leader" and increase their support for some form of income redistribution.

This argument, however, is inconsistent with the evidence shown in Figure 8.12. If income-based differences in attention to politics are driving patterns documented in Figure 8.13, then polarization on racial issues should also differentially affect high- and low-income respondents. I also ran the same analysis looking at support for reducing immigration levels: If cognitive (dis)engagement is driving the drop in the income gradient, then we would expect to see the same results for policy issues other than income redistribution. As Figure 8.14 shows, this is not the case: Both high- and low-income Republicans have picked up on elite cues and increase their opposition to immigration. While cognitive engagement likely plays a role, it cannot account for such differences across redistributive and nonredistributive issues.

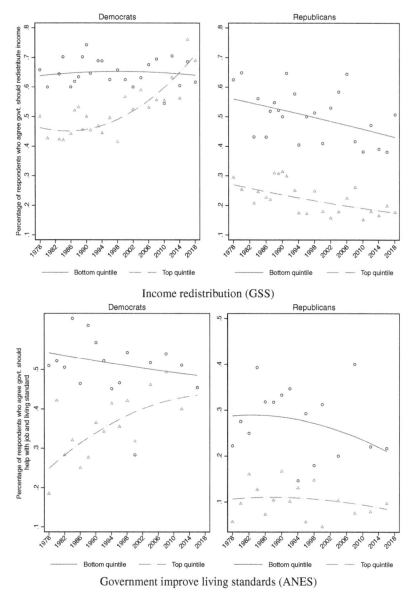

Income redistribution (GSS)

Government improve living standards (ANES)

Figure 8.13 Explaining the declining income gradient in the United States
Plots changes in percentage agreement by partisanship and income levels. The top panel uses the item available in the GSS while the bottom panel uses the item available in the ANES. For information on the income variable, see Appendix A1.1. GSS item wording: see Chapter 1. ANES item wording: "Some people feel the government in Washington should see to it that every person has a job and a good standard of living (1). Others think the government should just let each person get ahead on their own (7). Where would you place yourself?" People who pick 1-3 are recoded as 1, 0 otherwise.
Source: GSS longitudinal dataset, weighted and ANES longitudinal dataset, weighted.

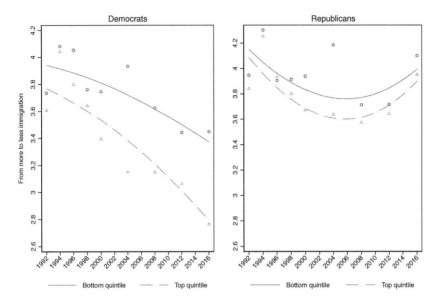

Figure 8.14 Support for reducing immigration levels in the United States by income and partisanship

Plots changes in average answer to the following question: "Do you think the number of immigrants from foreign countries who are permitted to come to the United States to live should be increased a lot, increased a little, left the same as it is now, decreased a little, or decreased a lot?" For information on the income variable, see Appendix A1.1.

Source: ANES longitudinal dataset, various years from 1988 to 2016, weighted.

United States: To Sum Up

As with Great Britain, aggregate attitudinal trends in the United States point to a key role for partisan dynamics. Polarization, especially on *redistribution to* issues, has created conditions favorable to both partisan sorting along reciprocity beliefs and belief change along partisan lines. The timing of major jumps in attitudinal trends echoes key legislative battles, especially under the Clinton and Obama administrations. Again, while aggregate trends reflect short- and long-term changes in partisan competition, there remains significant heterogeneity within parties. As is the case for low-income Republicans, people can resist aligning their policy preferences with their fairness beliefs. Rooted in fairness concerns, the altruism of high-income democrats stands out. Fiscal policy, discussed in Chapter 7 using the French case, likely plays a key role. Indeed, in contrast to France, an increase in taxes is not a credible threat in the United States. In such a context, where altruism is "cheap," high-income "bleeding heart liberals" are more likely to translate a left-wing shift in reciprocity beliefs into higher support for redistribution, specifically *redistribution to* policies.

Reverse Causality

In both Great Britain and the United States, mass belief change mirrors partisan dynamics. But who exactly is in the driver seat? When it happens, mass attitudinal change likely plays a role in partisan strategic repositioning. Still, as I argued throughout, there is no evidence that mass belief change precedes changes in partisan dynamics. Instead, the latter's timing is set by a bundle of interacting factors, including election timing or the internal struggles between different types of party activists (Bawn et al., 2012; Rodden, 2019).

In light of the nature of fairness reasoning and fairness beliefs, the fact that belief change follows and does not precede strategic repositioning is unsurprising. Fairness beliefs are not a bundle of objective statements about the status quo; they are composed of subjective evaluations of the extent to which the status quo aligns with shared norms of fairness. A change in aggregate fairness beliefs implies that a subset of individuals update their fairness evaluations in unison. This is only possible under the coordinated and mobilizing impact of electoral and partisan competition, explaining why partisan dynamics matter for explaining the timing and direction of mass attitudinal change in fairness beliefs.

Nevertheless, this does not mean that voters' fairness beliefs mirror elite dynamics in a purely top-down fashion. First, people's discursive context is shaped by factors other than partisan dynamics. I focus on the latter only to the extent that it captures systemic changes in the discursive context, one that will affect enough people to be picked up in aggregate data. Second, my emphasis is on partisan *dynamics* between two or more political parties. These dynamics are the outcome of many interacting factors, which no single party fully controls. For example, while both the New Labour in the United Kingdom and the SPD in Germany have engaged in "liberalizing" labor market reforms, the SPD was confronted with the rise of a radical left party following this policy shift, explaining why this Third-way shift has had very different attitudinal implications in Germany compared to those observed in Great Britain. Third, in the beginning of the chapter, I hypothesized a push and pull between (1) changes in the discursive context – which affect the types of fairness claims people are exposed to –, and (2) individual characteristics that affect the likelihood of "accepting" some fairness claims and "rejecting" others. In other words, while partisan dynamics create the conditions for belief change (among other factors), not everyone updates. In the remaining chapters, I focus my attention on this individual-level mechanism, starting with proportionality beliefs (Chapter 9) before turning to reciprocity beliefs (Chapter 10).

Long-Term Trends in Fairness Beliefs Beyond Great Britain and the United States

In the American and British cases, the conditions for a change in fairness beliefs appear to be met. What about other countries? Unfortunately, with the exception of Great Britain, researchers lack longitudinal data on fairness beliefs. As a very rough proxy, I rely on cohort differences. A cohort's average fairness score on a given scale is the sum of the score this cohort started with and change occurring between then and when beliefs are measured. A difference between two cohorts is thus due to (1) a difference in baseline beliefs and/or (2) a difference in cumulative change, that is, belief change. No difference between two cohorts suggests similar average baseline beliefs and only limited cumulative change, that is, beliefs stability. How common is this latter pattern?

To answer this question, I focus on the ESS. To address sample size limits, I pool two waves of data collected around the same period (within an eight-year window) and examine how beliefs differ across cohorts.[22] First, I examine between-cohort differences in answers to three survey items available in the ESS that proxy – if imperfectly – for proportionality beliefs. One is the traditional redistribution item, as well as respondents' agreement with the following two statements: "For a society to be fair, differences in people's standard of living should be small" and "Large differences in people's incomes are acceptable to properly reward differences in talents and efforts." I combine answers to these items into one additive score that I then standardize. For expository purposes, if two countries show similar patterns, I present the results for the pooled data. Based on Figure 8.15, we can say that stability is the norm. Scandinavian countries are an exception; though the difference between the cohort with the lowest score and that with the highest score is substantively small (0.2 SD).

Figure 8.16 examines reciprocity beliefs, focusing on three items also available in both the 2008 and 2016 waves of the ESS. Respondents are asked whether they agree or disagree with the following claims: "Most unemployed

---

[22] This analysis assumes that an eight-year window is small enough to minimize period effects. The smaller the window, the better. If I were to pool data from the early 1990s and late 2000s to maximize cohort sizes (a twelve-year window or more), a risk would be that the beliefs of older (younger) cohorts are shaped by period-specific factors that occurred in the 1990s (2000s). Because younger cohorts are oversampled in the 2000s data and older cohorts in the 1990s data, differences between the two would be hard to interpret.

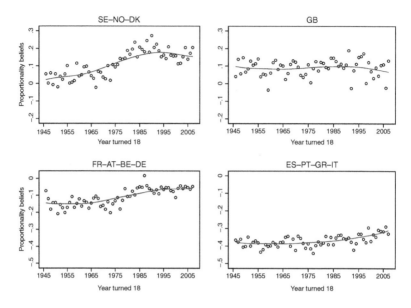

Figure 8.15 Proportionality beliefs: Cross-country generational analysis
Plots average values of proxies of proportionality beliefs by birth cohort. Higher
values indicate more tolerance toward large income differences. See text for item
wording.
Source: ESS 2008 and 2016.

people do not really try to find a job." "Many manage to obtain benefits/services
they are not entitled to" and "Social benefits/services make people less willing
to care for one another." Cohort differences point to substantive differences between people socialized in the 1940s and people socialized in the 1970s. In
contrast, differences between cohorts who came of age in the 1970s and those
who came of age in the 2000s are small in Germany, France and Southern
European countries. Scandinavian countries are again the exception. Given important period effects (the right-wing shift in reciprocity beliefs peaked in 2008
and was followed by a continuous shift to the left), the pattern for Great Britain
should be interpreted with care. Figure 8.6, which reproduces the analysis using two waves of the BSAS from the early 2000s, reveals a pattern similar to
the one documented for Scandinavian countries.

This analysis is only exploratory and should not be given too much weight.
Still, we can tentatively conclude that, in line with findings from Great Britain
and the United States, most of the action appear to be around reciprocity beliefs. The left-wing shift observed between cohorts coming of age before the
1980s coincides with the expansion of the welfare state, as well as a shift away

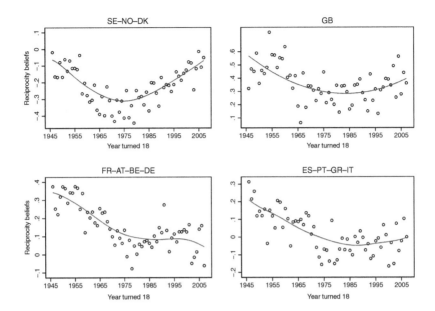

Figure 8.16 Reciprocity beliefs: Cross-country generational analysis
Plots average values of proxies of reciprocity beliefs by birth cohort. Higher values indicate more anti-*redistribution to* reciprocity beliefs. See text for item wording.
Source: ESS 2008 and 2016.

from authoritarian values (Inglehart, 1997). This suggests that positive rhetoric around an expanding welfare state, combined with a liberal shift in values, provided conditions conducive to a left-wing shift in reciprocity beliefs. In other words, belief change tends to coincides with large institutional upheavals such as the creation and expansion of the welfare state in the 1950s–1960s. Evidence of a complementary relationship between institutional change on the one hand, and fairness beliefs on the other, aligns with the argument presented in Chapter 2. Like Great Britain, Scandinavian countries exhibit a more recent anti-redistribution generational shift in fairness beliefs. Understanding the mechanisms underpinning this shift is unfortunately beyond the scope of this book.

Summary and Next Steps

I have shown that the changes in support for redistribution documented in Chapter 1 in Great Britain and the United States, are best interpreted as changes in support for *redistribution to* policies motivated by reciprocity concerns; not changes in *redistribution from* policies rooted in proportionality concerns. I also found that the decline in the income gradient in the United States is mostly driven by a subset of high-income respondents who have increased their support for *redistribution to* policies out of fairness concerns. In Great Britain, while the income gap in support for redistribution – as traditionally measured – is stable, the income gap in support for cuts to welfare is growing. These contrasting patterns, I show, can be plausibly tied to differences in partisan dynamics, which play out differently depending on people's income levels.

Based on the argument presented in this book, these partisan dynamics amount to a worse-case scenario for observing any of the implications of the benchmark model discussed in Chapter 1. In both countries, *redistribution from* policies are rarely debated and proportionality concerns rarely raised by political elites. Instead, the action has been mostly on the *redistribution to* front in the form of welfare-to-workfare reforms, sharp disagreement over coverage expansion and immigrant inclusions. These policy innovations tap into deeply held disagreements over the boundaries of social solidarity, themselves based on disagreements over perceptions of violations of the reciprocity norm. When this happens, the activation of reciprocity beliefs, especially among high-income individuals, produces attitudinal changes that have little to do with common expectations of a pro-redistribution turn among those who stand to benefit from redistribution. However, despite similar rhetoric and policy proposals (with Tony Blair borrowing heavily from Bill Clinton), differences in long-term partisan dynamics outweigh similarities, leading to belief polarization along partisan lines in the United States and to a right-wing shift in fairness beliefs, especially reciprocity beliefs, in Great Britain.

In Chapters 9 and 10, I further zoom in on the belief change pathway, starting with proportionality beliefs, before turning to reciprocity beliefs.

9

How Proportionality Beliefs Form

Based on the argument presented in Chapter 8, the correlation between proportionality beliefs and people's economic conditions has at least two origins. First, it emerges because exposure to different types of fairness claims is not random. If people closer to the bottom of the economic ladder are more likely to be exposed to claims that the status quo is unfair as prescribed by the proportionality norm, then they are also more likely to form beliefs in line with such claims. Second, the correlation emerges because economic conditions predict which claims people, conditional on exposure, are more likely to accept or reject. For example, if low-income individuals, when exposed to claims that the status quo is fair, are more likely to resist incorporating such claims into their own proto-ideological worldview, then they are also less likely to form such beliefs. Conversely, if people closer to the top of the economic ladder are both more likely to be exposed to claims that the status quo is fair and more likely to accept and incorporate such claims into their own "basket of considerations," then we should expect a correlation between income and proportionality beliefs.

In this chapter, I focus my analysis on the individual-level resistance/acceptance mechanism. Using British panel data collected over more than a decade, I show that individuals experiencing hardship are more likely to resist right-wing claims regarding the fairness of markets and income differences. Jointly, results from Chapters 8 and 9 highlight the push and pull between contextual and individual factors. They suggest that the relative stability of mass proportionality beliefs in Great Britain is plausibly the result of both "benign neglect" on the part of political elites – due, in the British case, to what I called convergence by omission – and mass resistance to right-wing, anti-redistribution proportionality rhetoric.

This chapter draws on an article co-authored with Anja Neundorf.[1] To pre-
serve the book's stylistic coherence, I use the singular throughout, but the
reader should keep in mind that this chapter is a joint project that owes a lot
to Anja's theoretical insights, deep knowledge of the literature and empirical
skills.

Stability as Resistance: Proportionality Beliefs and the Role of Material Self-interest

By altering the range of fairness considerations available to citizens, political
elites – amplified by media and other arenas of debate – increase the likelihood
that people will be exposed to new political messaging and new considerations
about the state of the world. In many cases, these changes are temporary, coin-
ciding with the passing of a specific bill or the aftermath of an economic event
such as the Great Recession. Partisan dynamics such as partisan convergence or
polarization can make such changes lasting, at least in the medium term. This
creates ideal conditions for belief change.

Partisan dynamics in Great Britain are not conducive to a pro-redistribution
shift in proportionality beliefs. Indeed, the ideological convergence between the
two main parties has decreased the relative share of traditional left-wing fairness considerations available in the political debate and increased centrist and
right-wing ones associated with both mainstream parties. From the perspective
of individual respondents, this has two implications. First, fewer individuals are
exposed to new left-wing fairness considerations. Second, more individuals are
exposed to right-wing fairness considerations.

When exposed to claims and considerations about the fairness of income
inequality and economic institutions, people on the losing end of the economic race and experiencing hardship face a tension between claims that the
status quo is fair, as prescribed by the proportionality norm, and wanting to
reach the conclusion that they are themselves hardworking individuals who deserve better. High-income individuals face no such tension. In their case, the
tension emerges when faced with claims and considerations that income inequality and economic institutions are unfair: Agreeing with such claims is

---

[1] The argument and evidence were previously published in *Political Behavior* under the titled
"Elite Cues and Economic Policy Attitudes: The Mediating Role of Economic Hardship"
(Cavaillé and Neundorf, 2022). The chapter only reproduces a subset of the article's overall
results. The article is licensed under a Creative Commons Attribution 4.0 International License
that permits use, sharing, adaptation, distribution and reproduction in any medium or format.
To view a copy of this licence, visit http://creativecommons.org/licenses/by/4.0/.

in tension with wanting to reach the conclusion that they deserve their economic success. As discussed in Chapter 4, correlational evidence suggests that people solve these tensions in a self-serving manner: Economic "losers" are less likely than economic "winners" to believe that effort pays and that resources are fairly distributed.[2] When it comes to the proportionality norm, people tend to prefer considerations that resonate with their own experience and help maintain their own self-esteem (DeScioli and Kurzban, 2009). Why this self-serving reasoning does not extend to reciprocity beliefs is something I will tackle in Chapter 10.

Assuming that people are exposed to a range of left- and right-wing fairness considerations on *redistribution from* issues, I consequently expect people experiencing hardship to be more likely to accept left-wing consonant considerations and resist right-wing dissonant ones. If, as in the British context, people are mostly exposed to right-wing considerations, hardship's main effect will be one of resistance to right-wing dissonant considerations. As a shorthand, I call this prediction the *resistance hypothesis*.

To test this hypothesis, I use panel data and examine the effect of material hardship on proportionality beliefs. To document the push and pull between the discursive context and individual economic conditions, I focus on a period of significant right-wing shift in elite discourse, specifically 1997, the year the Labour Party ran for office on its "New Labour" platform. In line with evidence from Chapter 8, I expect a right-wing shift in *aggregate* proportionality beliefs, especially so among people closer to the Labour Party. In line with the resistance hypothesis, I expect those who have experienced a negative economic shock to be less likely to experience a right-wing shift in proportionality beliefs.

Empirical Strategy

Before explaining the empirical strategy, I describe the data and the variables used in the analysis. I use the British Household Panel Survey (BHPS). The BHPS is an annual survey that provides high-quality socioeconomic data at the individual and household levels. It consists of a nationally representative sample of about 5,500 households recruited in 1991.[3] The panel ends in 2008 and covers the period preceding and following the 1997 elections, when the Labour

---

[2] Relatedly, Marshall (2016), using a plausibly exogenous variation in education-level and income, finds that more education and higher income result in more right-wing answers to the type of survey items used to measure proportionality beliefs.

[3] For more information about the BHPS, visit www.iser.essex.ac.uk/bhps. The data can be downloaded from https://beta.ukdataservice.ac.uk/datacatalogue/studies/study?id=5151.

Party moved to the right on economic issues.[4] To measure proportionality beliefs, I rely on the following items:

A. Ordinary people do not get their fair share nation's wealth.
B. There is one law for the rich and one for the poor.
C. Private enterprise solves economic problems.
D. Public services ought to be state owned.
E. Government has an obligation to provide jobs.
F. Strong trade unions protect employees.

Answers to these items were measured on seven occasions between 1991 and 2007. I have recoded them such that higher values indicate a more right-wing answer. Two items tap into proportionality beliefs, three ask about government intervention in the economic realm, and one asks about the role of trade unions. In other words, at least four items do not directly capture proportionality beliefs. As I show in Appendix A9.1 using the 1991 wave of the BSAS, these latter four items correlate with both proportionality beliefs and reciprocity beliefs. In other words, people who support strong government intervention over private enterprise are much more likely to believe that income differences are unfair and that "private" enterprise does not deliver fair outcomes. They are also more likely to express the type of moral hazard concerns that underpin reciprocity beliefs. This speaks against combining these items into an additive score. Indeed, a change in the score driven by these specific four items would be difficult to interpret. As I discuss when describing the empirical strategy, I rely on a measurement strategy that assesses patterns of answers to all six items, ensuring that attitudinal change, per this measure, is not driven by a specific subset of items. Throughout, I interpret a right-wing shift in patterns of answers as an anti-redistribution shift in proportionality beliefs.[5]

---

[4] Due to the different party systems in Wales, Scotland and Northern Ireland, I only keep individuals living in England. Given the emphasis on economic conditions, I restrict the BHPS sample to the working age population (16–65 years old). I exclude pensioners and respondents in full-time education from the analysis as income shocks are more difficult to measure for these groups.

[5] Note that this conceptual ambiguity does not affect the general interpretation of the results presented in this chapter. Indeed, these survey items directly ask about "Old" Labour issues, including conflict between management and labor, disagreement over the fairness of market economies and government intervention in the economy to help the "little guy." These are precisely the issues the "New" Labour dropped from its political platform starting in the mid-1990s. These items are thus ideal for documenting the impact of a change in the discursive context. Still, given that proportionality beliefs are imperfectly measured, individual-level estimates regarding the effect of hardship should be interpreted as informative of the *existence* of the resistance mechanism. Documenting *effect sizes* on proportionality beliefs per se would require different survey questions.

In order to measure changes in material hardship (whether positive or negative), I use two sets of variables. One set identifies people who experienced a substantial changes in their objective economic situation from one wave to the next, that is, an increase/drop of at least 25% in income, as well as a change in employment status (loosing or finding a job). The other set captures a subjective change in economic security from one wave to the next (a change in reported job security and subjective evaluation of one's financial situation). I rely on these subjective measures to compensate for the limitation of objective measures, which assume that the same objective income shock is experienced as hardship by all respondents. However, given that some shocks are expected, not all objective changes in economic conditions are experienced as hardship. In addition, subjective measures can help account for unobserved factor (e.g., private wealth) that shape whether an individual experiences an observed income shock as hardship or not.

To test the resistance hypothesis, I also need to distinguish between people more likely to be exposed to Labour rhetoric because they feel closer to the Labour Party. At each wave, respondents were asked which party they feel closest to. Using data collected before 1997, I code as Labour sympathizers people who report feeling closer to the Labour Party at least once (40%) and do the same for people who feel closer to the Conservative Party (36%).[6]

The resistance hypothesis seeks to test the effect of hardship on attitudinal stability. An empirical test of this hypothesis faces two challenges. One challenge is to distinguish between durable change (i.e., a change in the set of considerations people sample from) and temporary change (i.e., a change in the particular considerations that happen to be "on top" of individuals' basket at a given point in time due, for example, to framing effects). The other challenge is to identify the specific impact of hardship on stability, net of other stability-promoting mechanisms discussed in Chapter 8. Examples of such competing mechanisms include a lack of exposure to political discourse and people's tendency to discount claims and considerations that do not align with the considerations they already hold (see page 166).

To model stability, I rely on a first-order Markov transition process in which latent beliefs at time t are a function of previously held latent beliefs at time $t-1$ and measurement error that is assumed to be time invariant for reasons of identification. Latent beliefs are modeled as a categorical variable (i.e., a finite number of latent classes). The model's transition dynamics are parametrized by a multinomial logit model that estimates the probability of switching from

---

[6] Note that individuals who report a different party affiliation from one wave to the next is negligible (less than 5%).

one latent class to another and allows this probability to vary between survey waves.

For each wave, the measurement part of the model estimates membership probability in N classes. Comparing the model fit between models of varying class sizes (from one to five), I ultimately settle on a model with three latent classes.[7] One class comprises individuals who answer the six survey items in a consistently left-wing fashion. The second one comprises individuals who answer in a consistently right-wing fashion. Finally, a third category includes individuals who do not appear to be committed to one position over the other, a group I describe as ambivalent centrists.[8] In other words, the model distinguishes between (1) people who tend to believe that the status quo is unfair according to the proportionality norm and have a propensity to support *redistribution from* policies, (2) people who tend to believe that the status quo is fair according to the proportionality norm and have a propensity to oppose *redistribution from* policies and (3) people who cannot be classified as either because of the mix of proportionality considerations they hold. This categorical multi-item approach emphasizes qualitative differences in patterns of answers (e.g., consistent versus ambivalent). Under the reasonable assumption that switching from one latent class to another is both meaningful and durable, this measurement strategy seeks to leverage durable change over temporary change.

I expect beliefs to be, on average, persistent, meaning that the baseline probability of switching away from a given latent class is low. Changes in the discursive context increase – through exposure – the probability of a switch from one latent class to another. This is captured in the model by allowing the probability of switching between latent classes to vary over time. In the British context, I expect response patterns to exhibit a right-wing shift starting in 1997. The shift should be larger among individuals who feel closer to the Labour Party. Given that Labour voters tend to have more left-wing proportionality beliefs to start with, I expect an increase in the probability of switching from being consistently left-wing to being an ambivalent centrist.

To test for the resistance hypothesis, I further extend the model to capture the effect of a *change* in a respondent's material conditions (relative to no change) on the probability of switching from one latent class to another. Empirically, I expect the probability of shifting to the right to be lower for people experiencing hardship. Readers unfamiliar with latent Markov models can refer themselves to Appendix A9.3. Before moving forward with the analysis, a quick

---

[7] Model fit greatly improves when hypothesizing the existence of three different classes, and only marginally improves when fitting models for more than three latent classes.

[8] The estimates from the latent class measurement model are shown in Appendix A9.2.

word on why I did not choose more mainstream modeling strategies. In previous chapters, I have averaged multiple survey items into an index using weights recovered from a factor analysis (Ansolabehere, Rodden and Snyder, 2008). As previously mentioned, given some of the limits of the items available in the BHPS, I opted against this measurement strategy. I have other reasons to prefer the categorical measurement model used in this chapter. With a continuous outcome, researchers most often rely on OLS regressions with year and individual fixed effects. As demonstrated in the online appendix, with this empirical strategy, I can show that people who experience a change in their material circumstances from good to worse are also more likely to move from right to left on such a continuous indicator (see also Cavaillé and Neundorf, 2022). However, compared to my preferred modeling strategy, these more common specifications offer an inadequate test of the resistance hypothesis. Indeed, estimating the effect of hardship on attitudinal *stability* requires a modeling strategy that can distinguish between persistence that is not tied to hardship on the one hand, and hardship-induced resistance on the other. This is exactly what the model used here does. Traditional linear regression techniques are less well suited for this purpose. For example, in the context of an OLS regression with individual fixed effects (the gold standard when using panel data), if a given respondent does not have any variation from wave to wave, then he or she contributes nothing to the estimation.[9]

Results

Table 9.1 shows that, on average, close to half of the sample can be classified as having response patterns falling clearly on one of the two sides of the fairness cleavage (20% mostly pro-*redistribution from*, 22% mostly anti-*redistribution from*). The other half are classified as ambivalent, suggesting a more diverse mix of proportionality concerns, with some pointing to the status quo as fair and others pointing to the status quo as unfair.[10] Leveraging the panel structure of the data, I first examine how transition rates across latent classes differ.

---

[9] Another benefit of the modeling strategy described in this chapter is that it estimates the effect of hardship separately for each transition probability, meaning that the effect of hardship on moving from left wing to ambivalent centrist is allowed to differ from the effect of hardship on moving from ambivalent centrist to right wing. In contrast, linear models commonly used with panel data can only safely recover the effect of hardship averaged across different attitudinal "starting points," which biases the estimates downward.

[10] Mechanically, as the number of measurement items decreases, so does the size of the ambivalent category. Furthermore, as previously mentioned, these items only indirectly capture proportionality beliefs. I consequently refrain from interpreting these raw numbers in terms of the existing share of people with "mostly fair/unfair" proportionality beliefs.

Table 9.1 *Estimated mean transition probabilities*

Latent Cat.[t]	Latent Cat.[t-1]		
	Left wing	Ambi. centrist	Right wing
Proportion	*0.20*	*0.57*	*0.22*
Left wing	0.87	0.03	0.00
Centrist	0.12	0.94	0.01
Right wing	0.00	0.02	0.99

Table 9.1 shows that virtually nobody switches from left- to right-wing response patterns (or vice versa). In line with expectations, a switch from one consistent response category to another is very rare: The apple rarely falls far from the tree. In contrast, the probability of switching from left-wing to ambivalent is 12% on average.

Once I allow transition rates to vary by year, I find that the transition rate from left wing to ambivalent doubles in 1997 at around 25% (see Figure 9.1.A). For comparison, Figure 9.1.B plots the proportion of ambivalent centrists who shift to more consistently left- or right-wing response patterns from one wave to the next. As expected, there are virtually no ambivalent centrists that became more left wing. Among people classified as left wing by this measurement model, only one in ten feels close to the Conservative Party, while eight in ten feel close to the Labour Party and one in ten does not identify with any of the two main parties. In other words, this shift to the center suggests that Labour voters are "following the leader" (Lenz, 2013).[11]

Next, I examine whether individual material conditions shape response patterns in line with the resistance hypothesis. I expect material self-interest to manifest itself as resistance to partisan rhetoric among left-wing respondents, most of whom identify with the Labour Party. Specifically, I expect individuals experiencing hardship to be more likely to *resist* transitioning away from the consistently left-wing latent class. Results are presented in Table 9.2 and Figure 9.2.

Table 9.2 reports the estimates of a series of multinomial logistic regression models. The ambivalent centrist category (at time *t*) constitutes the reference

---

[11]　To investigate whether the year 1997 produced a more general change in political attitudes, no matter the issue and irrespective of a change in elite discourse, I replicate the analysis using gender attitudes as the outcome of interest. Gender issues were not politicized in the 1997 election and finding similar variations in patterns of answers to questions about gender would cast doubt on the previous results. As documented in the online appendix, there is no meaningful variations in gender attitudes over time.

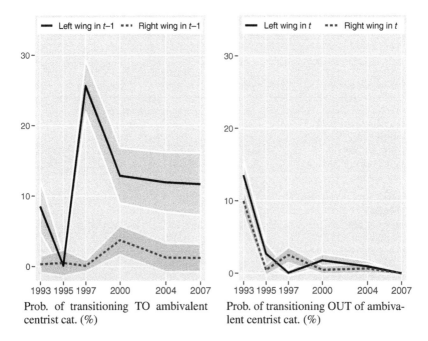

Figure 9.1 Time-varying predicted probabilities of attitudinal change
Plots the predicted probability of becoming an ambivalent centrist (left panel) or
no longer being an ambivalent centrist (right panel). For the underlying model, see
Appendix A9.3.
Source: BHPS, 1991–2007.

category.[12] This means that the estimates in the left-wing (right-wing) column
model the probability of becoming or remaining left wing (right wing) relative
to the probability of remaining or becoming more ambivalent. Substantively,
the results fit expectations: Those who experience hardship (compared with
those who have stable economic conditions) are more likely to become – or
remain – consistently left wing, namely, to hold proportionality beliefs that
incline them to support *redistribution from* policies. They are also less likely to
become – or remain – consistently right wing.

Logistic coefficients cannot be easily interpreted and compared (see Paolino,
2020). Furthermore, the estimates presented in Table 9.2 are average effects
across the whole time period and do not convey the interaction between period-
specific changes in elite discourse and material self-interest. In Figure 9.2, I

---

[12] Indeed, the ambivalent-centrist category is the "cross-road" category, meaning the category
people experiencing attitudinal change have to either transition into, or transition out of.

Table 9.2 *Belief change and material conditions*

IV: Material interest	Left wing		Right wing	
	Coefficient	Standard error	Coefficient	Standard error
	Objective material conditions			
Unemployment (ref: employed)				
Unemp in t and $t-1$	0.250	0.173	−0.659**	0.253
Became unemployed in t	0.322*	0.138	−0.037	0.253
Found job in t	0.178	0.136	−0.290	0.202
Income change (ref: no change)				
Drop by at last 25%	0.209**	0.084	0.032	0.131
Increase by at last 25%	−0.058	0.064	0.119	0.107
	Subjective material conditions			
Job security (ref: no change)				
Got worse	0.373***	0.095	−0.514***	0.134
Got better	0.136	0.091	0.217	0.182
Financial situation (ref: no change)				
Worse off	0.342***	0.081	−0.432***	0.117
Better off	0.092	0.073	−0.075	0.129

$^*p < .05,\ ^{**}p < .01\ ^{***}p < .001$.
The results are based on separate multinomial logistic regression for each set of material interest variables. All variables are measured as the time difference between two surveys that included the economic attitude items. N = 5,745.
Source: BHPS 1991–2007.

consequently focus on predicting transition rates from left wing to ambivalent response at different levels of hardship.

As shown in Figure 9.2, individuals who have experienced an economic shock are also more likely to remain consistently left-wing. For example, in 1997, individuals who have experienced no change in their perceived financial security have a transition probability away from left-wing economic attitudes of around 35%. In the case of individuals who experienced a worsening of their financial security, this probability hovers around 15%. In other words, economic hardship increases attitudinal stability. This finding supports the resistance hypothesis: Individual-level experiences with economic hardship mediate how individuals react to changes in the discursive context triggered, in this case, by a change in political elites' electoral strategies.

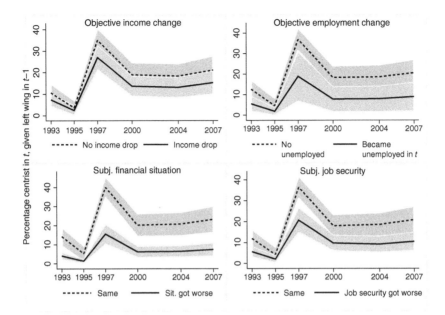

Figure 9.2 Resistance to right wing claims by economic condition
Plots the predicted probability of transitioning from left wing to centrist by economic conditions. For the underlying model, see Appendix A9.3.
Source: BHPS 1991–2007.

The strategic repositioning of the Labour Party in 1997 raises two possible concerns for this analysis. One is partisan cheerleading: Respondents more likely to "follow" might also be reporting improved conditions just to cast a positive light on the Labour Party (Bullock and Lenz, 2019).[13] Notice, however, that most of the action in Table 9.2 is among people who reported a *worsening* of their economic conditions. This suggests that partisan cheerleading is not driving our results. If this was the case, respondents reporting improved conditions should be driving our results. Another related concern is the role of switchers, who might be Blair enthusiasts engaging in Blair-specific cheerleading. Indeed, the Labour Party's strategic repositioning toward the center attracted a new type of voters: In this panel, 23% of people who declared a proximity to the Labour Party in 1997 had never expressed such sympathies in past waves. Still, remember that my argument and results emphasize leftwing respondents becoming more ambivalent: The overwhelming majority of

---

[13] This assumes partisan cheerleading affects egocentric evalutations not just sociotropic ones. To the best of my knowledge, the existing evidence only concerns sociotropic evalutations.

switchers do not have left-wing economic preferences to start with, making it extremely unlikely that this group's enthusiasm for Blair explains these findings.[14] Finally, because I am relying on panel data, there is also no concern that compositional changes are driving these results.

The Origins of Proportionality Beliefs: A Few Take Aways

These findings speak to debates on economic shocks and mass opinion change. A common expectation is that adverse economic events, such as the Great Recession, will be followed by left-wing shifts in mass economic policy preferences, especially among those experiencing hardship. Based on the model tested in this book, political economists need to take seriously the mediating role of partisan competition and its impact on the discursive context, distinguishing between favorable and unfavorable supply-side dynamics. Indeed, the latter can mute (or in some conditions de-multiply) the effect of economic hardship. For example, if, as it happened during the Great Recession, mainstream parties all emphasize austerity measures and spending cuts, pro-redistribution shifts in proportionality beliefs are less likely to materialize. More generally, as I discuss in the conclusion, in light of long-term elite convergence on economic issues, as well as the organizational decline of institutions that target left-wing messaging to economically insecure workers (e.g., trade unions or communist parties), expectations of a left turn underpinned by a left-wing shift in perceptions that market capitalism is inherently unfair are likely misplaced.

One can conjecture that the correlation between individual socioeconomic conditions and proportionality beliefs is the combined outcome of (1) legacies of previous episodes of class-based mobilizations and (2) incremental belief change among socially mobile individuals. Class-based mobilization targeted different socioeconomic groups with consonant proportionality consideration, providing ideal conditions for the formation of pro-redistribution proportionality beliefs among low-income individuals. These beliefs are then passed on through socialization. Because upward mobility depends on parental background, people socialized into left-wing proportionality beliefs are themselves more likely to be poor, explaining how the original correlation can persist across generations even without class-based mobilization (O'Grady, 2019). As upwardly mobile individuals move up the income and occupational ladder, they become more likely to be exposed to right-wing consideration and more likely

---

[14] Out of more than 5,000 observations, only 101 can be reasonably classified as both switcher and consistently left wing on economic issues.

to incorporate them in light of their own improved economic conditions. In line with this argument, Helgason and Rehm (2022) find that "core political values" (akin to what I have called proportionality beliefs) change in expected ways, "slowly but systematically as income evolves over the life cycle."

Summary and Next Steps

Proportionality beliefs form at the intersection of the discursive context and people's own economic experiences. An increase in pro-redistribution proportionality beliefs requires a favorable discursive context, one that exposes people to left-wing rhetoric regarding the fairness of economic institutions. Material hardship, in turn, mediates the impact of the discursive context. In Great Britain, it has arguably fed resistance to right-wing proportionality considerations and contributed, alongside the relative depoliticization of *redistribution from* issues, to the stability of proportionality beliefs.

Extrapolating to reciprocity beliefs, this suggests that the anti-redistribution shift observed in Great Britain has at least two sources: (1) a more consequential anti-redistribution discursive shift – discussed in Chapter 8 – and (2) lower individual-level resistance to anti-redistribution considerations regarding moral hazard and the prevalence of free riding. Chapter 10 focuses on explaining and documenting the latter.

Appendix

A9.1 Measuring Proportionality Beliefs Using BHPS Items

With the exception of the item asking about trade unions, the 1991 wave of the BSAS includes items similar to the ones asked in the BHPS, namely items 7, 8, 9, 11 and 12 in Table A9.1. I can consequently run an EFA on these items, alongside BSAS proportionality items used in other chapters of the book, namely, items 10 through 14 in Table A9.1. Items 11 and 12 are available in both the BSAS and the BHPS. I find that items 7–14 all load on the same dimension, with factor loadings ranging from 0.35 to 0.41 (not shown).

Using the 1991 wave of the BSAS, I can also examine how the items specific to the BHPS, that is, items 7–9, relate to both the proportionality and reciprocity latent dimensions. Table A9.1 reports factor loadings from a CFA. As found in Chapter 3 using data from the 2000s and 2010s, results show that the two latent dimensions are only weakly correlated. Allowing items 7–9 to load on both dimensions significantly improves the model fit. As a result, I do not combine these items into a linear scale to avoid giving too much weight to change tied to this subset of items.

Table A9.1 *Interpreting BHPS items: Evidence from the BSAS*

	Item Wording	Recip.	Prop.
1	The welfare state encourages people to stop helping each other	0.43	
2	If welfare benefits weren't so generous, people would learn to stand on their own two feet	0.88	
3	Many people who get welfare don't really deserve any help	0.75	
4	Most unemployed people could find a job if they really wanted one	0.67	
5	Most people on the dole are fiddling	0.70	
6	Benefits for unemployed people: too low and cause hardship vs. too high and discourage job seeking	0.59	
7	Private enterprise is the best way to solve Britain's problems	0.22	0.24
8	It is NOT the government's responsibility to provide jobs for everyone who wants one	0.17	0.24
9	Government should sell off more national industries	0.31	0.24
10	Management will always try to get the better of employees if it gets the chance		0.55
11	There is one law for the rich one for the poor		0.77
12	Ordinary people do not get their fair share of nation's wealth		0.74
13	Government should redistribute income from the better off to those who are least well-off		0.70
14	The gap between high and low incomes is too large		0.35
	Correlation coefficient between factors (95% CI)	0.23	[0.13–0.28]
	Standardized root mean squared residual		0.052
	Sample size		975

Higher (lower) values imply more right-wing (left-wing) answers. The results are based on a CFA. Final model relaxes the assumption that the error terms for items 7 and 9, and items 11 and 13, are uncorrelated. Additional goodness-of-fit measures: CFI $= 0.95$, RMSEA $= 0.051$.
Source: BSAS 1991.

A9.2 Latent Class Model

Table A9.2 provides a comparison of fit between models with one up to five classes. The model fit greatly improves if one hypothesizes the existence of three different classes. The rate at which the BIC changes clearly decreases

Table A9.2 *Measurement model: Model-fit comparison*

# Latent classes	LogLik	BIC	AIC	Npar
1	−327,148	654,511	654,344	24
2	−309,464	619,447	619,045	58
3	−303,215	607,360	606,639	104
4	−299,631	600,710	599,586	162
5	−297,338	596,748	595,140	232

above three classes. Increasing the number of latent classes beyond three only results in the breakdown of the nonideologue residual category, while the proportion of the sample composed of left- and right-wingers stays the same. I therefore limit the latent classes to three. The estimates from the latent class measurement model are shown in Table A9.3. The entries are the estimated response probabilities for each categorical answer of the survey items for people in that class.

Individuals in classes 1 and 3 have mirroring response patterns. For instance, individuals in class 1 have a probability of 0.67 of agreeing or agreeing strongly with the claim that public services should be state owned. Individuals in class 3 have a probability of disagreeing or disagreeing strongly of 0.62. This pattern is the same for all questions except for questions A and B, which show a strong bias in favor of a left-wing answer. These two questions were the only one where disagreeing was associated not with an economically conservative but an economically leftist position, potentially explaining this bias. However, overall, individuals in class 3 are still much less likely to take on a left-wing position on these two questions (0.38 versus 0.95 for individuals in class 1 for item A). I consequently identify individuals in class 1 as holding left-wing attitudes on economic and redistributive issues and individuals in class 3 as holding right-wing attitudes. Of interest is the very low probability of the left-wingers to ever take a "neither–nor" position (response category 3).

Latent class 2 stands out for its low probability of taking end-of-scale positions (response category 1 or 5) on any of the six items. These individuals have a higher propensity of rejecting both extreme liberal and conservative positions. There is a left bias in this category, confirming here the claim that, on average, the British population is in favor of government intervention and is aware of social inequality.

Table A9.3 *Estimates from the latent class measurement model*

	Latent Class			Overall
	Left wing	Ambivalent centrist	Right wing	
Proportion	*0.20*	*0.58*	*0.22*	
Item A				
1	0.40	0.06	0.03	0.12
2	0.55	0.54	0.40	0.51
3	0.04	0.26	0.31	0.23
4	0.00	0.13	0.25	0.13
5	0.00	0.01	0.01	0.01
Mean	1.65	2.48	2.81	2.38
Item B				
1	0.12	0.03	0.00	0.04
2	0.51	0.30	0.06	0.29
3	0.32	0.47	0.34	0.41
4	0.05	0.19	0.50	0.23
5	0.00	0.01	0.10	0.03
Mean	2.30	2.87	3.64	2.93
Item C				
1	0.46	0.09	0.04	0.15
2	0.51	0.55	0.39	0.51
3	0.03	0.21	0.25	0.18
4	0.00	0.14	0.28	0.15
5	0.00	0.01	0.04	0.02
Mean	1.58	2.44	2.90	2.37
Item D				
1	0.16	0.05	0.01	0.06
2	0.51	0.33	0.11	0.32
3	0.25	0.35	0.28	0.31
4	0.08	0.25	0.50	0.27
5	0.00	0.02	0.10	0.04
Mean	2.26	2.87	3.59	2.91
Item E				
1	0.13	0.06	0.00	0.06
2	0.53	0.40	0.08	0.36
3	0.17	0.21	0.13	0.19
4	0.16	0.30	0.62	0.35
5	0.01	0.02	0.16	0.05
Mean	2.39	2.83	3.85	2.97
Item F				
1	0.23	0.08	0.01	0.09
2	0.60	0.48	0.14	0.43
3	0.13	0.26	0.24	0.23
4	0.03	0.17	0.48	0.21
5	0.00	0.02	0.14	0.04
Mean	1.97	2.56	3.61	2.68

A9.3 Modeling Within-Person Dynamics

The analysis uses a first-order Markov transitioning structure, where the state at time t is a function of the state at time $t - 1$. Such a latent Markov model is specified as

$$P(y_{it}|x_{i0}) = \sum_{\theta_0=1}^{T} \cdots \sum_{\theta_T=1}^{T} P(\theta_0|x_{i0}) \sum_{t=1}^{T} P(\theta_t|\theta_{t-1}) \sum_{t=1}^{T} P(y_{it}|\theta_t). \quad (1)$$

This model specifies the categorical-level variable measuring latent economic attitudes θ_t, to be a function of previously held latent attitudes θ_{t-1} and a level of measurement error that is assumed to be time invariant for reasons of identification. Note that model 1 includes covariates x_{i0} on the initial state of economic policy preferences θ_0, when respondents first entered the panel. These account for observed characteristics that predict the probability that a respondent has economically left- or right-wing preferences in the first place (see Cavaillé and Neundorf, 2022 for more detail).

The model's transition dynamics are parametrized by a multinomial logit model that estimates the probability of being in state r instead of s – being for instance classified as left-winger instead of an ambivalent centrist – as a function of overall intercepts and time effects. The β coefficients are set to zero for $r = s$:

$$\log \left[\frac{P(\theta_t = r|\theta_{t-1} = s)}{P(\theta_t = s|\theta_{t-1} = s)} \right] = \beta_{0rs} + \beta_{1rst} \text{time}_{it}. \quad (2)$$

These specifications yield a time-heterogeneous Markov transition structure in which transition probabilities in and out of the latent classes of policy preferences differ between survey waves, allowing us to examine the temporal fit between documented changes in the discursive context and preference change (or stability) from one wave to the next. To test the resistance hypothesis, the model is extended to include covariates w_{it} that measure changes in a respondent's material conditions as follows:

$$\log \left[\frac{P(\theta_t = r|\theta_{t-1} = s)}{P(\theta_t = s|\theta_{t-1} = s)} \right] = \beta_{0rs} + \beta_{1rst} \text{time}_{it} + \beta_{rs} w_{it}. \quad (3)$$

10

The Nature and Origins of Reciprocity Beliefs

What explains the British Public's receptivity to negative rhetoric about the unfair allocation of social benefits? What differentiates people who embrace such rhetoric from people who resist it? Answering these questions requires unpacking the nature and origins of reciprocity beliefs.

Reciprocity beliefs represent a challenge for researchers. As documented in Chapter 4, in contrast to proportionality beliefs, when it comes to explaining differences in reciprocity beliefs, economic conditions and material self-interest have limited explanatory power. Indeed, with the exception of being unemployed, the probability of benefiting from *redistribution to* policies does not predict reciprocity beliefs. Instead, I found a puzzling and robust correlation between reciprocity beliefs on the one hand, and LAVs on the other. Why are answers to questions about law and order or discipline in school informative of answers to questions about moral hazard and the deservingness of able-bodied beneficiaries of social solidarity? This chapter seeks to answer this question.

I hypothesize that, underpinning the correlation between reciprocity beliefs and LAVs is a disagreement over how to best respond to social dilemmas. A social dilemma is a situation in which everyone would collectively be better-off cooperating; yet, the dominant strategy is to defect. People with more authoritarian response patterns to LAV items have a preference for maximizing cooperation by minimizing instances in which people who free ride on the collective effort unfairly walk away unpunished. When forming reciprocity beliefs, people with authoritarian values face a tension between wanting to reach the conclusion that punishment is needed to minimize free riding and information about the true prevalence of free riding. Faced with conflicting information, people with more authoritarian response patterns to the LAV items will overweigh evidence of free riding and moral hazard. The converse is true of people with more liberal values. They have a preference for minimizing instances in which people are unfairly punished despite being cooperators. This will lead them to underweight evidence of free riding and moral hazard. In a discursive context rich in claims about moral hazard, welfare abuse and opportunistic behavior, people with more authoritarian response patterns will be more likely to incorporate such claims into their own basket of fairness considerations, and people with more liberal response patterns will be more likely to resist them.

Using observational and experimental survey data collected in Great Britain, I find evidence that "authoritarians" and "liberals"[1] differ in how they weigh one type of error (i.e., failing to punish a free rider) against another (i.e., wrongly punishing a cooperator). I also show that changes in reciprocity beliefs are tied to more stable differences in LAVs. Furthermore, compared with other countries, Great Britain appears more authoritarian than not, providing a plausible explanation for why the British public has been receptive to rhetoric emphasizing moral hazard and free riding.

Reciprocity Beliefs through the Prism of Cooperation and Social Dilemmas

As discussed in Chapter 2, the reciprocity norm is a social technology useful in situations in which there is a tension between the individual interest and the collective interest. People, I hypothesize, differ fundamentally in how they approach such situations. As a result, they tend to also differ in how they would like to see the reciprocity norm enforced. To understand these differences, a brief review of public good games in behavioral economics is helpful.

The Social Solidarity Problem and How to Solve It

To study how members of a group can overcome social dilemmas, behavioral economists have relied on an ideal-typical game called the public goods game (PGG), which was reviewed in detail in Chapter 2. In its baseline form, the PGG captures the group's joint failure to solve a social dilemma. Everyone would be better-off cooperating, but failure to develop the shared understanding that all will cooperate ultimately means that, in line with the tit-for-tat logic of the reciprocity norm, nobody does. Once the option to punish others is introduced, convergence toward full cooperation happens through a four-step process. First, cooperation is jump-started by a group of high contributors with optimistic priors about others' willingness to cooperate. Second, the threat of

---

[1] I use these expressions as a shorthand to describe individual-level differences captured using questions about law and order and discipline in school.

punishment limits the share of individuals who decide to free ride in the first place and increases the share of individuals who believe that others will cooperate. Third, with punishment, a subset of individuals (which may or may not include the trusting individuals in round one) pay the price of punishing people who free ride, forcing this latter group to change their behavior. Fourth, after punishment is observed, it leads more players to update their priors about the relative share of cooperators and free riders. Core to this dynamic is a shared understanding of the reciprocity norm, the existence of individuals with optimistic priors regarding others' likelihood of cooperating and the existence of individuals willing to punish even at a personal cost.

The mechanisms that contribute to a cooperative equilibrium in a PGG are far from capturing the full complexity of all the social mechanisms that sustain large-scale social solidarity. Yet they provide a blueprint for identifying a key set of behavioral traits relevant to how people reason about social dilemmas. One such trait is whether someone starts by expecting the best from others or whether they start by expecting the worst, something often described as differences in *generalized trust*. According to work on generalized trust, people differ significantly on this point (Ostrom and Walker, 2003). Such differences have also been documented not only across individuals but also across cultural groups (Barrett et al., 2016; Henrich et al., 2001).

Recent work, building on evidence that cooperation is deeply intertwined with group membership (see Chapter 2 for a review), has helpfully revisited this literature with an emphasis on group boundaries. The generalized trust literature assumes that, when exposed to a random sample of individuals, people vary in their average baseline trust that others will cooperate. In contrast, Enke, Rodríguez-Padilla and Zimmermann (2022) argue that there is no such thing as generalized trust: What varies is how far people are willing to extend their trust. For some people, trust remains constant with social distance. For others, it declines with social distance.[2] As a shorthand, I call these differences, differences in *boundaries of trust*.

Another parameter, which has received less attention, is the willingness to pay to see free riders identified and punished. A socially optimal outcome is one in which nobody free rides. As shown by Eleonor Ostrom, in a small enough

---

[2] Enke, Rodríguez-Padilla and Zimmermann (2022) document these individual-level differences using both hypothetical dollars and trust points. Respondents are asked to split the dollars (points) between a randomly selected person who lives in their own country and someone who is a member of a specific group. Groups are assigned randomly and include the respondent's extended family, neighbors, friends of the family, colleagues, members of the same organization, or people who share the respondent's hobbies, religious beliefs, age, political views, and race. The authors find large individual-level differences that are highly predictive of attitudes toward foreign aid or border control.

group, this can be achieved without centralized monitoring. Part of the reason is that a subset of individuals appears especially sensitive to free riding and more willing to sacrifice their own time and resources to identify and punish free riders. In large welfare states, monitoring is performed by a central bureaucracy. The latter can make mistakes, such as unfairly denying benefits to some (unfair punishment of someone deserving) or unfairly granting benefits to others (unfair rewards going to someone undeserving). There is a trade-off between the two types of errors meaning that attempts to minimize one can end up increasing the other (Dickson, Gordon and Huber, 2009). People, I hypothesize, differ in terms of their *error sensitivity*, defined as their marginal rate of substitution between unfair punishment and unfair rewards. Put differently, the presence of free riders is likely to be more "painful" for some people than for others, making them more willing to "pay" for actions that will minimize the prevalence of free riding by making it harder and more risky to shirk, even if it means some cooperators are unfairly caught in the process.

These differences have been famously documented in the case of the criminal justice system (Xiong, Greenleaf and Goldschmidt, 2017). While some fret over innocents found guilty – an unfair punishment – others abhor the thought that guilty individuals could be found innocent – an unfair reward. A key assumption in this chapter is that these differences extend to all contexts approximating a social dilemma, that is, a situation in which an individual can win big by playing it selfish (stealing, lying or shirking), especially if others are being prosocial (trusting, helping and contributing).

Jointly, differences in generalized trust, boundaries of trust and error sensitivity shape how people approach social dilemmas. On one end of the spectrum, people display low generalized trust, narrow boundaries of trust and a higher sensitivity to unfairly rewarding free riders. On the other end, people display high generalized trust, expansive boundaries of trust and a higher sensitivity to unfairly punishing cooperators. Next, I connect these differences to differences in LAVs.

Liberal–Authoritarian Values as Proxies

In the previous section, I described two ideal-typical approaches to social dilemmas. Anyone having taken an introductory course in political theory might recognize the famous contrast between a Hobbesian approach to the social contract and other approaches put forward by liberal philosophers. Isaiah Berlin, for example, talks of "philosophers with an optimistic view of human nature," among which he includes Locke and Smith, who believe "that there should be a large area for private life over which neither the State nor any other authority must be allowed to trespass." He contrasts this group to Hobbes "and those who agreed with him" who, concerned with men's ability to "destroy one another, and mak[e] social life [im]possible," favor instituting "greater safeguards [...] to keep them in their places," even if this means "increasing the area of centralized control and decreasing that of the individual" (Berlin, 1958, p. 7). While Hobbesian thinkers are concerned with protecting the group from individuals' selfish impulses (i.e., minimizing free riding with an emphasis on punishment, or negative reciprocity), Liberals see a more pressing problem to address; namely carving a space for individual autonomy to minimize the claims made by the group on their own members (i.e., minimizing unfair punishment with an emphasis on positive reciprocity).

Social psychologists have shown that these scholarly debates over order-promoting institutions and principles echo differences found in the general public. Findings from Moral Foundation Theory are here particularly helpful. Indeed, a close read of Jonathan Haidt's work on morality suggests that people systematically differ in terms of the "moral matrices" they rely on to navigate social dilemmas.[3] Moral Foundation Theory scholars describe two ideal-typical mindsets that echo the Hobbesian versus Liberal distinction. One mindset, they argue, is built on the belief that "suppressing selfishness" requires "strengthening groups and institutions" and "binding individuals into roles and duties in order to constrain their imperfect natures." This binding approach rests on a pessimistic understanding of human nature and focuses on the "group as the locus of moral value" (Graham, Haidt and Nosek, 2009, p. 1030). The other mindset seeks to favor prosocial behavior by "protecting individuals directly (often using the legal system) and by teaching individuals to respect the rights of other individuals" (Shweder et al., 1997; Turiel, 1983). Such a perspective is rooted in a more optimistic conception of human nature, according to which humans are inherently prosocial once protected from harm and injustice. In line with this research, I expect differences in patterns of answer to questions about punishment and discipline (central to LAV indices) to capture broad differences between Hobbesian-binding and Liberal-individualizing orientations to social dilemmas.

These differences in orientations to social dilemmas can also explain why, as discussed in Chapter 4, answers to LAV and anti-immigration items are strongly correlated. First, people with narrow boundaries of trust are more

---

[3] In this approach, the moral domain is defined as "interlocking sets of values, practices, institutions, and evolved psychological mechanisms that work together to suppress or regulate selfishness and make social life possible" (Graham, Haidt and Nosek, 2009, p. 70). In other words, "moral matrices" help suppress free riding and encourage cooperative behavior to overcome social dilemmas.

likely to be hostile to open borders. Second, people with low trust and more sensitive to unfair rewards will be more likely to perceive open borders and an open welfare state as sources of moral hazard. As a result, they will also be more likely to mistrust immigrants and be dissatisfied with existing migration flows.

In the following section, I propose evidence in support of this interpretative framework. There is extensive evidence that people differ in terms of baseline trust and that the effect of social distance on trust varies across individuals (Enke, Rodríguez-Padilla and Zimmermann, 2020, 2022). As a result, I focus on documenting the often overlooked existence of differences in error sensitivity. First, I use observational data to test for the existence of a latent domain-invariant preference for minimizing some types of errors over others. I also examine whether people who are more sensitive to unfairly rewarding free riders are also more likely to rank as authoritarian on the LAV dimension. Second, I manipulate the perceived cost of free riding and examine whether differences in error sensitivity and LAVs help predict people's response to this manipulation. In both cases, I use survey data collected in June-July 2019 from a sample of British respondents.[4]

Differences in Error Sensitivity

To examine if people have preferences over the type of error to minimize, I start by leveraging patterns of answers to questions about unfair rewards and unfair punishment across distinct institutional domains. If someone is more sensitive to one type of error in one domain, then she should also be more sensitive to the same type of error in other domains. To examine this expectation, I asked respondents a set of survey questions about error types covering *five* institutional domains. For expository purposes, I start by listing these items using the example of social transfers and errors in granting/denying benefits:

> The Department for Work and Pension (the DWP) is in charge of paying social benefits to people who qualify. When giving social benefits, the DWP can make mistakes. But which mistake do you think is WORSE?

> Deny benefits to someone who qualifies.
> Give benefits to someone who does not qualify.
> Both are equally bad.
> Do not know.

---

[4] Respondents were recruited online through Qualtrics and match the British population on education, age, gender and work status. The recruitement protocole was the same as the one used to create the Dynata sample (see Appendix A3.1). Note that this sample does not constitute a representative sample of the British population.

Thinking about mistakes the DWP makes when giving social benefits, which one do you think is MOST COMMON?

Deny benefits to someone who qualifies.
Give benefits to someone who does not qualify.
Both occur at similar rates.
Do not know.

This set of questions was repeated four more times, varying the institutional realm each time and minimizing differences in wording and structure. Specifically, I asked respondents about the following four institutions and related errors:

When granting refugee status, the Home Office can make mistakes. But which mistake do you think is worse? Most common?

 – Deny refugee status to an asylum seeker who qualifies.
 – Give refugee status to an asylum seeker who does not qualify.

(Start by defining blue-collar crimes.) When judging blue-collar crimes, all systems of justice make mistakes. But which mistake do you think is worse? Most common?

 – Convict an innocent person.
 – Let a guilty person go free.

(Start by defining white-collar crimes.) When judging white-collar crimes, all systems of justice make mistakes. But which mistake do you think is worse? Most common?

 – Convict an innocent person.
 – Let a guilty person go free.

When granting loans, all banks make mistakes. But which mistake do you think is worse? Most common?

 – Deny a loan to someone who qualifies.
 – Give a loan to someone who does not qualify.

As previously stated, if someone is more sensitive to one type of error in one domain, then she is also likely to be sensitive to the same type of error in another domain. If this is true in two domains, then this should be especially likely in a third domain and so on and so forth. Empirically, this implies that it is possible to model patterns of answers to the "which is worse?" items under the following assumptions: (1) Responses to all items are governed by a latent trait θ, and (2) as a person's locations on θ increase, the probability of choosing a given type of error as "worse" increases (or at least does not decrease). In practice, this amounts to fitting Mokken's monotonely homogeneous (MH) model to answers to the "which is worse?" items (more below). Failure to fit such a model would suggest that differences in error sensitivity do not shape responses to these items.

There remains the possibility that success in fitting such a model might just be an artifact of the question format, which encourages respondents to mechanically provide similar answers across domains. As a result, I fit the same model to the "most common?" items. If question wording is driving my results, then I should be able to fit the same model to the latter set of items. However, if my argument is correct, this should not be possible. Indeed, a domain-invariant dislike for one type of error over the other does not imply a domain-invariant propensity to assume that one type of error is more prevalent than the other. As argued in Chapters 8 and 9, not only are beliefs shaped by domain-invariant individual factors (such as error sensitivity or, in the case of proportionality beliefs, economic conditions), they are also shaped by domain-specific contextual factors (such as elite discourse or one's social context). The latter explains why, while error sensitivity does not vary across domains, perception of error prevalence does.

A word on the choice of the institutional domains that are listed above. The justice system items were designed to vary target groups, holding the institutional domain constant. If, instead of error sensitivity, negative (or positive) affect toward blue-and white-collar individuals shapes responses to the "which is worse?" items, then the correlation across the two items will be low, thus undermining my expectation regarding domain-invariant error sensitivity. The item on banking was designed to capture attitudes toward an issue where individual and collective interests do not clash: Cheating on one's loan application has little consequences for everyone's ability to get a loan and does not constitute free riding. Evidence that people answer questions about banking in similar ways as they answer questions about the justice system, immigration or social transfers would indicate that the patterns of answers might be, again, merely an artifact of the question format.

Let's start with simple descriptive statistics.[5] As shown in Table 10.1, up to three times more people chose the DNK response option when asked about error prevalence than when asked about which type of error is the worst. Between 40% and 60% of respondents think that both errors are equally bad.

To fit a Mokken's MH model, three assumptions need to hold: unidimensionality, monotonicity and local independence. Unidimensionality means that survey answers can be used to order respondents on a single latent dimension θ. Monotonicity means that the more θ increases, the more likely it is that a respondent provides responses typical of the higher attribute level. Local inde-

---

[5] For this analysis, I have dropped individuals who took the survey in less than 7 min. This duration represents the 10th percentile in terms of survey duration. However, I keep individuals who, despite being below this cut-off, have successfully answered the screening question. The final sample size is 1,688.

Table 10.1 *Error sensitivity and prevalence: Descriptive results*

Which one is **worse**?

	Undeserved punishment	Both	Undeserved rewards	DNK
Social benefits	0.41	0.44	0.13	0.02
Refugee program	0.23	0.41	0.31	0.05
Blue-collar crime	0.29	0.57	0.10	0.04
White-collar crime	0.27	0.55	0.14	0.04
Bank loans	0.09	0.52	0.35	0.04

Which one is **most common**?

	Undeserved punishment	Both	Undeserved rewards	DNK
Social benefits	0.35	0.32	0.23	0.09
Refugee program	0.18	0.37	0.34	0.12
Blue-collar crime	0.10	0.33	0.41	0.15
White-collar crime	0.09	0.31	0.44	0.16
Bank loans	0.23	0.34	0.31	0.12

Source: Qualtrics 2019.

pendence implies that, for individuals with the same θ value, answers to survey questions are uncorrelated. In this part of the analysis, I am most interested in the unidimensionality and monotonicity assumptions.

To test for unidimensionality, I use a procedure examining which items, if any, could be described using a Mokken scale. When applied to the "which is worse?" items, the algorithm returns one Mokken scale ($H = 0.35$) using all items with the exception of the banking item: Knowing that someone finds it worse to deny a loan to someone who meets the criteria versus grant a loan to someone who does not says nothing about θ. When applied to the "most common?" items, the algorithm returns two Mokken scales ($H = 0.39$ and 0.32), one combining the justice system items, and the other combining the refugee and social transfer items. Based on this first analysis, unidimensionality only applies to the "which is worse?" items, with the exception of the item on bank loans.

Next, I turn to the monotonicity assumption. Figure 10.1 shows cumulative trace lines of each of the remaining "which is worse?" items as a function of the sum of respondents' answer to the other three items. With the exception of a small kink for the "justice blue collar" item, higher scores imply a higher proportion of people who chose a higher attribute on the forth item, in this case choosing the response option stating that unfair rewards are worse. Appendix A10.1 shows the same analysis for the "most common?" items and reveals

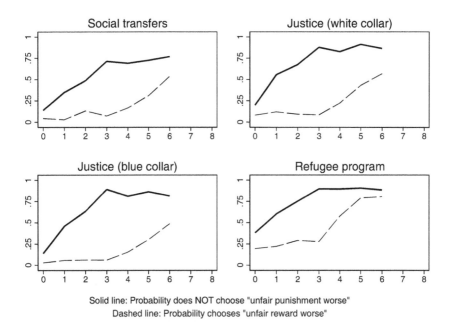

Solid line: Probability does NOT choose "unfair punishment worse"
Dashed line: Probability chooses "unfair reward worse"

Figure 10.1 Testing for monotonicity using "Which is worse?" items
For a given X-axis score, plots the share that does NOT choose "unfair punishment
is worse" (solid line) and the share that chooses "unfair reward is worse" (dashed
line). X-axis scores are the sum of the answers to the other three items. The score
ranges from 0 ("unfair punishment is worse" on all three) to 6 ("unfair reward is
worse" on all three).
Source: Qualtrics 2019.

repeated violations of the monotonicity assumption. Specifically, a higher score
on three items does not imply a higher likelihood of choosing the response
option stating that undeserved rewards are more common.

Jointly, these results suggest the existence of individual differences in error sensitivity. In light of the difficulty of fitting a similar model to the "most
common?" items, these results do not appear to be an artifact of survey design.
I now turn to examining the relationship between error sensitivity and LAVs.
To do so, I run a confirmatory factor analysis (CFA) to estimate the correlation between the latent factors shaping answers to the "which is worse" items
and to the LAV items.[6] Based on this analysis, I find a correlation of 0.51. At
first sight, these results are unsurprising. Indeed, someone who favors the death
penalty should be especially sensitive to the guilty failing to be punished. What

_____

[6] See Chapter 3 for more information on CFA.

is more difficult to explain is the connection between LAVs and error sensitivity in the realm of immigration and social insurance. Specifically, why would someone who favors the death penalty also be more sensitive to unfair rewards in the realm of social benefits? What connects discipline in schools to unfair rewards in the realm of immigration and criminal justice? I have proposed a possible reason for these relationship, and tested one observable implication, namely the existence of a domain-invariant preference for minimizing unfair rewards or unfair punishments. In the next section, I turn to another test of this framework, one specifically focused on the realm of social benefits.

Error Sensitivity, Resource Pooling and Resource Scarcity

I have argued that people differ in how they approach situations in which individual "selfish" behavior can undermine the collective interest. To further test this hypothesis, I manipulated perceptions of scarcity with regards to shared resources. When shared resources are scarce, free riding accelerates their depletion. I expect sensitivity to unfair rewards (i.e., the failure to punish free riders) over unfair punishment (i.e., punishing cooperators) to predict how people reason about access to shared resources in a context of scarcity. Simply put, given that scarcity increases free riding's collective cost, I expect people to increase their support for punishing such behavior. This increase should be the largest among those most sensitive to free riding.

In Great Britain, the National Health Service (NHS) is an ideal case to test this expectation. The NHS is a shared resource that is routinely presented as overused and overstretched. I experimentally primed respondents to think about the finances of the NHS and examined the manipulation's effect on support for universal access to the NHS. Specifically, I randomly varied the order of two blocks of survey questions. One block – the *scarcity* block – first reminded respondents that "(the) NHS is paid for by taxes and is free for all" and that "(b)ecause of growing demands on the NHS, many worry that the NHS will soon not have enough money and resources to provide everyone with the treatment they need when they need it." Then respondents were asked their opinion on the likelihood that, in the next decade, taxes to fund the NHS would go up, the quality of care will go down and co-pay will be introduced. The overwhelming majority of respondents provided pessimistic responses with regards to the NHS' fiscal health. The other block – the *exclusion* block – asked respondents who they thought should be denied access to the NHS. First, respondents were reminded that "priority access to care mostly depends on the seriousness of a patient's condition." They were then asked whether they thought other factors should be taken into consideration beyond a patient's condition. The response options were as follow: "YES, it would be right to limit someone's access to priority care if ..."[7]

They can afford to pay for similar treatment in the private sector
Their illness is due to a heavy smoking or drinking habit
They are not British citizens
They have contributed little in taxes
They are illegal immigrants
Some other reason
NO, access to priority care should ONLY be decided by the seriousness of someone's condition

In this analysis, I am particularly interested in the immigrant, smoker and low tax-contributor categories. Members of these categories can be construed as suspicious undeserving free riders. Research repeatedly finds that being an immigrant counts as a negative when assessing the deservingness of a welfare recipient.[8] Smokers and people who do not pay enough taxes can also be denied access because they "take more than they contribute," doing so out of personal choice (i.e., choosing not to stop smoking and choosing not to work, respectively).

People who saw the *scarcity* block first are the treatment group. People who saw the *exclusion* block first are the control group. The order manipulation increases the perceived cost of free riding in the treatment group compared to the control group. I expect fewer people to support universal access in the treatment group and I expect respondents in this group to want to deny priority care to a larger category of "undeserving" individuals. I have designed the outcome of interest to capture the treatment's effect on both the extensive margin – someone who flips from supporting unconditional access to supporting some conditionality – and the intensive margin – someone who already supports some conditionality, and wants to increase this level further

---

[7] Unless they chose the "NO" response option, respondents could pick more than one factor. Across treatment and control, the category least likely to be denied priority access are high-income individuals (16%). In total, 60% of respondents chose to exclude one or both categories of immigrants. With regard to smokers, on average, 28% elected to exclude this group. This number is 18% for people who have not paid enough in taxes.

[8] Historically, the British welfare state was explicitly designed for citizens only. More generally, as argued in Chapter 2, group boundaries are constitutive of social solidarity. On the one hand, membership (i.e., group boundaries) facilitates resource pooling. On the other, resource pooling is what gives membership its value. In light of this, it is unsurprising that immigrants are perceived to have the weakest claim to shared resources.

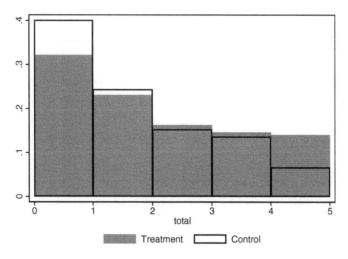

Figure 10.2 Number of groups denied priority access
Plots the distribution of the outcome by treatment condition. Interpretation: 5%
of respondents in the control group chose to exclude all five groups from priority
access. This share rose to 15% in the treatment group.
Source: Qualtrics 2019.

by excluding more categories of recipients.[9] If people with a more Hobbesian
approach to social dilemmas have a stronger dislike for "unfairly rewarding the
undeserving," then I expect larger treatment effects for individuals with more
authoritarian responses to LAV items. I repeat the same analysis using – instead
of LAV scores – an index combining the error sensitivity items discussed
earlier.[10]

Figure 10.2 compares the total number of groups excluded (none, 1 and up to
5) in the control and treatment groups. Individuals who have to first think about
the financial state of the NHS are less likely to support universal access. On
average, 0.35 more groups are denied priority access in the treatment condition

[9] This design decision is particularly important given that, as a baseline, Hobbesians are more
exclusionary than Liberals. In the case of Liberals, who tend to express high support for
universalism as a baseline, the treatment is likely to work on the extensive margin. Hobbesians,
in contrast, already support excluding immigrants. In their case, the treatment will work on the
intensive margin. Failure to capture both could produce results that are difficult to interpret.

[10] Reliance on this index assumes local independence, which is a strong assumption to make. In
the absence of a purposefully developed measure of error sensitivity, results presented next
need to be interpreted with caution, and interpreted alongside the analysis relying on LAV
items.

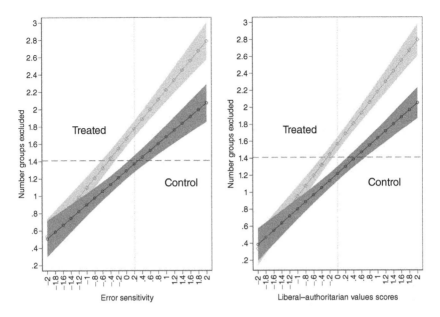

Figure 10.3 Number of groups denied priority access: Heterogeneity analysis
Plots the predicted number of groups excluded, by treatment condition and by error sensitivity (or LAVs). Predicted values were computed after regressing number of groups excluded on error sensitivity (or LAVs), interacted with the treatment dummy. See text for X-axis variables. Larger values on the X-axis indicates higher sensitivity to unfair rewards and more authoritarian LAVs. The horizontal line captures the average number of groups excluded. The vertical line plots the median error sensitivity and grid preferences score.
Source: Qualtrics 2019.

($t = 4.69$) relative to the control. Next, I examine if the effect size varies with error sensitivity and LAVs. As shown in Figure 10.3, people identified as more authoritarian and more sensitive to people getting undeserved rewards are both more likely, as a baseline, to exclude more groups and also more affected by the treatment.

A closer analysis of the data (see Appendix A10.2) shows that answers to the exclusion questions are nested, meaning that people who chose to exclude smokers or people who did not pay enough in taxes also exclude immigrants. The reverse, however, is not true. In other words, people who exclude three or more groups are mostly extending their punitive behavior to groups beyond immigrants. This means that the results are not driven by anti-immigrant sentiment alone.

Turtles All the Way Down?

The argument presented above raises one important question: Where do Hobbesian-binding versus Liberal-individualizing orientations to social dilemmas come from? A natural tendency is to tie these orientations to fundamental personal traits such as personality types (e.g., the "authoritarian personality"). In other words, people are born closer to one side of the spectrum than the other.[11] Such explanation of the origins of Hobbesian-binding versus Liberal-individualizing orientations raises the question of the origins of personality traits. In other words, emphasizing individual personality traits runs the risk of infinite regress.

I prefer to more cautiously tie these differences to group-specific ecological factors and class socialization. Research on class and parenting styles (Gelfand, 2019), or evidence that economic insecurity affects preferred "leadership style" (Ballard-Rosa et al., 2021; Safra et al., 2017) align with this interpretation. Relatedly, the evidence presented in Chapter 4 showing that social distance measures are highly correlated with both LAVs and reciprocity beliefs further points to the importance of socialization and sorting.

The Formation of Reciprocity Beliefs

I have argued that, when answering questions about sentencing, discipline in school, moral hazard or recipients' moral failings, respondents are tapping into a set of considerations and ideas that differ in systematic ways across respondents depending on how they reason about how to best maximize cooperation and minimize free riding.

How do these differences affect belief formation? As showed in Chapter 9 using the example of proportionality beliefs, when faced with new considerations regarding the fairness of the status quo, people can choose to accept them (i.e., incorporate them into their own basket of considerations) or reject them (i.e., resist incorporating them). In the case of reciprocity beliefs, people with Hobbesian-binding orientations will pay more attention to discursive cues that emphasize free riding and favor considerations that align with their emphasis on punishment (i.e., considerations that punishment is fair because free riding is prevalent). People with Liberal-individualizing orientations will have the opposite response. This mechanism contributes to the correlation between LAV items on the one hand, and free riding beliefs on the other.

---

[11] Haidt argues that their coexistence within the human population has provided humans with evolutionary advantages.

Replicating the longitudinal analysis presented in Chapter 9 requires panel data that both includes repeated measures of reciprocity beliefs and LAVs, and covers a major change in the discursive context. I was unable to identify a dataset that meets these criteria. The analysis presented next is consequently only suggestive. I first examine evidence that changes in reciprocity beliefs are tied to more stable differences in LAVs. I also compare Great Britain to other countries, to see if British respondents are more Hobbesian than not, potentially explaining their receptivity to rhetoric emphasizing moral hazard and free riding.

Explaining the Conservative Shift in Reciprocity Beliefs: The Hobbesians Strike back?

First, I examine whether people's LAV scores are more stable than their reciprocity beliefs score using a pseudo-cohort analysis. Figure 10.4 plots changes in reciprocity beliefs and LAV scores[12] broken down by birth cohort. The left panel documents a general conservative shift alongside generational differences in average reciprocity beliefs. The right panel shows that, in contrast, LAV scores, while different on average across generations, are much more stable.

Note that I have dropped observations collected in 2015, 2016 and 2017, three years during which the authoritarian score exhibits a marked liberal shift. This period overlaps with the Brexit upheaval. Remainers (i.e., people who oppose Great Britain's exit from the E.U.) appear to have reacted to the new status quo by expressing much less ethnocentric attitudes on items asking about "traditional British values" (an item included in the LAV index). To assess whether these changes in patterns of answers are temporary or not, more than three waves of data are needed.[13]

When it comes to Hobbesian-binding versus Liberal-individualizing orientations to social dilemmas, how does Great Britain compare to other advanced postindustrial democracies? To answer this question, I turn to cross-national data on LAVs. The 2008 wave of the ESS includes the following item: "People who break the law should be given much harsher sentences than they are these days."[14] This item reflects both an individual's desire for more punishment of

---

[12] To measure individual differences in LAVs, I use the same items on sentencing and discipline at school described in Chapter 4.

[13] This recent shifts also highlights the limits of using this index to proxy for differences in how people approach social dilemmas. While it is beyond the scope of this book to engage in such measurement exercise, I hope to have provided enough evidence to encourage future research in that direction.

[14] Cross-national value surveys, such as the World Value Survey, ask questions that, while correlated with LAVs, only provide imperfect substitutes for the type of Hobbesian or Liberal

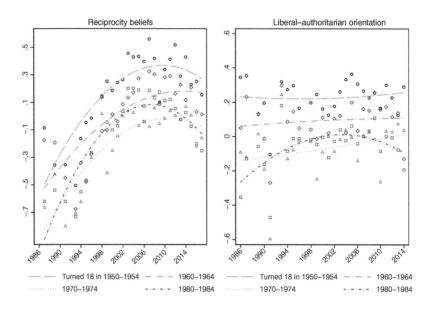

Figure 10.4 Reciprocity beliefs and LAVs: Pseudo-cohort analysis
Plots the average reciprocity beliefs (left panel) and LAV scores (right panel) for
people in a given cohort and in a given survey year.
Source: BSAS, longitudinal dataset. The 2015, 2016 and 2017 waves have been
dropped; see text for more information.

deviance and her belief about the current status quo (as not punishing enough).
Answers to this item are highly correlated with answers to the ESS items used
in the previous chapters to measure reciprocity beliefs. In Great Britain, for
example, moving from strongly agree to strongly disagree on this punishment
item implies a shift in reciprocity beliefs equal to two standard deviations of the
reciprocity beliefs score. Furthermore, this one single item explains 20 percent
of the variance in the reciprocity score.

Figure 10.5 plots the percentage of respondents who offer a liberal response
to this question (i.e., disagree). As you can see, Great Britain differs from other
"old" Western democracies in that regard, scoring as low as countries that only
recently democratized. Figure 10.6 uses cohort analysis to proxy for long-term
trends. For expository purposes, I pool data from countries with similar average

mindsets I have described in this chapter. Indeed, questions on gender, gay rights or
institutional trust are known to be correlated with LAVs, yet provide only indirect evidence
with regards to attitudes toward law and order, as well as discipline in school.

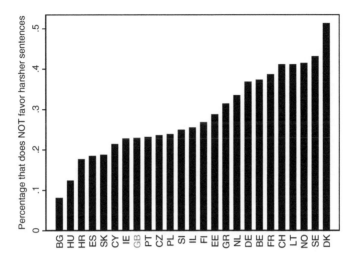

Figure 10.5 Cross-country differences in liberal attitudes on sentencing
Plots the share of people who oppose harsher sentencing by group of countries.
Item wording: "People who break the law should be given much harsher sentences
than they are these days," coded as 1 if disagree and 0 if agree or neither agree nor
disagree.
Source: ESS 2008.

responses.[15] Great Britain stands out for not exhibiting the liberalizing trends of
countries like France or Germany: The young and the old barely differ in their
attitudes to sentencing. In Scandinavian countries, between-cohort differences
are also limited but with one major difference: These countries are much less
punishing to start with.

Earlier, I argued that one major difference between authoritarians and liberals
is error sensitivity. The BSAS includes a question asking whether it is
worse to "convict an innocent," "release a guilty" or "cannot choose." Figure
10.7, left panel, plots the share of individuals who pick the first response option
by survey year. The between-cohort differences are available in the right panel,
with each cohort representing a 5-year bin. This figure shows evidence of a
decreasing concern for unfair punishment (wrongly convicting an innocent) in
favor of a rising concern for unfair rewards (letting the guilty go free).

[15] Before doing so, I also examine if these countries exhibit roughly the same between-cohort
differences.

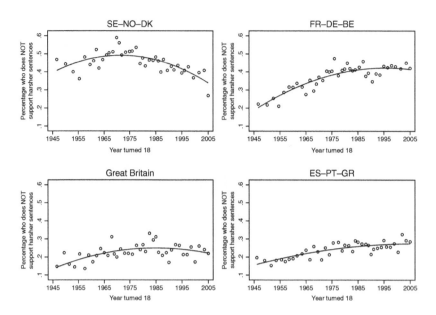

Figure 10.6 Liberal attitudes on sentencing by cohort
Plots the share of people in a given cohort that oppose harsher sentencing.
Item wording: "People who break the law should be given much harsher sentences
than they are these days," coded as 1 if disagree and 0 if agree or neither agree nor
disagree.
Source: ESS 2008.

Considered jointly, the evidence presented above suggests that Thatcher was
in friendly territory when deciding to politicize the issue of free riding. Great
Britain appears more Hobbesian than other countries in Europe. Furthermore,
evidence of an inter-generational liberal shift is limited to people who came
of age in the 1960s and 1970s. In contrast, in continental Europe, each new
generation is less authoritarian than the one that came before.

Summary and Next Steps

This chapter, jointly with Chapter 9, has provided preliminary evidence of the
push-and-pull between the discursive context and individual attributes, including economic conditions and Hobbesian/Liberal approaches to social dilemmas. In the British context, this push-and-pull has resulted in a conservative
shift in reciprocity beliefs and relatively stable proportionality beliefs. Specifically, Great Britain has combined an Hobbesian culture with a discursive context conducive to the formation of pessimistic beliefs regarding the prevalence

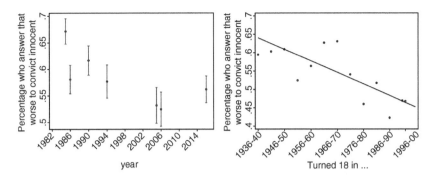

Figure 10.7 Liberal attitudes on conviction mistakes: Overtime change
Plots changes in the share of people who find it worse to convict an innocent, by
year (left panel) and by cohort (right panel). The right panel uses data collected in
2005–2006. Results are similar if pooling the 1985 and 1986 waves (with slightly
different cohorts). Item wording: "All systems of justice make mistakes, but which
do you think is worse: to convict an innocent person, to let a guilty person go free,
can't choose."
Source: BSAS longitudinal dataset.

of free riding and, consequently, a decline in support for *redistribution to*
policies.

Materialist explanations of fairness beliefs have a hard time accounting for
the formation of reciprocity beliefs. In this chapter, I provided a first step in
laying out a non-materialist explanation that can account for the correlation between LAVs and reciprocity beliefs. To do so, I took stock of the reciprocity
norm's role in the monitoring of free riding in contexts of interdependence (see
Chapter 2) and developed my argument accordingly. Based on the evidence presented here, this line of inquiry provides some explanatory power. As discussed
in Chapter 4, other lines of inquiry emphasizing the key role of anti-immigrant
sentiment or status threat carry only limited explanatory power.

There is still a lot to unpack with regards to the nature and determinants
of fairness beliefs and reciprocity beliefs in particular. I hope the argument
and evidence provided in this book will encourage some readers to explore
new avenues of research. For now, it is time to conclude my inquiry into the
dynamics of mass attitudes toward redistribution.

Appendix

A10.1 Perceptions of Error Prevalence across Institutions

Are people who are more likely to perceive one type of error as more prevalent in one arena, also more likely to do so in other arenas? According to

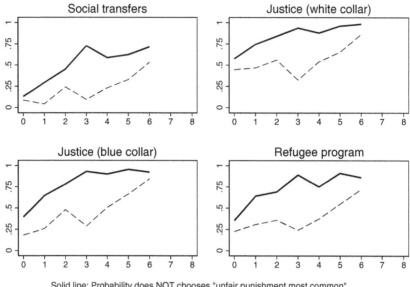

Figure A10.1 Testing for monotonicity using "Most common?" items
For a given X-axis score, plots the share that does NOT choose "unfair punishment is worse" (solid line) and the share that chooses "unfair reward is worse" (dashed line). X-axis scores are the sum of the answers to the other three items. It ranges from 0 ("unfair punishment is worse" on all three) to 6 ("unfair reward is worse" on all three).
Source: Qualtrics 2019.

Figure A10.1, the answer is negative: as the kinks in the trace lines show, the monotonicity assumption does not hold.

A10.2 Assessing the Pecking Order

As Figure 10.3 shows, people with the most authoritarian values both exclude more people at baseline and are more affected by the treatment. Specifically, among people who are most liberal (1 SD below the mean), only 3% choose three groups or more to exclude. This is true in both the control and treatment groups. Among people who are most authoritarian (1 SD above the mean), 33% choose three groups or more to exclude in the control group (11% choose four or more) and 44% do the same in the treatment group (28% choose four or more).

People who choose to exclude three groups or more appear to follow an implicit pecking order: virtually all mention illegal immigrants (95%) and those without citizenship (90%). The next most mentioned category is smokers (75%), followed by people who have not paid much in taxes (52%) and the rich (41%).

Comparing people who pick three categories with people who pick four categories, most of the difference comes from the smoker, low tax contribution and rich categories. For example, 98% (94%) of people who pick four categories mention illegal immigrants (noncitizens), compared to 92% (88%) who pick three categories. In contrast, the percentages for the smoker (no tax contribution) categories are 74% (73%) and 33% (33%) respectively.

These numbers suggest that the larger effect sizes for authoritarians are not driven by people choosing, under scarcity, to exclude non-natives. Indeed, authoritarians already exclude these categories in the control group. Note that the design does not allow me to disentangle between the increase tied to the smoker and to the no tax contribution categories on the one hand, and the increase tied to wanting to exclude rich people on the other.

Conclusion

The public's reaction to rising inequality has perplexed many. Some commentators find it surprisingly muted. Others, following Donald Trump's election and *Brexit*, worry that the public's reaction, while forceful, is misguided. Immigrants and racial minorities, they fear, have become easy scapegoats for voters left behind by globalization and technological change. In this concluding chapter, I start by summarizing this book's main contributions to our understanding of this multifaceted response to rising inequality. I then highlight important take aways for policymakers and researchers. I conclude with informed – if more speculative – insights regarding the future of redistributive politics in postindustrial democracies.

The Missing Left Turn

In light of dramatic increases in income inequality, why aren't voters asking for more income redistribution? To answer this question, I proposed a theoretical framework with at least two legs to stand on. One is a theory of fairness reasoning that highlights the filtering and anchoring role of fairness beliefs, defined as people's summary assessments of the status quo as deviating from what is prescribed by the proportionality and reciprocity norms. Following a deep dive into the structuring role of fairness beliefs, I argued against thinking of demand for redistribution in the singular. Instead, I distinguished between attitudes toward policies that *redistribute to* those who cannot provide for themselves. Taking stock of the reciprocity norm's role in the monitoring of free riding, I also proposed a non-materialist explanation of the formation of reciprocity beliefs, highlighting an overlooked relationship between second-dimension attitudes and attitudes toward *redistribution to* policies. The framework's second leg examined how fairness reasoning and material self-interest interact.

I showed how material self-interest helps explain deviations from what fairness reasoning prescribes. Material self-interest also affects how proportionality beliefs form, explaining why fairness reasoning contributes to the formation of *redistribution from* policy preferences that tend to align with people's objective material self-interest.

This framework provided the micro-foundations for my analysis of the "missing left turn" in high-inequality postindustrial democracies. Based on this argument, the benchmark model's expectation of change in the face of rising inequality is misplaced. The complementary relationship between fairness beliefs and existing levels of redistribution mean that, of all the factors conducive to a mass increase in support for *redistribution from* and *redistribution to* policies, income inequality is among the least consequential. That's because fairness beliefs that justify low levels of redistribution will also favor limited attitudinal reactions to growing inequality, while fairness beliefs that justify high levels of redistribution will have the opposite effect. With fairness reasoning in the picture, baseline expectations are turned on their heads: Countries that are more likely to experience an increase in income inequality are also those least likely to interpret this growth as unfair.

To understand attitudinal stability and change, I consequently downplayed the role of income inequality and highlighted the key role of institutional design, fiscal policy and partisan dynamics, which jointly affect which types of fairness beliefs matter, how much they matter and how they change. I found little evidence that these contextual factors have combined to increase demand for redistribution in countries most affected by rising inequality, explaining the public's overall muted response.

Fairness reasoning also sheds a new light on coalitions that support *redistribution to* policies. It highlights the central role of "economic winners" who believe that *redistribution to* policies are fair and recipients deserving. Fairness reasoning, in combination with material self-interest, also helps understand how institutional design shapes the size of this coalition and how fiscal stress can weaken it.

In many European countries, budgetary constraints and high levels of public debt following the Great Recession have rekindled the debate over the size of the welfare state. Mainstream models predict that high-income groups will be more likely to turn against a bankrupt welfare state for fear of having to foot the bill. My framework predicts strong heterogeneity among the rich, with high-income "bleeding heart" liberals central to coalitions opposing retrenchment. The centrality of bleeding heart liberals to anti-retrenchment coalitions increases with benefit targeting: When transfers are targeted to the least well-off, high-income individuals who are concerned about free riding support retrenchment, increasing the importance of bleeding heart liberals for limiting cuts in social spending. Yet, in a context of fiscal stress, this altruistic support can also weaken. While low-income voters, who vote against their interest to "punish" undeserving recipients, have attracted most of the attention, my findings indicate that bleeding heart liberals require as much, if not more, attention from researchers.

In light of fairness beliefs' filtering role, understanding how they form and change is key to understanding the long-term dynamics of mass attitudes toward redistributive social policies. A change in aggregate fairness beliefs, I have argued, requires (1) a discursive shock that repeatedly exposes people to critical claims about the fairness of the status quo and (2) a large subset of individuals predisposed to incorporate these critical statements. In other words, it requires a situation in which contextual-pull and individual-push factors align to promote mass belief change. These conditions, I showed, are met in the United States and Great Britain, though only for reciprocity beliefs. In the United States, this perfect storm has led to partisan polarization, with Republicans and Democrats diverging on their understanding of how to best implement social solidarity. In Great Britain, convergence through cooptation and omission has provided conditions favorable to an anti-redistribution shift in reciprocity beliefs. Of course, this very simple model of belief formation leaves many stones unturned including the conditions conducive to large discursive shocks. I will come back to these questions later in this conclusion when discussing next steps for research and the future of redistributive politics.

Populist Movements Left and Right

The book's conceptualization of fairness reasoning and emphasis on material stakes – as shaped by individuals and institutional factors policies – not only speaks to aggregate attitudinal trends, it also sheds a new light on populist movements that sprung following the Great Recession. It helps understand why the Great Recession did not only benefit left-wing movements and why this differed accross postindustrial democracies.

Occupy Wall Street, the Tea Party and *Les Gilets Jaunes* all expressed distributional concerns worded as a critique of the fairness of the status quo. These movements differed with regard to the type of fairness norm emphasized and fairness belief expressed, with implications regarding the policies each group has advocated. To simplify somewhat, *Les Gilets Jaunes* and Occupy Wall Street were expressing dissent in the face of perceived violations of the proportionality norm. Occupy Wall Street protesters clamored for *redistribution to* policies that would prevent income and wealth accumulation among the "1%." *Les Gilets Jaunes* faced more favorable conditions than Occupy Wall Street: As shown in Chapter 3, a majority of French voters are predisposed to see the status quo as unfairly deviating from what the proportionality norm prescribes. The reverse is true in the United States, explaining why Occupy Wall Street had a more limited impact.

Les Gilets Jaunes also included a large set of far-right voters expressing reciprocity concerns over free riding, particularly immigrants' unfair access to social benefits. Because members of the movement were united in their proportionality beliefs, the movement evolved into a more traditional, if highly disorganized, populist far-left movement.[1] Still, reciprocity beliefs are important to understand who *Les Gilets Jaunes* supporters sided with in the ballot box: People with right-wing reciprocity beliefs were more likely to side with Marine Le Pen's far-right *Rassemblement National* than with Jean-Luc Melanchon's far-left *France Insoumise*. As discussed in Chapter 6, explaining these differences in terms of differences in anti-immigrant sentiment overlooks important features of the far-right's electoral success in Europe, specifically, a shift from niche parties loosely committed to small government to mainstream parties presenting themselves as the protectors of the welfare state. Against predictions that immigration through the rise of far-right parties would transform the welfare state, it is the welfare state that has transformed far-right parties.

While the *Gilets Jaunes* and the Occupy protesters were looking to the top of the income distribution, the Tea Party supporters were looking down and sideways (Hochschild, 2018), objecting to seeing their taxes used to fund transfers to minority groups through the Affordable Care Act and reward people who took on too much debt before the recession. They were expressing frustration over perceived violations of the reciprocity norm. In line with the claim that fairness concerns take a back seat when material stakes are transparent and consequential, this frustration only extended to the redistributive features of social policy. Social insurance in the form of Medicare or Medicaid, which also benefited members of the Tea Party, were given a pass, something Donald Trump, who promised to leave Social Security and Medicare untouched, understood better than other members of the Republican Party committed to sweeping entitlement reforms. One might speculate that this type of right-wing movement is itself a child of the welfare state. Absent the latter, such fairness grievances are less likely to emerge and capture the national stage.

---

[1] An important follow-up project for ethnographers might be to trace the critical junctures during which these reciprocity issues could have taken over but were ultimately kept at bay.

Take Away for Policymakers

The argument presented in this book has implications for several policy debates that have dominated policy making circles either recently or in the past decades. One debate is the call to emulate Scandinavian countries' flexicurity model. Another is a cluster of welfare reforms, most common in the 1990s and 2000s, which were designed to "end welfare as we know it" and ultimately produce a public more supportive of anti-poverty efforts.

Scandinavian countries' low level of income inequality combined with high economic dynamism have caught policymakers' interest. Most recently, Jean Tirole, a leading French economist has recommended countries with high unemployment such as France implement reforms inspired by the Scandinavian flexicurity model, combining reforms that move labor market institutions closer to the "ideal market" with generous unemployment insurance for thus commodified workers (Méda, 2012). Such calls are routinely dismissed by opponents as failing to account for enabling factors specific to Scandinavian countries such as an export-led growth model most common in small countries or comparatively higher levels of ethnic homogeneity. Others have argued that the Scandinavian model succeeds only because others do not follow it: Given complementaries between growth models, the Scandinavian model cannot be exported *ad infinitam* (Acemoglu, Robinson and Verdier, 2017). This book suggests another reason: The flexicurity model assumes a very specific combination of fairness beliefs that few postindustrial countries share. First, reforms that commodify labor are more likely to be accepted if people believe that patterns of job retention and job loss are "fair." In a market economy, "fair" means that they are based on merit. In a knowledge economy, "fair" means that they are based on the supply and demand of skills that are themselves accessible through an educational system that also rewards merit. Second, reforms that increase transfers to the unemployed assume a shared understanding that the unemployed are deserving, and that this expansion will not encourage and reward "idleness." As shown in Chapter 3, Scandinavian countries stand out as believing that, in their country, effort pays and free riding is limited. Now imagine trying to advocate for such reforms in a country like France that holds the exact opposite beliefs: These reforms will poll poorly. A combination of vocal opposition from those directly affected by the reform and bad polling will be enough to block proposed reform packages. This has been a recurrent pattern in France since the mid-1990s.

The flexicurity example suggests that policymakers invest more time understanding and measuring mass fairness beliefs. Welfare reform is an instance in which politicians, consciously or not, did exactly that. Not only did they register fairness concerns, they tried to change fairness beliefs, specifically reciprocity beliefs. Welfare reforms implemented by Clinton in the mid-1990s were designed to target transfers to the truly "deserving" and minimizing moral hazard by incentivizing work. The expectation was that, by shifting from welfare to workfare, voters would associate the poor with work, update their beliefs about the modal recipient and come to embrace generous transfers through these new programs. Yet, the reform had no long-term effects on welfare policy preferences, perceptions of welfare recipients and attitudes toward the poor (Soss and Schram, 2007, p. 116).[2] In Great Britain, a similar reform shifted reciprocity beliefs in the *opposite* direction. The argument presented in this book suggests several reasons for this failure. One is that it overlooks the stabilizing properties of fairness beliefs, in general, and reciprocity beliefs, in particular: As proto-ideologies rooted in moral mindsets, reciprocity beliefs are hard to change. Another reason is that, in the case of fairness belief formation and change, Bayesian updating is the exception, not the norm. Welfare reforms, by calling attention to free riding and moral hazard, ended up favoring the formation of anti-redistribution reciprocity beliefs among people morally predisposed to worry about free riding and moral hazard.

Studying the Demand Side of Redistributive Politics: Implications for Research

The community of scholars interested in the topic investigated in this book is large and vibrant. While I do not expect readers from this community to agree with everything argued in this book, I hope to have convinced them of several insights relevant for future research in that field. One is the need to invest more time better matching research questions to concepts of interest, and concepts of interest to the adequate measurement strategies. Currently, there is too much conceptual ambiguity when it comes to the study of economic and redistributive preferences. Ideally, researchers should specify more clearly whether their research question requires measuring support for a specific redistributive policy (e.g, one mentioned in a bill proposal) or measuring latent predispositions to support a type of redistributive policy. If the goal is to measure the former, then the wording should reflect this specificity, asking explicitly about pre-distribution policies, progressive taxation, the generosity of means-tested

---

[2] According to Soss and Schram (2007), at best, the reform "made welfare less salient as a basis for party evaluation," something to be expected given that the two parties were no longer distinguishable on this specific policy.

benefits or unconditional access to non-means-tested ones. If the goal is to measure a predisposition, then an index using multiple items tapping into fairness beliefs might be more suitable. Innovation with regard to measurement tools is a related next step. Instead of relying on the traditional redistribution item, researchers would benefit from developing new measurement tools asking about the different facets of redistributive policies.

The second insight is also methodological and speaks to the study of fairness reasoning more specifically. Fairness concerns are everywhere; yet their political impact remains difficult to document empirically. This book's argument suggests one way forward using large-N survey data. In a first step, researchers start by identifying a finite number of fairness norms used to justify (or criticize) major resource-allocation outcomes. One way to do so is through focus groups. In a second step, researchers develop pilot survey items aimed at measuring beliefs about the fairness of the status quo adapted to the norms uncovered in step 1. Using representative surveys and combining purposefully designed items developed in step 2 with a latent class measurement model, one will be able to distinguish people with "mostly fair" beliefs from those with "mostly unfair" beliefs and assess the relative size of people with a mixed basket of thoughts about the status quo. One might also examine the extent to which the distribution of fairness beliefs overlaps with politically relevant group boundaries. Such measurement exercise could help classify countries, or within countries, institutional arenas, in which fairness reasoning has status quo re-reinforcing or change-inducing properties.

The last two insights speak to how researchers theorize the micro foundations of policy preferences. Many students of public opinion tend to dismiss material self-interest as irrelevant. I hope this book has demonstrated the benefit of moving beyond the claim that material self-interest "does not matter." As I have shown throughout, material self-interest does matter in both direct and indirect ways, as shaped by situational and institutional factors. The issue is not whether it matters, but how and when does it matter.

This book also contributes to developing a more fully-fledged theory of the behavioral underpinnings of the "first" and "second dimensions" of politics in postindustrial democracies. In line with past studies, the evidence presented throughout the book suggests first-dimension attitudes find their roots in a traditional class cleavage pitting the winners against the losers of market capitalism. The proportionality norm and disagreement over the extent to which the economic system is truly meritocratic are what remains of this cleavage. For this first dimension, the assumption that people's beliefs and preferences are shaped by their economic position and class trajectory goes a long way.

In contrast, a clear conceptualization of the second dimension and a theory explaining where people fall on this dimension have proven more elusive. Consensus is often limited to the claim that the second dimension is "noneconomic."[3] While important predictors of second-dimension attitudes have been identified (e.g., education and city living), the mechanisms underpinning these correlations are highly debated (Ballard-Rosa et al., 2021; Maxwell, 2019). The relationship between reciprocity beliefs and second-dimension attitudes highlights the limits of conceptualizing second-dimension preferences as "noneconomic." Instead, I have proposed to revisit this dimension as rooted in disagreement over how to best address social dilemmas including the provision of social insurance. This suggests that noneconomic issues, such as abortion, gay rights or women's right, which do not have the features of a social dilemma, might be less constitutive of the second dimension than issues such as law and order, immigrants' access to the welfare state or workfare reforms.[4] The book only scratches the surface of a larger research agenda. I hope to have convinced my reader that this line of inquiry is worth investing precious time and resources.

The Future of Redistributive Politics

The framework presented in this book carries a few insights for the future of redistributive politics in postindustrial societies. Pro-redistribution platforms come in several flavors. One example of such platform is a call for a universal basic income (UBI). Such calls are commonly heard on the left of the American political landscape. The framework proposed in this book highlights a few facts that have remained unnoticed. First, this proposal often does not go hand-in-hand with a call for more *redistribution from* policies. To the contrary, UBI is often touted as the fair solution to rising inequality without having to interfere with market mechanisms. This reflects an underlying set of fairness beliefs rep-

---

[3] Some researchers boil the latter down to whatever noneconomic issue is most salient in their country and period of interest, for example, immigration (Ford and Jennings, 2020), nationalism (Shayo, 2009), abortion or gay rights (Weeden and Kurzban, 2014). Others emphasize the shared "cultural preferences" or "values" that underpin people's attitudes toward these issues, distinguishing between "cosmopolitan liberals" and "parochial authoritarians" (Kitschelt and Rehm, 2014). Other expressions include "communitarian" versus "liberal" (Bornschier, 2010), "materialist" versus "post-materialist" (Inglehart, 2007) or "open" versus "closed" (Johnston, Lavine and Federico, 2017).

[4] As shown by Busemeyer, Rathgeb and Sahm (2022), it is attitudes on these particular issues that distinguish far-right voters in Europe from others.

resentative of highly educated supporters of center-left parties: The belief that markets are fair according to the proportionality norm (the "winners" of technological change are fairly rewarded for their skill set), alongside the belief that the main beneficiaries of UBI are deserving because, for example, technological change and skill obsolescence are ineluctable. Trust in the beneficiaries of UBI also reflects this group's minimal concerns for moral hazard. Interestingly, the taxation side of UBI is rarely discussed. An honest discussion of the taxation level required for UBI could trigger a quick shift toward more self-interested opposition. Opinion formation on UBI is still ongoing, given that many voters are cross-pressured, framing, as well as credible information on future income gains and losses will have large implications for building a coalition favorable to such inequality-reducing proposal.

Another policy debate relevant for income redistribution is that around macroeconomic policy, especially following the COVID-19 pandemic. To mitigate the economic consequences of the pandemic, postindustrial democracies have turned to massive fiscal and monetary stimulus. Commentators disagree on how to best deal with the fiscal and inflationary fallouts. My argument and findings highlight one possible consequence of responding through higher interest rates and austerity measures, namely the erosion of mass support for social insurance's redistributive design, even in a context in which people hurt by the Covid-induced recession are deemed "deserving." Debt sustainability is likely to be a hot-button issue in the next decade, especially if interest rates go up and/or budget deficits become or persist as chronic. Understanding how this feeds back into redistributive politics is an important frontier for research. One way forward, as I have argued in this book, is a careful account of the role of uncertainty over the pocketbook consequences of macroeconomic policy for the future of pro-*redistribution to* coalitions.

These examples illustrate the fault lines inherent to pro-*redistribution to* coalitions. Thomas Piketty's most recent book, titled *Capitalism and Ideology*, is a perfect example of an attempt to build a redistributive platform centered on the *redistribution from* dimension and justified using references to the proportionality norm. In the book, Piketty defends a highly progressive income and wealth taxes used to fund a lump-sum universal transfer (i.e., "inheritance for all") accessible at the age of 25 years old. Favorable reviews of the book highlight how existing income and wealth distributions have little to do with effort and talent and commend the universal transfer as a way to move the status quo closer to "equal opportunity for all." Unfavorable reviews challenge this interpretation. According to Raghu Rajam, today's rich are self-made "working-rich," whose wealth derives from their "ability to put resources to good use."

Piketty's proposal is unjust and would lead to economic suicide.[5] Note how the efficiency/productivity counterargument is indistinguishable from the fairness argument: Arguing that Piketty's proposals have detrimental efficiency implications implicitly assumes that high-income workers are mostly being rewarded for their effort and talent. This debate focuses on perceived deviations from what the proportionality norm prescribes. It overlooks an important fact: Within the general public, those who would support Piketty's proposal out of proportionality concerns (the status quo is unfair) might, in response to the lump-sum unconditional transfer, ultimately oppose it out of reciprocity concerns.

History points to another hurdle for this type of pro-*redistribution from* platform: References to the proportionality norm are often not enough. According to Scheve and Stasavage (2016), it is only when the rich can be convincingly portrayed as free riding on the collective effort that support for *redistribution from* policies increases. Progressive taxation, they argue, "saw its heyday in the twentieth century, when compensatory arguments for taxing the rich focused on unequal sacrifice in mass warfare" (p. 288). Total warfare constitutes a social dilemma: Citizens' individual interest is to defect, at the expense of the collective. In line with the reciprocity principle, citizens' willingness to contribute their blood to the war effort is conditional on the belief that everyone is engaged in a similar sacrifice, that is, nobody is free riding (Levi, 1991). In such a context, large economic profits are perceived to violate the reciprocity norm: They reflect an actors' selfish economic gains at the expense of the collective (ultimate) sacrifice. In other words, the ability to frame high-income earners as war profiteers who violate the reciprocity norm helps explain why some countries were able to introduce wealth taxation, while others were not. In market societies, such framing requires mass warfare, which profoundly reconfigures the economic realm, from a sphere of legitimate selfish accumulation of income and wealth to an actor in the tool for collective survival. If Scheve and Stasavage are correct, Piketty's pro-*redistribution from* platform is unlikely to win over the public on proportionality concerns alone.

Warfare aside, a first step for political entrepreneurs seeking a shift to the left on the *redistribution from* policy dimension is its re-politicization. Absent the latter, people with pro-*redistribution from* proportionality beliefs are unlikely to be politically activated. Furthermore, without a favorable discursive context, economic grievances will remain latent, and people experiencing them will be

---

[5] Raghu Rajam, "Thomas Piketty's 'Capital and Ideology': Scholarship without Solutions," *Financial Times*, February 25, 2020.

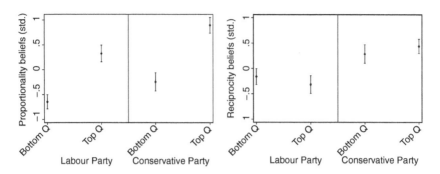

Figure C.1   Fairness beliefs in Great Britain by partisanship and income
Plots proportionality (left figure) and reciprocity (right figure) beliefs by parti-
sanship and income. Higher values indicate more anti-redistribution beliefs. See
Chapter 4 for item wording.
Source: BSAS longitudinal dataset.

unlikely to develop left-wing proportionality beliefs. In light of long-term elite
convergence on economic issues, as well as the organizational decline of institutions that target left-wing messaging to economically insecure workers,
such re-politicization appears unlikely. Another issue is the ideological tension
running through center-left and center-right electoral coalitions, which make it
difficult for political leaders to play the proportionality card. In contrast, parties
face a more homogeneous electorate on issues pertaining to the *redistribution
to* dimension of redistributive politics. Figure C.1 plots average proportionality and reciprocity beliefs by income quintile and partisanship in Great Britain.
In both parties, moving from the bottom-income to the top-income quintile is
associated with a 1 SD shift in proportionality beliefs (from less fair to more
fair). In contrast, there is no income gradient with regard to reciprocity beliefs. Here, the main difference is between parties, not within parties. As a result, parties are incentivized to politicize one type of debate over redistribution
(e.g., coverage extension, unemployment benefits, workfare, and poverty alle-
viation) at the expense of another (e.g., progressive taxation and regulation of
wage-setting practices). This does not bode well for income redistribution as,
mechanically, the latter types of policies are better than the former at decreasing
market inequality. Such tension over *redistribution from* policy issues is starker
in a two-party system, potentially explaining why rising market inequality has
gone mostly unchecked in Great Britain and the United States.

I started this book with the following question: Can an egalitarian turn in
mass attitudes toward redistributive policies provide a countervailing force to
rising inequality? Answering this question, it turns out, is not so simple. To do
so, I had to rethink what these attitudes are and how they change. On the basis

of this revision, one should not expect growing support for either *redistribution from* or *redistribution to* policies to be one of the driving forces behind policy change. The fact that voters do not lead by supporting status quo disrupting policies en masse does not imply that they will not follow. The next step is thus to better map the constraints faced by policymakers dedicated to income redistribution. In this concluding section, I have detailed some of the constraints imposed by voters. I look forward to seeing these insights incorporated into work focusing on factors beyond public opinion.

References

Acemoglu, Daron, James A. Robinson and Thierry Verdier. 2017. "Asymmetric growth and institutions in an interdependent world." *Journal of Political Economy* 125(5):1245–1305.

Acemoglu, Daron, Suresh Naidu, Pascual Restrepo and James A. Robinson. 2015. "Democracy, redistribution and inequality." In *Handbook of Income Distribution*, eds. Anthony B. Atkinson and Francois Bourguignon, Vol. 2. Elsevier, pp. 1885–1966.

Akbaş, Merve, Dan Ariely and Sevgi Yuksel. 2019. "When is inequality fair? an experiment on the effect of procedural justice and agency." *Journal of Economic Behavior & Organization* 161:114–127.

Akesson, Jesper, Robert W. Hahn, Robert D. Metcalfe and Itzhak Rasooly. 2022. "Race and redistribution in the United States: An experimental analysis." NBER Working Paper (w30426). www.nber.org/papers/w30426.

Alesina, Alberto and Edward L. Glaeser. 2006. *Fighting Poverty in the US and Europe: A World of Difference*. Oxford University Press.

Alesina, Alberto, Armando Miano and Stefanie Stantcheva. 2023. "Immigration and redistribution." *The Review of Economic Studies* 90(1):1–39.

Alesina, Alberto and Eliana La Ferrara. 2002. "Who trusts others?" *Journal of Public Economics* 85(2):207–234.

Alesina, Alberto and Eliana La Ferrara. 2005. "Preferences for redistribution in the land of opportunities." *Journal of Public Economics* 89(5–6):897–931.

Alesina, Alberto and George-Marios Angeletos. 2005. "Fairness and redistribution." *American Economic Review* 95(4):960–980.

Almås, Ingvild, Alexander Cappelen and Bertil Tungodden. 2020. "Cutthroat capitalism versus cuddly socialism: Are Americans more meritocratic and efficiency-seeking than Scandinavians?" *Journal of Political Economy* 128(5):1753–1788.

Almås, Ingvild, Alexander W. Cappelen, Erik Ø Sørensen and Bertil Tungodden. 2010. "Fairness and the development of inequality acceptance." *Science* 328(5982):1176–1178.

American National Election Studies. 2017. *ANES 2016 Time Series Study Initial Release* [dataset and documentation]. May 7, 2017 version. www.electionstudies.org

Andersen, Steffen, Seda Ertaç, Uri Gneezy, Moshe Hoffman and John A. List. 2011. "Stakes matter in ultimatum games." *American Economic Review* 101(7):3427–3439.

Ansolabehere, Stephen, Jonathan Rodden and James M. Snyder. 2008. "The strength of issues: Using multiple measures to gauge preference stability, ideological constraint, and issue voting." *American Political Science Review* 102(2):215–232.

Atkinson, Anthony Barnes. 2008. *The Changing Distribution of Earnings in OECD Countries*. Oxford University Press.

Autor, David. 2010. "The polarization of job opportunities in the US labor market: Implications for employment and earnings." *Community Investments* 23(2):11–16.

Axelrod, Robert. 1980. "More effective choice in the prisoner's dilemma." *Journal of Conflict Resolution* 24(3):379–403.

Axelrod, Robert and Douglas Dion. 1988. "The further evolution of cooperation." *Science* 242(4884):1385–1390.

Baldassarri, Delia and Andrew Gelman. 2008. "Partisans without constraint: Political polarization and trends in American public opinion." *American Journal of Sociology* 114(2):408–446.

Ballard-Rosa, Cameron, Mashail A. Malik, Stephanie J. Rickard and Kenneth Scheve. 2021. "The economic origins of authoritarian values: evidence from local trade shocks in the United Kingdom." *Comparative Political Studies* 54(13):2321–2353.

Barber, Michael, Nolan McCarty, Jane Mansbridge and Cathie Jo Martin. 2015. "Causes and consequences of polarization." In *Political Negotiation: A Handbook*, eds. Jane Mansbridge and Cathie Jo Martin. Brookings Institution Press, pp. 37–90.

Barrett, H. Clark, Alexander Bolyanatz, Alyssa N. Crittenden et al. 2016. "Small-scale societies exhibit fundamental variation in the role of intentions in moral judgment." *Proceedings of the National Academy of Sciences* 113(17):4688–4693.

Bartels, Larry. 2005. "Homer gets a tax cut: Inequality and public policy in the American mind." *Perspectives on Politics* 3(1):15–31.

Baumard, Nicolas. 2016. *The Origins of Fairness: How Evolution Explains Our Moral Nature*. Oxford University Press.

Bawn, Kathleen, Martin Cohen, David Karol, Seth Masket, Hans Noel and John Zaller. 2012. "A theory of political parties: Groups, policy demands and nominations in American politics." *Perspectives on Politics* 10(03):571–597.

Bechtel, Michael M. and Kenneth Scheve. 2014. "Who cooperates? Reciprocity, and the causal effect of expected cooperation in representative samples." *Journal of Experimental Political Science* 4(3):206–228

Bénabou, Roland and Jean Tirole. 2006. "Belief in a just world and redistributive politics." *The Quarterly Journal of Economics* 121(2):699–746.

Bénabou, Roland and Jean Tirole. 2011. "Identity, morals, and taboos: Beliefs as assets." *The Quarterly Journal of Economics* 126(2):805–855.

Bénabou, Roland and Jean Tirole. 2016. "Mindful economics: The production, consumption, and value of beliefs." *Journal of Economic Perspectives* 30(3):141–164.

Beramendi, Pablo and Philipp Rehm. 2016. "Who gives, who gains? Progressivity and preferences." *Comparative Political Studies* 49(4):529–563.

Berg, Joyce, John Dickhaut and Kevin McCabe. 1995. "Trust, reciprocity, and social history." *Games and Economic Behavior* 10(1):122–142.

Bergman, Manfred Max and Dominique Joye. 2001. "Comparing social stratification schemas: CAMSIS, CSP-CH, Goldthorpe, ISCO-88, Treiman, and Wright." *Cambridge Studies in Social Research.* Available at: www.sociology.cam.ac.uk/system/files/documents/cs10.pdf.

Berlin, Isaiah. 1958. *Two Concepts of Liberty: An Inaugural Lecture Delivered before the University of Oxford on 31 October 1958.* Oxford University Press, pp. 33–57.

Betz, Hans-Georg. 2016. "The Revenge of the Plouc: The Revival of Radical Populism Under Marine Le Pen in France." In *Economic Growth in Europe since 1945*, eds. Hanspeter Kriesi and Takis S. Pappas. ECPR Press.

Bicchieri, Cristina. 2005. *The Grammar of Society: The Nature and Dynamics of Social Norms.* Cambridge University Press.

Bicchieri, Cristina. 2016. *Norms in the Wild: How to Diagnose, Measure, and Change Social Norms.* Oxford University Press.

Binmore, Ken G. 1994. *Game Theory and the Social Contract: Just Playing*, MIT Press.

Blair, Tony and Gerhard Schroeder. 2000. "The third way/Die neue mitte." *Dissent* 47(2):51–65.

Blanchard, Olivier. 2019. "Public debt and low interest rates." *American Economic Review* 109(4):1197–1229.

Borghans, Lex, Anne C. Gielen and Erzo F.P. Luttmer. 2014. "Social support substitution and the earnings rebound: Evidence from a regression discontinuity in disability insurance reform." *American Economic Journal: Economic Policy* 6(4):34–70.

Bornschier, Simon. 2010. "The new cultural divide and the two-dimensional political space in Western Europe." *West European Politics* 33(3):419–444.

British Social Attitudes Survey, longitudinal survey. N.d. Cumulative file compiled by the authors NatCen Social Research [data collection]. UK Data Service [distributor]. https://ukdataservice.ac.uk.

Bullock, John and Gabriel Lenz. 2019. "Partisan bias in surveys." *Annual Review of Political Science* 22:325–342.

Busemeyer, Marius R., Philip Rathgeb and Alexander H.J. Sahm. 2022. "Authoritarian values and the welfare state: the social policy preferences of radical right voters." *West European Politics* 45(1):77–101.

Cappelen, Alexander W., Astri Drange Hole, Erik Ø Sørensen and Bertil Tungodden. 2007. "The pluralism of fairness ideals: An experimental approach." *American Economic Review* 97(3):818–827.

Cappelen, Alexander W., James Konow, Erik Ø Sørensen and Bertil Tungodden. 2013. "Just luck: An experimental study of risk-taking and fairness." *American Economic Review* 103(4):1398–1413.

Cappelen, Alexander W., Karl O Moene, Siv-Elisabeth Skjelbred and Bertil Tungodden. 2017. "The merit primacy effect." https://ssrn.com/abstract=2963504. Economics Discussion Paper No. 06/2017. NHH Department.

Card, David, Jörg Heining and Patrick Kline. 2013. "Workplace heterogeneity and the rise of West German wage inequality." *The Quarterly Journal of Economics* 128(3):967–1015.

Castel, Robert. 1995. *Les métamorphoses de la question sociale: une chronique du salariat.* Gallimard.

Caughey, Devin, Tom O'Grady and Christopher Warshaw. 2019. "Policy ideology in European mass publics, 1981–2016." *American Political Science Review* 113(3):674–693.

Cavaillé, Charlotte. 2022. "Why some care more about free riding than others and why it matters." IAST Working Paper No. 652.

Cavaillé, Charlotte and Karine Van der Straeten. 2023. "Immigration and Support for Redistribution: Lessons from Europe." *Journal of Economic Literature*. www.aeaweb.org/articles?id=10.1257/jel.20221708&&from=f.

Cavaillé, Charlotte and Anja Neundorf. 2022. "Elite cues and economic policy attitudes: The mediating role of economic hardship." *Political Behavior*. https://doi.org/10.1007/s11109-021-09768-w.

Cavaillé, Charlotte and Jeremy Ferwerda. 2023. "How distributional conflict over in-kind benefits generates support for far-right parties." *The Journal of Politics* 85(1):19–33.

Cavaillé, Charlotte and Kris-Stella Trump. 2015. "The two facets of social policy preferences." *Journal of Politics* 77(1):146–160.

Chase, Elaine and Robert Walker. 2013. "The co-construction of shame in the context of poverty: Beyond a threat to the social bond." *Sociology* 47(4):739–754.

Chetty, Raj. 2005. Why do unemployment benefits raise unemployment durations? Moral hazard vs. liquidity. www.nber.org/papers/w11760. *NBER Working Paper* (w11760).

Chong, Dennis and James N. Druckman. 2007. "Framing theory." *Annual Review of Political Science* 10:103–126.

Clasen, Jochen, Jon Kvist, Wim Van Oorschot, et al. 2001. "On condition of work: increasing work requirements in unemployment compensation schemes." In *Nordic Welfare States in the European Context*, eds. Johan Fritzell, Bjorn Hvinden, Mikko Kautto, Jon Kvist and Hannu Uusitalo. Routledge, pp. 33–57.

Conditions de vie et aspirations, 1979–2020. N.d. Credoc [producteur]. ADISP [diffuseur].

Converse Philip E. 2006. "The nature of belief systems in mass publics (1964)." *Critical Review* 18(1–3):1–74.

Costello, Anna B. and Jason W. Osborne. 2005. "Best practices in exploratory factor analysis: Four recommendations for getting the most from your analysis." *Practical Assessment Research and Evaluation* 10(7):1–9. https://doi.org/10.7275/jyj1-4868.

Cramer, Katherine J. 2016. *The Politics of Resentment: Rural Consciousness in Wisconsin and the Rise of Scott Walker*. University of Chicago Press.

Cruces, Guillermo, Ricardo Perez-Truglia and Martin Tetaz. 2013. "Biased perceptions of income distribution and preferences for redistribution: Evidence from a survey experiment." *Journal of Public Economics* 98:100–112.

Curry, Oliver Scott, Daniel Austin Mullins and Harvey Whitehouse. 2019. "Is it good to cooperate? Testing the theory of morality-as-cooperation in 60 societies." *Current Anthropology* 60(1):47–69.

Dahlberg, Matz, Karin Edmark and Helène Lundqvist. 2012. "Ethnic diversity and preferences for redistribution." *Journal of Political Economy* 120(1):41–76.

Dalton, Russell J. 2013. *The apartisan American: dealignment and changing electoral politics*. CQ Press.

Dassonneville, Ruth and Marc Hooghe. 2018. "Indifference and alienation: Diverging dimensions of electoral dealignment in Europe." *Acta Politica* 53(1):1–23.

De Koster, Willem, Peter Achterberg and Jeroen Van der Waal. 2013. "The new right and the welfare state: The electoral relevance of welfare chauvinism and welfare populism in the Netherlands." *International Political Science Review* 34(1):3–20.

DeScioli, Peter and Robert Kurzban. 2009. "Mysteries of morality." *Cognition* 112(2):281–299.

Dickson, Eric S., Sanford C. Gordon and Gregory A. Huber. 2009. "Enforcement and compliance in an uncertain world: An experimental investigation." *The Journal of Politics* 71(4):1357–1378.

Downs, Anthony. 1957. "An economic theory of political action in a democracy." *Journal of Political Economy* 65(2):135–150.

DREES, Barometre d'opinion. N.d. Drees [producteur]. ADISP [diffuseur]. https://drees2-sgsocialgouv.opendatasoft.com/explore/dataset/431_le-barometre-d-opinion/information/.

Druckman, James N., Erik Peterson and Rune Slothuus. 2013. "How elite partisan polarization affects public opinion formation." *American Political Science Review* 107(1):57–79.

Durante, Ruben, Louis Putterman and Joël Van der Weele. 2014. "Preferences for redistribution and perception of fairness: An experimental study." *Journal of the European Economic Association* 12(4):1059–1086.

Emmenegger, Patrick, Silja Häusermann, Bruno Palier and Martin Seeleib-Kaiser. 2012. *The Age of Dualization: The Changing Face of Inequality in Deindustrializing Societies*. Oxford University Press.

Enders, Adam M. and Jamil S. Scott. 2019. "The increasing racialization of American electoral politics, 1988-2016." *American Politics Research* 47(2):275–303.

Enke, Benjamin, Ricardo Rodríguez-Padilla and Florian Zimmermann. 2020. "Moral universalism and the structure of ideology." *NBER Working Paper* (w27511). www.nber.org/papers/w27511.

Enke, Benjamin, Ricardo Rodríguez-Padilla and Florian Zimmermann. 2022. "Moral universalism: Measurement and heterogeneity." *Management Science* 68(5): 3590–3603.

Esping-Andersen, G. 1990. *The Three Worlds of Welfare Capitalism*. Polity Press.

European Social Survey, Round 4 Data. 2008. Data file edition 4.5. Sikt - Norwegian Agency for Shared Services in Education and Research, Norway – Data Archive and distributor of ESS data for ESS ERIC. http://dx.doi.org/10.21338/NSD-ESS4-2008.

European Social Survey, Round 8 Data. 2016. Data file edition 2.2. Sikt - Norwegian Agency for Shared Services in Education and Research, Norway – Data Archive and distributor of ESS data for ESS ERIC. http://dx.doi.org/10.21338/NSD-ESS8-2016.

European Social Survey, Round 9 Data. 2018. Data file edition 3.1. Sikt - Norwegian Agency for Shared Services in Education and Research, Norway – Data Archive and distributor of ESS data for ESS ERIC. http://dx.doi.org/10.21338/NSD-ESS9-2018.

European Social Survey, Rounds 1 through 9 Data. 2022. Data file generated by combining data from individual rounds Sikt – Norwegian Agency for Shared Services in Education and Research, Norway – Data Archive and distributor of ESS data for ESS ERIC. www.europeansocialsurvey.org/data/.

Evans, Geoffrey, Anthony Heath and Mansur Lalljee. 1996. "Measuring left-right and libertarian-authoritarian values in the British electorate." *British Journal of Sociology* 47(1):93–112.

Evans, Geoffrey and James Tilley. 2012. "How parties shape class politics: Explaining the decline of the class basis of party support." *British Journal of Political Science* 42(1):137–161.

Ewald, François. 2014. *L'Etat providence*. Grasset.

Falk, Armin, Ernst Fehr and Urs Fischbacher. 2003. "On the nature of fair behavior." *Economic Inquiry* 41(1):20–26.

Farber, Henry S., Daniel Herbst, Ilyana Kuziemko and Suresh Naidu. 2021. "Unions and inequality over the twentieth century: New evidence from survey data." *The Quarterly Journal of Economics* 136(3):1325–1385.

Fehr, Ernst and Klaus M. Schmidt. 2006. "The economics of fairness, reciprocity and altruism–experimental evidence and new theories." In *Handbook of the Economics of Giving, Altruism and Reciprocity*, eds. Serge-Christophe Kolm and Jean Mercier Ythier, Vol. 1. Elsevier Science, pp. 615–691.

Fehr, Ernst and Simon Gächter. 2000. "Cooperation and punishment in public goods experiments." *American Economic Review*. 90(4):980–994

Fischbacher, Urs and Simon Gachter. 2010. "Social preferences, beliefs, and the dynamics of free riding in public goods experiments." *American Economic Review* 100(1):541–556.

Fischbacher, Urs, Simon Gächter and Ernst Fehr. 2001. "Are people conditionally cooperative? Evidence from a public goods experiment." *Economics Letters* 71(3): 397–404.

Fong, Christina. 2001. "Social preferences, self-interest, and the demand for redistribution." *Journal of Public Economics* 82(2):225–246.

Fong, Christina M. and Erzo F. P. Luttmer. 2009. "What determines giving to Hurricane Katrina victims? Experimental evidence on racial group loyalty." *American Economic Journal: Applied Economics* 1(2):64.

Fong, Christina M. and Panu Poutvaara. 2019. "Redistributive politics with target-specific beliefs." *IFO Working Paper* No. 297. www.ifo.de/DocDL/wp-2019-297-fong-poutvaara-redistributive-politcs.pdf.

Fong, Christina M., Samuel Bowles and Herbert Gintis. 2006. "Strong reciprocity and the welfare state." *In Handbook of the Economics of Giving, Altruism and Reciprocity*, ed. Serge-Christophe Kolm and Jean Mercier Ythier, Vol. 2. Elsevier, pp. 1439–1464.

Ford, Robert and Will Jennings. 2020. "The changing cleavage politics of Western Europe." *Annual Review of Political Science* 23:295–314.

Forst, Rainer. 2014. *Justification and Critique: Towards a Critical Theory of Politics*. Polity.

Friedman, Milton. 1962. *Capitalism and Freedom*. University of Chicago press.

Frohlich, Norman, Joe Oppenheimer and Anja Kurki. 2004. "Modeling other-regarding preferences and an experimental test." *Public Choice* 119(1–2):91–117.

Galbraith, John K. 1967. *The New Industrial State*. Houghton Mifflin.

Ganzeboom, Harry B.G. 2015. "International Social Survey Programme: Social Inequality IV - ISSP 2009." GESIS Data Archive, Cologne. ZA5995 Data file Version 1.0.0.

Garthwaite, Kayleigh. 2016. "Stigma, shame and'people like us': An ethnographic study of foodbank use in the UK." *Journal of Poverty and Social Justice* 24(3):277–289.

Gelfand, Michele. 2019. *Rule Makers, Rule Breakers: Tight and Loose Cultures and the Secret Signals that Direct Our Lives.* Scribner.

Georgiadis, Andreas and Alan Manning. 2012. "Spend it like Beckham? Inequality and redistribution in the UK, 1983–2004." *Public Choice* 151(3–4):537–563.

Gilens, Martin. 1999. *Why Americans Hate Welfare: Race, Media, and the Politics of Antipoverty Policy.* University of Chicago Press.

Gintis, Herbert. 2016. "Homo Ludens: Social rationality and political behavior." *Journal of Economic Behavior & Organization* 126:95–109.

Gintis, Herbert, Samuel Bowles, Robert T. Boyd, et al. 2005. *Moral Sentiments and Material Interests: The Foundations of Cooperation in Economic Life.* MIT Press.

Goren, Paul. 2001. "Core principles and policy reasoning in mass publics: A test of two theories." *British Journal of Political Science* 31(1):159–177.

Graham, Jesse, Jonathan Haidt and Brian A. Nosek. 2009. "Liberals and conservatives rely on different sets of moral foundations." *Journal of Personality and Social Psychology* 96(5):1029.

Gramsci, Antonio. 1971. *Selections from the Prison Notebooks*, ed. and transl. Quentin Hoare and Geoffrey Nowell Smith. Lawrence and Wishart.

Grasso, Maria Teresa, Stephen Farrall, Emily Gray, Colin Hay and Will Jennings. 2019. "Thatcher's children, Blair's babies, political socialization and trickle-down value change: An age, period and cohort analysis." *British Journal of Political Science* 49(1):17–36.

Gross, Justin H. and Daniel Manrique-Vallier. 2014. "A mixed membership approach to the assessment of political ideology from survey responses." In *Handbook of Mixed Membership Models and Their Applications*, eds. Edoardo M. Airoldi, David M. Blei, Elena A. Erosheva and Stephen E. Fienberg. CRC Press, Routledge Handbooks Online.

Gubrium, Erika K. and Ivar Lødemel. 2013. "'Not good enough': Social assistance and shaming in Norway." In *The Shame of It: Global Perspectives on Anti-poverty Policies*, eds. Erika K. Gubrium, Sony Pellissery and Ivar Lødemel. Policy Press, pp. 85–110.

Güth, Werner, Rolf Schmittberger and Bernd Schwarze. 1982. "An experimental analysis of ultimatum bargaining." *Journal of Economic Behavior & Organization* 3(4):367–388.

Haderup Larsen, Mikkel and Merlin Schaeffer. 2020. "Healthcare chauvinism during the COVID-19 pandemic." *Journal of Ethnic and Migration Studies* 47(7): 1455–1473.

Hall, Peter A. 1993. "Policy paradigms, social learning, and the state: The case of economic policymaking in Britain." *Comparative Politics* 25:275–296.

Hall, Peter A., Miles Kahler and David A. Lake. 2013. *The Political Origins of Our Economic Discontents.* Cornell University Press.

Hay, Colin. 2018. "The 'Crisis' of Keynesianism and the rise of neoliberalism in Britain: An ideational institutionalist approach." In *The Rise of Neoliberalism and Institutional Analysis*, eds. John L. Campbell and Ove K. Pedersen. Princeton University Press, pp. 193–218.

Helgason, Agnar Freyr and Philipp Rehm. 2022. "Long-term income trajectories and the evolution of political attitudes." *European Journal of Political Research* 62(1): 264–284.

Henrich, Joseph, Robert Boyd, Samuel Bowles, Colin Camerer, Ernst Fehr, Herbert Gintis and Richard McElreath. 2001. "In search of *Homo economicus*: Behavioral experiments in 15 small-scale societies." *American Economic Review* 91(2):73–78.

Henry, P. J. and David O. Sears. 2009. "The crystallization of contemporary racial prejudice across the lifespan." *Political Psychology* 30(4):569–590.

Hetherington, Marc J. and Jonathan D. Weiler. 2009. *Authoritarianism and Polarization in American Politics*. Cambridge University Press.

Hochschild, Arlie Russell. 2018. *Strangers in Their Own Land: Anger and Mourning on the American Right*. The New Press.

Holland, Alisha C. 2018. "Diminished expectations: Redistributive preferences in truncated welfare states." *World Politics* 70(4):555–594.

Horton, Tim. 2010. "Solidarity lost? Labour and the politics of the welfare state." *The Political Quarterly* 81(1):S31–S45.

Hout Michael. 2004. "Getting the most out of the GSS income measures." *GSS Methodological Report* #101.

Hvidberg, Kristoffer B., Claus Kreiner and Stefanie Stantcheva. 2020. Social Position and fairness views. *NBER Working Paper* (w28099). www.nber.org/papers/w28099.

Inglehart, Ronald. 1997. *Modernization and Postmodernization: Cultural, Economic, and Political Change in 43 Societies*. Cambridge University Press.

Inglehart, Ronald. 2007. *Postmaterialist Values and the Shift from Survival to Self-Expression Values*. Princeton University Press.

Inglehart, R., Haerpfer, C., Moreno, A., et al. (eds.). 2020. *World Values Survey: All Rounds – Country-Pooled Datafile*. Madrid, Spain & Vienna, Austria: JD Systems Institute & WVSA Secretariat [Version: www.worldvaluessurvey.org/WVSDocumentationWVL.jsp].

ISSP Research Group. 2008. "International Social Survey Programme: Role of Government I-IV - ISSP 1985-1990-1996-2006." GESIS Data Archive, Cologne. ZA4747 Data file Version 1.0.0, https://doi.org/10.4232/1.4747.

ISSP Research Group (2014). "International Social Survey Programme: Social Inequality I-IV - ISSP 1987-1992-1999-2009." GESIS Data Archive, Cologne. ZA5890 Data file Version 1.0.0, https://doi.org/10.4232/1.11911.

ISSP Research Group. 2018. "International Social Survey Programme: Role of Government V - ISSP 2016." GESIS Data Archive, Cologne. ZA6900 Data file Version 2.0.0, https://doi.org/10.4232/1.13052.

ISSP Research Group. 2021. "International Social Survey Programme: Social Inequality V - ISSP 2019." GESIS Data Archive, Cologne. ZA7600 Data file Version 2.0.0, https://doi.org/10.4232/1.13829.

Iversen, Torben and David Soskice. 2001. "An asset theory of social policy preferences." *American Political Science Review* 95(4):875–894.

Jacobs, Alan M. and J. Scott Matthews. 2017. "Policy attitudes in institutional context: Rules, uncertainty, and the mass politics of public investment." *American Journal of Political Science* 61(1):194–207.

Jacoby, William G. 1991. "Ideological identification and issue attitudes." *American Journal of Political Science* 27(1):178–205.

Jaeger, Mads Meier. 2006. "Welfare regimes and attitudes towards redistribution: The regime hypothesis revisited." *European Sociological Review* 22(2):157–170.

Jaeger, Mads Meier. 2009. "United but divided: Welfare regimes and the level and variance in public support for redistribution." *European Sociological Review* 25(6):723–737.

Johnston, Christopher D., Howard G. Lavine and Christopher M. Federico. 2017. *Open versus Closed: Personality, Identity, and the Politics of Redistribution*. Cambridge University Press.

Kalyvas, Stathis N. 1994. "Hegemony breakdown: The collapse of nationalization in Britain and France." *Politics & Society* 22(3):316–348.

Kato, Junko. 2003. *Regressive Taxation and the Welfare State: Path Dependence and Policy Diffusion*. Cambridge University Press.

Kinder, Donald R. and David O. Sears. 1981. "Prejudice and politics: Symbolic racism versus racial threats to the good life." *Journal of Personality and Social Psychology* 40(3):414.

Kitschelt, Herbert. 1997. *The Radical Right in Western Europe: A Comparative Analysis*. University of Michigan Press.

Kitschelt, Herbert and Philipp Rehm. 2014. "Occupations as a site of political preference formation." *Comparative Political Studies* 47(12):1670–1706.

Kiviat, Barbara. 2019. "The moral limits of predictive practices: The case of credit-based insurance scores." *American Sociological Review* 84(6):1134–1158.

Kluegel, James R., Gyorgy Csepeli, Tamas Kolosi, Antal Orkeny and Maria Nemenyi. 1995. "Accounting for the rich and the poor: Existential justice in comparative perspective." In *Social Justice and Political Change, Public Opinion in Capitalist and Post-communist States*, eds. James R. Kluegel, David S. Mason and Bernd Wegener. Routledge, pp. 179–207.

Knight, Frank H. 2012. *Risk, Uncertainty and Profit*. Courier Corporation.

Konow, James. 2003. "Which is the fairest one of all? A positive analysis of justice theories." *Journal of Economic Literature* 41(4):1188–1239.

Konow, James, Tatsuyoshi Saijo and Kenju Akai. 2008. "Morals and mores? Experimental evidence on equity and equality from the US and Japan." www.dklevine.com/archive/refs4122247000000002055.pdf.

Kootstra, Anouk. 2016. "Deserving and undeserving welfare claimants in Britain and the Netherlands: Examining the role of ethnicity and migration status Using a Vignette Experiment." *European Sociological Review* 32(3):325–338.

Korpi, Walter and Joakim Palme. 1998. "The paradox of redistribution and strategies of equality: Welfare state institutions, inequality, and poverty in the Western countries." *American Sociological Review* 63(5):661–687.

Kriesi, Hanspeter, Edgar Grande, Martin Dolezal, Marc Helbling, Dominic Hoglinger, Swen Hutter and Bruno Wuest. 2012. *Political Conflict in Western Europe*. Cambridge University Press.

Kristov, Lorenzo, Peter Lindert and Robert McClelland. 1992. "Pressure groups and redistribution." *Journal of Public Economics* 48(2):135–163.

Kuziemko, Ilyana, Michael Norton, Emmanuel Saez and Stefanie Stantcheva. 2013. "How elastic are preferences for redistribution? Evidence from randomized survey experiments." *American Economic Review* 105(4):1478–1508.

Lambert, Paul S. and Ken Prandy. 2012. "CAMSIS project webpages: Cambridge Social Interaction and Stratification Scales." www.camsis.stir.ac.uk/.

Lamont, Michèle. 2002. *The Dignity of Working Men: Morality and the Boundaries of Race, Class, and Immigration.* Harvard University Press.

Lamont, Michèle and Virag Molnar. 2002. "The study of boundaries in the social sciences." *Annual Review of Sociology* 28:167–195.

Larsen, Christian Albrekt and Thomas Engel Dejgaard. 2013. "The institutional logic of images of the poor and welfare recipients: A comparative study of British, Swedish and Danish newspapers." *Journal of European Social Policy* 23(3):287–299.

Lenz, Gabriel S. 2009. "Learning and opinion change, not priming: Reconsidering the priming hypothesis." *American Journal of Political Science* 53(4):821–837.

Lenz, Gabriel S. 2013. *Follow the Leader?: How Voters Respond to Politicians' Policies and Performance.* University of Chicago Press.

Lerner, Melvin J. 1980. *The Belief in a Just World.* Springer.

Levendusky, Matthew. 2009. *The Partisan Sort: How Liberals Became Democrats and Conservatives Became Republicans.* University of Chicago Press.

Levi, Margaret. 1991. *Consent, Dissent, and Patriotism.* Cambridge University Press.

Levitt, Steven D. and John A. List. 2007. "What do laboratory experiments measuring social preferences reveal about the real world?" *Journal of Economic Perspectives* 21(2):153–174.

List, John A. 2007. "On the interpretation of giving in dictator games." *Journal of Political Economy* 115(3):482–493.

Lukes, Steven. 2004. *Power : A Radical View.* Macmillan International Higher Education.

Lupu, Noam and Jonas Pontusson. 2011. "The structure of inequality and the politics of redistribution." *American Political Science Review* 105(2):316–336.

Margalit, Yotam. 2013. "Explaining social policy preferences: Evidence from the Great Recession." *American Political Science Review* 107(1):80–103.

Marshall, John. 2016. "Education and voting conservative: Evidence from a major schooling reform in Great Britain." *The Journal of Politics* 78(2):382–395.

Martinsen, Dorte Sindbjerg. 2020. "Migrants' access to social protection in Denmark." In *Migration and Social Protection in Europe and Beyond (Volume 1)*, ed. Jean-Michel Lafleur and Daniela Vintila. Springer International Publishing, pp. 123–135.

Matsunaga, Masaki. 2010. "How to factor-analyze your data right: Dos, donts, and how-tos." *International Journal of Psychological Research* 3(1):97–110.

Matthijs, Matthias M. 2012. *Ideas and Economic Crises in Britain from Attlee to Blair (1945–2005).* Routledge.

Maxwell, Rahsaan. 2019. "Cosmopolitan immigration attitudes in large European cities: Contextual or compositional effects?" *American Political Science Review* 113(2):456–474.

McCarty, Nolan M., Keith T. Poole and Howard Rosenthal. 1997. *Income Redistribution and the Realignment of American Politics*. AEI Press Publisher for the American Enterprise Institute.

McCarty, Nolan M., Keith T. Poole and Howard Rosenthal. 2008. *Polarized America*. MIT Press.

McClendon Gwyneth. 2018. *Envy in Politics: How Envy, Spite, and the Pursuit of Admiration Influence Politics*. Princeton University Press.

Méda, Dominique. 2012. "La flexicurité à la française : un échec avéré." *Les Politiques Sociales* 3–4(2):86–97.

Meier, Stephan. 2007. "A survey of economic theories and field evidence on pro-social behavior." In *Economics and Psychology: A Promising New Cross-disciplinary Field*, ed. B. S. Frey & A. Stutzer. MIT Press, pp. 51–87.

Meltzer, Allan H. and Scott F. Richard. 1981. "A rational theory of the size of government." *The Journal of Political Economy* 89(5):914–927.

Mewes, Jan and Steffen Mau. 2012. "Unraveling working-class welfare chauvinism." In *Contested Welfare States: Welfare Attitudes in Europe and Beyond*, ed. Stefan Svallfors. Stanford University Press, pp. 119–157.

Milazzo, Caitlin, James Adams and Jane Green. 2012. "Are voter decision rules endogenous to parties' policy strategies? A model with applications to elite depolarization in post-Thatcher Britain." *The Journal of Politics* 74(1):262–276.

Miller, Charles E. and Samual S. Komorita. 1995. "Reward allocation in task-performing groups." *Journal of Personality and Social Psychology* 69(1):80.

Miller, Gary and Norman Schofield. 2003. "Activists and partisan realignment in the United States." *American Political Science Review* 97(2):245–260.

Moene, Karl O. and Michael Wallerstein. 2001. "Inequality, social insurance, and redistribution." *American Political Science Review* 95(04):859–874.

Mudge, Stephanie L. 2018. *Leftism Reinvented: Western Parties from Socialism to Neoliberalism*. Harvard University Press.

OECD. 2008. *Growing Unequal?: Income Distribution and Poverty in OECD Countries*. Organization for Economic Cooperation and Development.

O'Grady, Tom. 2019. "How do economic circumstances determine preferences? Evidence from long-run panel data." *British Journal of Political Science* 49(4): 1381–1406.

O'Grady, Tom. 2021. *The Transformation of British Welfare Policy: Politics, Discourse and Public Opinion*. Oxford University Press.

Ostrom, Elinor. 1998. "A behavioral approach to the rational choice theory of collective action: Presidential address, American Political Science Association, 1997." *American Political Science Review* 92(1):1–22.

Ostrom, Elinor and James Walker. 2003. *Trust and Reciprocity: Interdisciplinary Lessons for Experimental Research*. Russell Sage Foundation.

Oxoby, Robert J. and John Spraggon. 2008. "Mine and yours: Property rights in dictator games." *Journal of Economic Behavior & Organization* 65(3–4):703–713.

Paolino, Philip. 2020. "Predicted probabilities and inference with multinomial logit." *Political Analysis* 29(3):1–6.

Park, Alison, Elizabeth Clery, John Curtice, Miranda Phillips and David Utting. 2012. *British Social Attitudes 29*. London, NatCen Social Research .

Petersen, Michael Bang, Daniel Sznycer, Leda Cosmides and John Tooby. 2012. "Who deserves help? evolutionary psychology, social emotions, and public opinion about welfare." *Political Psychology* 33(3):395–418.

Pew Research Center. 2007. "1987-2007 Values Surveys Combined Dataset." www .pewresearch.org/politics/dataset/1987-2007-values-surveys-combined-dataset/.

Pierson, Paul. 2001. *The New Politics of the Welfare State*. Oxford University Press.

Piketty, Thomas. 2020. *Capital and Ideology*. Harvard University Press.

Polanyi, Karl. 1944. *The Great Transformation: The Political and Economic Origins of Our Time*. Beacon Press.

Poole, Keith T. and Howard Rosenthal. 1997. *Congress: A Political-economic History of Roll Call Voting*. Oxford University Press.

Przeworski, Adam and John Sprague. 1986. *Paper Stones: A History of Electoral Socialism*. University of Chicago Press.

Rehm, Philipp. 2009. "Risks and redistribution: An individual-level analysis." *Comparative Political Studies* 42(7):855–881.

Rehm, Philipp, Jacob S. Hacker and Mark Schlesinger. 2012. "Insecure alliances: Risk, inequality, and support for the welfare state." *American Political Science Review* 106(2):386–406.

Richardson, Heather Cox. 2004. *The Death of Reconstruction: Race, Labor, and Politics in the Post-civil War North, 1865–1901*. Harvard University Press.

Rodden, Jonathan A. 2019. *Why Cities Lose: The Deep Roots of the Urban-rural Political Divide*. Basic Books.

Rodden, Jonathan A. 2021. "Keeping your enemies close: Electoral rules and partisan polarization." In *Who Gets What? The New Politics of Insecurity*, ed. Frances McCall Rosenbluth and Margaret Weir. SSRC Anxieties of Democracy Cambridge University Press, pp. 129–160.

Roth, Christopher, Sonja Settele and Johannes Wohlfart. 2022. "Risk exposure and acquisition of macroeconomic information." *American Economic Review: Insights* 4(1):34–53.

Rueda, David. 2007. *Social Democracy Inside Out: Partisanship and Labor Market Policy in Advanced Industrialized Democracies*. Oxford University Press.

Rueda, David. 2018. "Food comes first, then morals: Redistribution preferences, parochial altruism, and immigration in Western Europe." *The Journal of Politics* 80(1):225–239.

Rueda, David and Daniel Stegmueller. 2015. "The externalities of inequality: Fear of crime and preferences for redistribution in Western Europe." *American Journal of Political Science* 60(2):472–489.

Rueda, David and Daniel Stegmueller. 2019. *Who Wants What? Redistribution Preferences in Comparative Perspective*. Cambridge University Press.

Runst, Petrik. 2018. "Does immigration affect demand for redistribution? An experimental design." *German Economic Review* 19(4):383–400.

Safra, Lou, Yann Algan, Teodora Tecu, Julie Grèzes, Nicolas Baumard and Coralie Chevallier. 2017. "Childhood harshness predicts long-lasting leader preferences." *Evolution and Human Behavior* 38(5):645–651.

Saint-Paul, Gilles. 1999. "Toward a theory of labor market institutions." https://papers .ssrn.com/sol3/papers.cfm?abstract_id=224564. *UPF Economics and Business Working Paper* Number 433.

Sands, Melissa L. 2017. "Exposure to inequality affects support for redistribution." *Proceedings of the National Academy of Sciences* 114(4):663–668.

Sands, Melissa L. and Daniel de Kadt. 2020. "Local exposure to inequality raises support of people of low wealth for taxing the wealthy." *Nature* 586(7828):257–261.

Scheidel, Walter. 2018. T*The Great Leveler: Violence and the History of Inequality from the Stone Age to the Twenty-first Century*. Princeton University Press.

Scheve, Kenneth and David Stasavage. 2006. "Religion and preferences for social insurance." *Quarterly Journal of Political Science* 1(3):255–286.

Scheve, Kenneth and David Stasavage. 2012. "Democracy, war, and wealth: Lessons from two centuries of inheritance taxation." *American Political Science Review* 106(1):81–102.

Scheve, Kenneth and David Stasavage. 2016. *Taxing the Rich: A History of Fiscal Fairness in the United States and Europe*. Princeton University Press.

Schram, Sanford F., Joe Brian Soss and Richard Carl Fording. 2010. *Race and the Politics of Welfare Reform*. University of Michigan Press.

Schumacher, Gijs and Kees Van Kersbergen. 2016. "Do mainstream parties adapt to the welfare chauvinism of populist parties?" *Party Politics* 22(3):300–312.

Schumpeter, Joseph A. 1950. *Capitalism, Socialism, and Democracy*. 3rd Ed. Harper.

Sears, David O. and Carolyn L. Funk. 1991. "The role of self-interest in social and political attitudes." *Advances in Experimental Social Psychology* 24(1):1–91.

Sears, David O., Colette Van Laar, Mary Carrillo and Rick Kosterman. 1997. "Is it really racism?: The origins of white Americans' opposition to race-targeted policies." *The Public Opinion Quarterly* 61(1):16–53.

Shayo, Moses. 2009. "A model of social identity with an application to political economy: Nation, class, and redistribution." *American Political Science Review* 103(2):147–174.

Sherman, Jennifer. 2009. *Those Who Work, Those Who Don't: Poverty, Morality, and Family in Rural America*. University of Minnesota Press.

Shweder, Richard A., Nancy C. Much, Manamohan Mahapatra and Lawrence Park. 1997. "The big three of morality (autonomy, community, divinity) and the big three explanations of suffering." *Morality and Health*, pp. 119–169.

Skitka, Linda J. and Philip E. Tetlock. 1993. "Providing public assistance: Cognitive and motivational processes underlying liberal and conservative policy preferences." *Journal of Personality and Social Psychology* 65(6):1205.

Skocpol, Theda and Vanessa Williamson. 2011. *The Tea Party and the Remaking of Republican Conservatism*. Oxford University Press.

Smith, Tom W., Peter Marsden, Hout Michael and Jibum Kim. N.d. General Social Surveys, 1972-2014 [machine-readable data file]. 1972-2014 [machine-readable data file] Principal Investigator, Tom W. Smith; Co-Principal Investigator, Peter V. Marsden; Co-Principal Investigator, Michael Hout; Sponsored by National Science Foundation. -NORC ed.- Chicago: NORC at the University of Chicago [producer and distributor].

Sniderman, Paul M. and John Bullock. 2004. "A consistency theory of public opinion and political choice: The hypothesis of menu dependence." In *Studies in Public Opinion*, ed. Willem E. Saris and Paul M. Sniderman. Princeton University Press, pp. 337–357.

Sniderman, Paul M., Michael Bang Petersen, Rune Slothuus and Rune Stubager. 2014. *Paradoxes of Liberal Democracy: Islam, Western Europe, and the Danish cartoon Crisis.* Princeton University Press.

Sombart, Werner. 1976. *Why Is There No Socialism in the United States?* Springer.

Soss, Joe and Sanford F. Schram. 2007. "A public transformed? Welfare reform as policy feedback." *American Political Science Review* 101(01):111–127.

Stoll, Heather. 2010. "Elite-level conflict salience and dimensionality in Western Europe: Concepts and empirical findings." *West European Politics* 33(3):445–473.

Svallfors, Stefan. 1997. "Worlds of welfare and attitudes to redistribution: A comparison of eight Western Nations." *European Sociological Review* 13(3):283–304.

Svallfors, Stefan. 2012. "Welfare attitudes in context." In *Contested Welfare States*, ed. Stefan Svallfors. Stanford University Press, pp. 222–240.

Sznycer, Daniel, Maria Florencia Lopez Seal, Aaron Sell, Julian Lim, Roni Porat, Shaul Shalvi, Eran Halperin, Leda Cosmides and John Tooby. 2017. "Support for redistribution is shaped by compassion, envy, and self-interest, but not a taste for fairness." *Proceedings of the National Academy of Sciences* 114(31):8420–8425.

Thévenot, Laurent and Luc Boltanski. 1991. *De la justification. Les économies de la grandeur.* Gallimard.

Tomasello, Michael. 2016. *A Natural History of Human Morality.* Harvard University Press.

Tomasello, Michael and Amrisha Vaish. 2013. "Origins of human cooperation and morality." *Annual Review of Psychology* 64:231–255.

Torfing, Jacob. 1999. "Workfare with welfare: Recent reforms of the Danish welfare state." *Journal of European Social Policy* 9(1):5–28.

Trump, Kris-Stella. 2018. "Income inequality influences perceptions of legitimate income differences." *British Journal of Political Science* 48(4):929–952.

Turiel, Elliot. 1983. *The Development of Social Knowledge: Morality and Convention.* Cambridge University Press.

University of Essex, Institute for Social and Economic Research. 2021. *British Household Panel Survey: Waves 1–18, 1991–2009.* [data collection]. 8th Edition. UK Data Service. SN: 5151, http://doi.org/10.5255/UKDA-SN-5151-2.

Vogel, Steven K. 2018. *Marketcraft: How Governments Make Markets Work.* Oxford University Press.

Wallerstein, Michael and Bruce Western. 2000. "Unions in decline? What has changed and why." *Annual Review of Political Science* 3(1):355–377.

Walzer, Michael. 1983. *Spheres of Justice: A Defense of Pluralism and Equality.* Basic books.

Weeden, Jason and Robert Kurzban. 2014. *The Hidden Agenda of the Political Mind: How Self-Interest Shapes Our Opinions and Why We Won't Admit It.* Princeton University Press.

Wegener, Bernard and David Mason. 2010. "International Social Justice Project, 1991 and 1996." Inter-university Consortium for Political and Social Research [distributor].

Weil, David. 2014. *The Fissured Workplace.* Harvard University Press.

Wilensky, Harold L. 1974. *The Welfare State and Equality.* University of Caliornia Press.

Wilensky, Harold L., Gregory M. Luebbert, Susan Reed Hahn and Adrienne M. Jamieson. 1985. *Comparative Social Policy: Theories, Methods, Findings*. University of Caliornia Press.

Xiong, Moulin, Richard G. Greenleaf and Jona Goldschmidt. 2017. "Citizen attitudes toward errors in criminal justice: Implications of the declining acceptance of Blackstone's ratio." *International Journal of Law, Crime and Justice* 48:14–26.

Zaller, John R. and Stanley Feldman. 1992. "A simple theory of the survey response: Answering questions versus revealing preferences." *American Journal of Political Science* 36(3):579–616.

Zaller, John R. 1992. *The Nature and Origins of Mass Opinion*. Cambridge University Press.

Index

Note: Page references in **bold** denote tables or figures. Footnote references are in the form *pgnfn* (e.g. 5n6 is footnote 6 on page 5). Footnotes are numbered sequentially by chapter.

Pepper D. Culpepper, *Quiet Politics and Business Power: Corporate Control in Europe and Japan*

Sarah Zukerman Daly, *Organized Violence after Civil War: The Geography of Recruitment in Latin America*

Christian Davenport, *State Repression and the Domestic Democratic Peace*

Donatella della Porta, *Social Movements, Political Violence, and the State*

Alberto Diaz-Cayeros, *Federalism, Fiscal Authority, and Centralization in Latin America*

Alberto Diaz-Cayeros, Federico Estévez, and Beatriz Magaloni, *The Political Logic of Poverty Relief: Electoral Strategies and Social Policy in Mexico*

Jesse Driscoll, *Warlords and Coalition Politics in Post-Soviet States*

Thad Dunning, *Crude Democracy: Natural Resource Wealth and Political Regimes*

Thad Dunning et al., *Information, Accountability, and Cumulative Learning: Lessons from Metaketa I*

Gerald Easter, *Reconstructing the State: Personal Networks and Elite Identity*

Antje Ellerman, *The Comparative Politics of Immigration: Policy Choices in Germany, Canada, Switzerland, and the United States*

Margarita Estevez-Abe, *Welfare and Capitalism in Postwar Japan: Party, Bureaucracy, and Business*

Henry Farrell, *The Political Economy of Trust: Institutions, Interests, and Inter-Firm Cooperation in Italy and Germany*

Karen E. Ferree, *Framing the Race in South Africa: The Political Origins of Racial Census Elections*

M. Steven Fish, *Democracy Derailed in Russia: The Failure of Open Politics*

Robert F. Franzese, *Macroeconomic Policies of Developed Democracies*

Roberto Franzosi, *The Puzzle of Strikes: Class and State Strategies in Postwar Italy*

Timothy Frye, *Building States and Markets After Communism: The Perils of Polarized Democracy*

Mary E. Gallagher, *Authoritarian Legality in China: Law, Workers, and the State*

Geoffrey Garrett, *Partisan Politics in the Global Economy*

Scott Gehlbach, *Representation through Taxation: Revenue, Politics, and Development in Postcommunist States*

Edward L. Gibson, *Boundary Control: Subnational Authoritarianism in Federal Democracies*

Jane R. Gingrich, *Making Markets in the Welfare State: The Politics of Varying Market Reforms*

Miriam Golden, *Heroic Defeats: The Politics of Job Loss*

Yanilda María González, *Authoritarian Police in Democracy: Contested Security in Latin America*

Jeff Goodwin, *No Other Way Out: States and Revolutionary Movements*

Merilee Serrill Grindle, *Changing the State*

Anna Grzymala-Busse, *Rebuilding Leviathan: Party Competition and State Exploitation in Post-Communist Democracies*

Anna Grzymala-Busse, *Redeeming the Communist Past: The Regeneration of Communist Parties in East Central Europe*

Frances Hagopian, *Traditional Politics and Regime Change in Brazil*

Mark Hallerberg, Rolf Ranier Strauch, and Jürgen von Hagen, *Fiscal Governance in Europe*

Henry E. Hale, *The Foundations of Ethnic Politics: Separatism of States and Nations in Eurasia and the World*

For EU product safety concerns, contact us at Calle de José Abascal, 56–1°, 28003 Madrid, Spain or eugpsr@cambridge.org.

www.ingramcontent.com/pod-product-compliance
Ingram Content Group UK Ltd.
Pitfield, Milton Keynes, MK11 3LW, UK
UKHW010249140625
459647UK00013BA/1758